GPU Pro 360

Guide to Image Space

GPU Pro 360

Guide to Image Space

Edited by Wolfgang Engel

CRC Press
Taylor & Francis Group
Boca Raton London New York

CRC Press is an imprint of the
Taylor & Francis Group, an **informa** business

AN A K PETERS BOOK

CRC Press
Taylor & Francis Group
6000 Broken Sound Parkway NW, Suite 300
Boca Raton, FL 33487-2742

© 2019 by Taylor & Francis Group, LLC
CRC Press is an imprint of Taylor & Francis Group, an Informa business

No claim to original U.S. Government works

Printed in Canada on acid-free paper

International Standard Book Number-13: 978-1-138-48432-0 (Paperback)
International Standard Book Number-13: 978-1-138-48435-1 (Hardback)

Library of Congress Cataloging-in-Publication Data

Names: Engel, Wolfgang F., editor.
Title: GPU pro 360 guide to image space / [edited by] Wolfgang Engel.
Description: First edition. | Boca Raton, FL : CRC Press/Taylor & Francis Group, 2018. | Includes bibliographical references and index.
Identifiers: LCCN 2018020104| ISBN 9781138484320 (pbk. : acid-free paper) |
   ISBN 9781138484351 (hardback : acid-free paper)
Subjects: LCSH: Computer graphics. | Digital images. | Graphics processing units--Programming.
Classification: LCC T385 G6888345 2018 | DDC 006.6--dc23
LC record available at https://lccn.loc.gov/2018020104

Visit the eResources: www.crcpress.com/9781138484320

Visit the Taylor & Francis Web site at
http://www.taylorandfrancis.com

and the CRC Press Web site at
http://www.crcpress.com

Contents

Introduction

In this book we will cover various algorithms that operate primarily in image space. Graphics programmers chose to work in image space for a number of reasons. Some techniques naturally map this space while others seek to exploit screen space because it offers an implicit LOD and visibility is handled automatically. The variety of algorithms in this section, drawing from several subfields of computer graphics, speaks to the power and convenience of working in screen space.

The first chapter, "Anisotropic Kuwahara Filtering on the GPU," by Jan Eric Kyprianidis, Henry Kang, and Jürgen Döllner, describes a very interesting method for creating abstracted, non-photorealistic images by applying an anisotropic Kuwahara filter. The authors demonstrate a GPU implementation of the filter, which can be used for post-processing pre-rendered images to make them more artful. It could also be used in real time for creating stylized games.

Our next chapter tackles the challenge of antialiasing geometric edges in rendered scenes. As Hugh Malan discusses in his chapter, "Edge Antialiasing by Post-Processing," standard multi-sampled antialiasing has a number of downfalls, one of which is that it is difficult to incorporate into a deferred renderer. This chapter provides a screen-space solution for antialiasing and is compatible with rendering engines that make use of deferred shading.

In "Environment Mapping with Floyd-Steinberg Halftoning," written by László Szirmay-Kalos, László Szécsi, and Anton Penzov, an algorithm is presented for computing importance samples using the GPU. This algorithm uses a clever application of a classic halftoning technique and is useful for accelerating the importance-sampling step in high quality environment-mapped lighting.

Next, Thomas Engelhardt and Carsten Dachsbacher cover an algorithm for computing occluded sets in their chapter "Hierarchical Item Buffers for Granular Occlusion Culling." This technique demonstrates a method for computing sets of visible and occluded objects entirely on the GPU, thus allowing a renderer to skip objects that will not be visible in the final image.

Depth of field is a very important visual element in many games and feature films. Artists can use depth of field to direct the viewer's eyes to a certain part of the screen or to provide a dramatic transition. In "Realistic Depth of Field in

Postproduction," by David Illes and Peter Horvath, a high quality depth-of-field implementation suitable for GPU acceleration is described.

In a more traditional screen space approach, "Real-Time Screen Space Cloud Lighting," Kaori Kubota discusses an efficient but visually compelling method for simulating lit clouds. Physically based cloud lighting algorithms are very computationally demanding. This chapter takes the approach of recreating the look of cloud lighting without depending on expensive, physically based simulation.

In "Screen-Space Subsurface Scattering," by Jorge Jimenez and Diego Gutierrez, the authors present an interesting twist on subsurface scattering; they describe a way to compute it in screen space. Some of the benefits of computing subsurface scattering in screen space are that it provides an implicit level of detail (objects farther from the viewer appear smaller on screen), and it dramatically decreases the number of draw calls and number of render targets necessary with more traditional texture-space algorithms.

The next chapter is "The Skylanders SWAP Force Depth-of-Field Shader," by Michael Bukowski, Padraic Hennessy, Brian Osman, and Morgan McGuire. It describes the depth-of-field shader used in production at Vicarious Visions for the Skylanders series of games. Their technique generates very convincing near and far out-of-focus areas completely in image space without any additional scene rendering.

"Simulating Partial Occlusion in Post-Processing Depth-of-Field Methods," by David C. Schedl and Michael Wimmer, uses the ideas similar to order independent transparency methods to store multiple depth layers of the rendered scene. Having the multiple depth layers allows for more realistic rendering of the out-of-focus areas of the scene.

"Second-Depth Antialiasing," by Emil Persson, discusses a novel semi-analytical antialiasing method that uses the regular depth buffer and a new second-depth depth buffer to precisely identify the geometry edges and the amount of antialiasing they need. The author provides detailed implementation information, performance analysis, and full source code in the book's web materials.

The next chapter is "Practical Framebuffer Compression," by Pavlos Mavridis and Georgios Papaioannou. Authors describe a lossy buffer compression method based on the principles of chrominance subsampling. The method provides a practical way of reducing bandwidth and improving associated performance, which are required in the modern high-resolution games. It allows for direct rendering into two channel render targets including alpha blending. The authors discuss multiple methods of reconstruction of the regular RGB data.

"Coherence-Enhancing Filtering on the GPU," by Jan Eric Kyprianidis and Henry Kang, shows CUDA implementation of a fully automatic image filter, which aggressively smooths out the less important image regions while preserving the important features. The authors provide extensive background for the filtering along with very detailed implementation guidelines.

"Screen-Space Grass," by David Pangerl, describes an efficient and unique method for drawing background grass. This technique utilizes a very fast screen space technique and presents a novel solution to the otherwise very difficult problem of drawing many thousands or even millions of grass instances.

Next, João Raza and Gustavo Nunes present "Screen-Space Deformable Meshes via CSG with Per-Pixel Linked Lists." This chapter provides a method by which ordinary geometric meshes may be cut and deformed dynamically in screen space. The chief strength of their technique is in its generality and applicability to many interesting scenarios that come up in games and other real-time applications such as damage deformation, rigid object fracture, and destruction.

Our final chapter, "Bokeh Effects on the SPU" by Serge Bernier, offers a bokeh-style depth-of-field rendering technique that is optimized for the PS3's SPUs. Depth of field is an important visual tool in games and other interactive media. This new technique is exciting in that it provides a "next-generation" camera lens effect on a current generation platform.

Web Materials

Example programs and source code to accompany some of the chapters are available on the CRC Press website: go to https://www.crcpress.com/9781138484320 and click on the "Downloads" tab.

The directory structure follows the book structure by using the chapter numbers as the name of the subdirectory.

General System Requirements

The material presented in this book was originally published between 2010 and 2016, and the most recent developments have the following system requirements:

- The DirectX June 2010 SDK (the latest SDK is installed with Visual Studio 2012).

- DirectX 11 or DirectX 12 capable GPUs are required to run the examples. The chapter will mention the exact requirement.

- The OS should be Microsoft Windows 10, following the requirement of DirectX 11 or 12 capable GPUs.

- Visual Studio C++ 2012 (some examples might require older versions).

- 2GB RAM or more.

- The latest GPU driver.

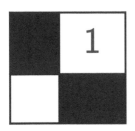

1

Anisotropic Kuwahara Filtering on the GPU

Jan Eric Kyprianidis, Henry Kang, and
Jürgen Döllner

1.1 Introduction

Photorealistic depictions often contain more information than necessary to communicate the intended information. Artists therefore typically remove detail and use abstraction for effective visual communication. A typical approach to

Figure 1.1. Original image (left). Output of the anisotropic Kuwahara filter (right). A painting-like flattening effect is generated along the local feature directions, while preserving shape boundaries.

automatically create stylized abstractions from images or videos is the use of an *edge-preserving* filter. Popular examples *of* edge-preserving filters used for image abstraction are the *bilateral* filter [Tomasi and Manduchi 98] and *mean shift* [Comaniciu and Meer 02]. Both smooth low-contrast regions while preserving high-contrast edges. Therefore they may fail for high-contrast images, where either no abstraction is performed or relevant information is removed because of the thresholds used. They also often fail for low-contrast images, where typically too much information is removed.

An edge-preserving filter that overcomes this limitation is the *Kuwahara filter* [Kuwahara et al. 76]. Based on local area flattening, the Kuwahara filter properly removes details even in a high-contrast region, and protects shape boundaries even in low-contrast regions. Hence it helps to maintain a roughly uniform level of abstraction across the image, while providing an overall painting-style look. Unfortunately the Kuwahara filter is unstable in the presence of noise and suffers from block artifacts. Several extensions and modifications have been proposed to improve the original Kuwahara filter. A discussion can be found in [Papari et al. 07].

In this chapter we present an implementation of the anisotropic Kuwahara filter [Kyprianidis et al. 09]. The anisotropic Kuwahara filter is a generalization of the Kuwahara filter that avoids artifacts by adapting shape, scale, and orientation of the filter to the local structure of the input. Due to this adaption, directional image features are better preserved and emphasized. This results in overall sharper edges and a more feature-abiding painterly effect.

1.2   Kuwahara Filtering

The general idea behind the Kuwahara filter is to divide the filter kernel into four rectangular subregions which overlap by one pixel. The filter response is then defined by the mean of a subregion with minimum variance (Figure 1.2).

Let $f\colon \mathbb{Z}^2 \longrightarrow \mathbb{R}^3$ denote the input image, let $r > 0$ be the radius of the filter and let $(x_0, y_0) \in \mathbb{Z}^2$ be a point. The rectangular subregions are then given by

$$
\begin{aligned}
W_0 &= [x_0 - r, x_0] \times [y_0, y_0 + r], \\
W_1 &= [x_0, x_0 + r] \times [y_0, y_0 + r], \\
W_2 &= [x_0, x_0 + r] \times [y_0 - r, y_0], \\
W_3 &= [x_0 - r, x_0] \times [y_0 - r, y_0].
\end{aligned}
$$

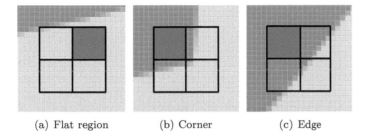

(a) Flat region   (b) Corner   (c) Edge

Figure 1.2. The Kuwahara filter divides the filter kernel into four rectangular subregions. The filter response is then defined by the mean of a subregion with minimum variance.

Let $|W_k| = (r+1)^2$ be the number of pixel in each subregion. The mean (average) of a subregion W_k is then defined as:

$$m_k = \frac{1}{|W_k|} \sum_{(x,y) \in W_k} f(x,y).$$

The variance is defined as the average of the square of the distance of each pixel to the mean:

$$
\begin{aligned}
s_k^2 &= \frac{1}{|W_k|} \sum_{(x,y) \in W_k} \big(f(x,y) - m_k\big)^2 \\
&= \frac{1}{|W_k|} \sum_{(x,y) \in W_k} f^2(x,y) - m_k.
\end{aligned}
$$

Assuming that the variances of the color channels do not correlate, we define the variance of the subregion W_k to be the sum of the squared variances of

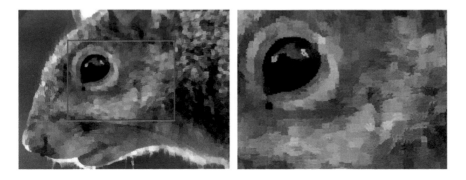

Figure 1.3. Output of the Kuwahara filter.

```glsl
uniform sampler2D src;
uniform int radius;

void main (void) {
  vec2 src_size = textureSize2D(src, 0);
  vec2 uv = gl_FragCoord.xy / src_size;
  float n = float((radius + 1) * (radius + 1));

  vec3 m[4];
  vec3 s[4];
  for (int k = 0; k < 4; ++k) {
    m[k] = vec3(0.0);
    s[k] = vec3(0.0);
  }

  struct Window { int x1, y1, x2, y2; };
  Window W[4] = Window[4](
    Window( -radius, -radius,      0,      0 ),
    Window(       0, -radius, radius,      0 ),
    Window(       0,       0, radius, radius ),
    Window( -radius,       0,      0, radius )
  );

  for (int k = 0; k < 4; ++k) {
    for (int j = W[k].y1; j <= W[k].y2; ++j) {
      for (int i = W[k].x1; i <= W[k].x2; ++i) {
        vec3 c = texture2D(src, uv + vec2(i,j) / src_size).rgb;
        m[k] += c;
        s[k] += c * c;
      }
    }
  }

  float min_sigma2 = 1e+2;
  for (int k = 0; k < 4; ++k) {
    m[k] /= n;
    s[k] = abs(s[k] / n - m[k] * m[k]);

    float sigma2 = s[k].r + s[k].g + s[k].b;
    if (sigma2 < min_sigma2) {
      min_sigma2 = sigma2;
      gl_FragColor = vec4(m[k], 1.0);
    }
  }
}
```

Listing 1.1. Fragment shader implementation of the Kuwahara filter.

the color channels:

$$\sigma_k^2 = s_{k,r}^2 + s_{k,g}^2 + s_{k,b}^2. \tag{1.1}$$

Now, the output of the Kuwahara filter is defined as the mean of a subregion with minimum variance:

$$F(x_0, y_0) := m_i, \quad i = \operatorname{argmin}_k \sigma_k.$$

In Figure 1.3 the output of an image processed with the Kuwahara filter is shown. Clearly noticeable are the artifacts in the output. These are due to the use of rectangular subregions. In addition, the subregion selection process is unstable if noise is present or subregions have the same variance. This results in randomly chosen subregions and corresponding artifacts. A more detailed discussion of limitations of the Kuwahara filter can be found in [Papari et al. 07]. An implementation of the Kuwahara filter is shown in Listing 1.1.

1.3 Generalized Kuwahara Filtering

Several attempts have been made to address the limitations of the Kuwahara filter. In this section we present an implementation of the generalized Kuwahara filter, which was first proposed in [Papari et al. 07]. To overcome the limitations of the unstable subregion selection process, a new criterion is defined. Instead of selecting a single subregion, the result is defined as the weighted sum of the means of the subregions. The weights are defined based on the variances of the subregions. This results in smoother region boundaries and fewer artifacts. To improve this further, the rectangular subregions are replaced by smooth weighting functions over sectors of a disc (Figure 1.4). As can be seen in Figure 1.5, this significantly improves the quality of the output.

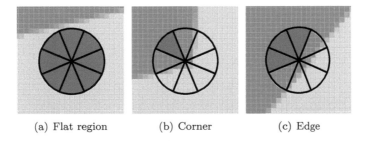

(a) Flat region   (b) Corner   (c) Edge

Figure 1.4.   The generalized Kuwahara filter uses weighting functions defined over sectors of a disc. The filter response is defined as a weighed sum of the local averages, where more weight is given to those averages with low standard deviation.

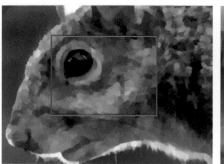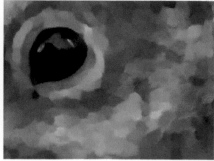

Figure 1.5. Output of the generalized Kuwahara filter.

We begin with the construction of the weighting functions. We divide the plane into N equal sectors by defining characteristic functions which are 1 over the sector and 0 otherwise:

$$\chi_k(x,y) = \begin{cases} 1 & \frac{(2k-1)\pi}{N} < \arg(x,y) \le \frac{(2k+1)\pi}{N} \\ 0 & \text{otherwise} \end{cases} \quad k = 0, \ldots, N-1.$$

Let

$$G_\sigma(x,y) = \frac{1}{2\pi\sigma^2} \exp\left(-\frac{x^2 + y^2}{2\sigma^2}\right)$$

be the Gaussian with standard deviation σ. To define smooth weighting functions, the characteristic functions of the different sectors χ_k are first convolved and then multiplied with a Gaussian:

$$w_k = \left(\chi_k \star G_{\sigma_s}\right) \cdot G_{\sigma_r} \tag{1.2}$$

The convolution smooths the characteristic functions such that they slightly overlap. The multiplication achieves a decay with increasing radius. Since $\sum_k w_k(x,y) = G_{\sigma_r}(x,y)$ for $(x,y) \in \mathbb{Z}^2$ the sum of the w_k is equivalent to a Gaussian filter.

Let f denote the input image. The weighted mean at a point $(x_0, y_0) \in \mathbb{Z}^2$ is then defined by

$$m_k = \sum_{(x,y)\in\mathbb{Z}^2} f(x,y)\, w_k(x - x_0, y - y_0),$$

and the weighted variance is given by

$$s_k^2 = \sum_{(x,y)\in\mathbb{Z}^2} \left(f(x,y) - m_k\right)^2 w_k(x - x_0, y - y_0)$$

$$= \sum_{(x,y)\in\mathbb{Z}^2} f^2(x,y)\, w_k(x - x_0, y - y_0) - m_k.$$

```
uniform sampler2D src;
uniform sampler2D K0;
uniform int N;
uniform int radius;
uniform float q;

const float PI = 3.14159265358979323846;

void main (void) {
  vec2 src_size = textureSize2D(src, 0);
  vec2 uv = gl_FragCoord.xy / src_size;

  vec4 m[8];
  vec3 s[8];
  for (int k = 0; k < N; ++k) {
    m[k] = vec4(0.0);
    s[k] = vec3(0.0);
  }

  float piN = 2.0 * PI / float(N);
  mat2 X = mat2(cos(piN), sin(piN), -sin(piN), cos(piN));

  for ( int j = -radius; j <= radius; ++j ) {
    for ( int i = -radius; i <= radius; ++i ) {
      vec2 v = 0.5 * vec2(i,j) / float(radius);
      if (dot(v,v) <= 0.25) {
        vec3 c = texture2D(src, uv + vec2(i,j) / src_size).rgb;
        for (int k = 0; k < N; ++k) {
          float w = texture2D(K0, vec2(0.5, 0.5) + v).x;

          m[k] += vec4(c * w, w);
          s[k] += c * c * w;

          v *= X;
        }
      }
    }
  }

  vec4 o = vec4(0.0);
  for (int k = 0; k < N; ++k) {
    m[k].rgb /= m[k].w;
    s[k] = abs(s[k] / m[k].w - m[k].rgb * m[k].rgb);

    float sigma2 = s[k].r + s[k].g + s[k].b;
    float w = 1.0 / (1.0 + pow(255.0 * sigma2, 0.5 * q));

    o += vec4(m[k].rgb * w, w);
  }
  gl_FragColor = vec4(o.rgb / o.w, 1.0);
}
```

Listing 1.2. Fragment shader implementation of the generalized Kuwahara filter.

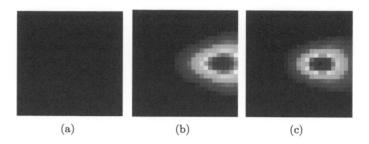

$$\text{(a)} \qquad\qquad\qquad\qquad \text{(b)} \qquad\qquad\qquad\qquad \text{(c)}$$

Figure 1.6. Approximation of the weighting function w_0 for $N = 8$: (a) characteristic function χ_0; (b) characteristic function χ_0 convolved with Gaussian function G_{σ_s}; (c) finally, multiplication with Gaussian function G_{σ_r}.

Let σ be defined as in Equation (1.1). We set

$$\alpha_k = \frac{1}{1 + \left(255 \cdot \sigma_k^2 \right)^{q/2}},$$

and define the output of the filter by

$$F(x_0, y_0) := \frac{\sum_k \alpha_k \, m_k}{\sum_k \alpha_k}. \tag{1.3}$$

The definition of the weighting factors α_k ensures that more weight is given to sectors with low standard deviation, i.e., those that are more homogeneous. This is similar to the approach of [Papari et al. 07], but avoids the indetermination, when some of the s_k are zero. The parameter q controls the sharpness of the output. We use $q = 8$ in our examples.

The weighting functions w_k are difficult to compute, because their computation requires convolution. A closed form solution is currently not known. Since the w_k do not depend on the pixel location, a straight forward approach would be to precompute them. We use a slightly different approach in our implementation, where all w_k are derived by bilinear sampling a texture map. We use this approach because it will easily generalize to anisotropic filtering which will be discussed in the next section. Let

$$R_\varphi = \begin{pmatrix} \cos\varphi & -\sin\varphi \\ \sin\varphi & \cos\varphi \end{pmatrix}.$$

be the rotation matrix that performs a rotation by the angle φ in counter-clockwise order. Since $\chi_k = \chi_0 \circ R_{-2\pi k/N}$, and since Gaussian functions are rotational invariant, we have

$$w_k = \left((\chi_0 \star G_{\sigma_s}) \cdot G_{\sigma_r} \right) \circ R_{-2\pi k/N}$$
$$= w_0 \circ R_{-2\pi k/N}.$$

Here, $\circ$ denotes composition of functions. For our implementation (Listing 1.2) we sample w_0 into a texture map K_0 of size 32×32. The sampling is performed using Equation (1.2) with

$$\sigma_r = \frac{1}{2} \cdot \frac{K_{\text{size}} - 1}{2} = 7.75,$$
$$\sigma_s = 0.33 \cdot \sigma_r,$$

and the origin moved to the center of the texture map. Figure 1.6 illustrates the different steps of the computation. Now suppose that $r > 0$ denotes the desired filter radius. Then the weighting functions w_k can be approximated by

$$w_k(x,y) = K_0 \left(\begin{pmatrix} 0.5 \\ 0.5 \end{pmatrix} + \frac{R_{-2\pi k/N}(x,y)}{2r} \right).$$

1.4   Anisotropic Kuwahara Filtering

The generalized Kuwahara filter fails to capture directional features and results in clustering artifacts. The anisotropic Kuwahara filter addresses these limitations by adapting the filter to the local structure of the input. In homogeneous regions the shape of the filter should be a circle, while in anisotropic regions the filter should become an ellipse whose major axis is aligned with the principal direction of image features (Figure 1.7). As can be seen in Figure 1.8, this avoids clustering and moreover creates a painterly look for directional image features (Figure 1.1).

Figure 1.9 shows an overview of the algorithm. We begin with calculating the structure tensor and smooth it with a Gaussian filter. Local orientation and a measure for the anisotropy are then derived from the eigenvalues and eigenvectors of the smoothed structure tensor. Finally, the actual filtering is performed.

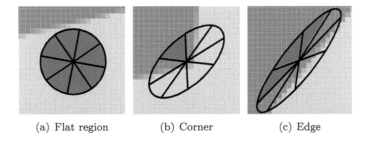

(a) Flat region   (b) Corner   (c) Edge

Figure 1.7. The anisotropic Kuwahara filter uses weighting functions defined over an ellipse, whose shape is based on the local orientation and anisotropy. The filter response is defined as a weighed sum of the local averages, where more weight is given to those averages with low standard deviation.

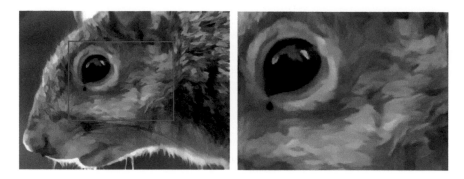

Figure 1.8. Output of the anisotropic Kuwahara filter.

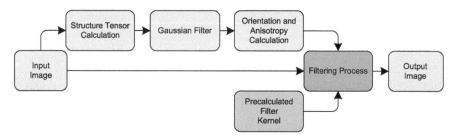

Figure 1.9. Schematic overview of the anisotropic Kuwahara filter.

1.4.1   Orientation and Anisotropy Estimation

The local orientation and anisotropy estimation is based on the *eigenvalues* and *eigenvectors* of the structure tensor [Brox et al. 06]. We calculate the structure tensor directly from the RGB values of the input [Kyprianidis and Döllner 08]. Let f be the input image and let

$$S_x = \frac{1}{4}\begin{pmatrix} +1 & 0 & -1 \\ +2 & 0 & -2 \\ +1 & 0 & -1 \end{pmatrix} \quad \text{and} \quad S_y = \frac{1}{4}\begin{pmatrix} +1 & +2 & +1 \\ 0 & 0 & 0 \\ -1 & -2 & -1 \end{pmatrix}$$

be the horizontal and vertical convolution masks of the Sobel filter. Then, approximations of the partial derivatives of f can be calculated by

$$f_x = S_x \star f \quad \text{and} \quad f_y = S_y \star f,$$

where $\star$ denotes convolution. The structure tensor of f is then defined by

$$(g_{ij}) = \begin{pmatrix} f_x \cdot f_x & f_x \cdot f_y \\ f_x \cdot f_y & f_y \cdot f_y \end{pmatrix} =: \begin{pmatrix} E & F \\ F & G \end{pmatrix}.$$

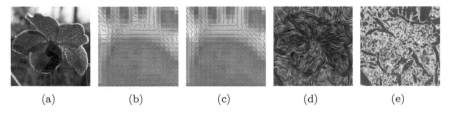

(a)   (b)   (c)   (d)   (e)

Figure 1.10. (a) Original image. (b) Eigenvectors of the structure tensor. (c) Eigenvectors of the smoothed structure tensor. (d) Visualization of the eigenvectors of the smoothed structure tensor using line integral convolution. (e) Anisotropy (blue=low, red=high).

Here, · denotes the scalar product. The eigenvalues of the structure tensor correspond to the squared minimum and maximum rate of change of f. The eigenvectors correspond to the respective directions. Selecting the eigenvector corresponding to the minimum rate of change gives a vector field. As shown in Figure 1.10(b) this vector field has discontinuities. In order to smooth the vector field, smoothing of the structure tensor is performed. The result of applying a Gaussian filter is shown in Figure 1.10(c). Smoothing the structure tensor is a linear operation on the tensor, but the effect on the eigenvectors is highly nonlinear and corresponds geometrically to principal component analysis. In our examples, we use a Gaussian filter with standard deviation $\sigma = 2.0$. Note that we do not normalize the tensor. Therefore, structure tensors corresponding to edges with large gradient magnitude get more weight during smoothing. Hence, orientation information of edges is distributed into the neighborhood of the edges (Figure 1.10(d)).

The eigenvalues of the structure tensor are non-negative real numbers and are given by

$$\lambda_{1,2} = \frac{E + G \pm \sqrt{(E - G)^2 + 4F^2}}{2}.$$

The eigenvector oriented in direction of the minimum rate of change is given by

$$t = \begin{pmatrix} \lambda_1 - E \\ -F \end{pmatrix}.$$

We define local orientation by

$$\varphi = \arg t.$$

To measure the amount of anisotropy, we use the approach proposed in [Yang et al. 96]:

$$A = \frac{\lambda_1 - \lambda_2}{\lambda_1 + \lambda_2}.$$

The anisotropy A ranges from 0 to 1, where 0 corresponds to isotropic and 1 corresponds to entirely anisotropic regions (Figure 1.10(e)).

```
uniform sampler2D src;

void main (void) {
  vec2 src_size = textureSize2D(src, 0);
  vec2 uv = gl_FragCoord.xy / src_size;
  vec2 d = 1.0 / src_size;

  vec3 c = texture2D(src, uv).xyz;
  vec3 u = (
            -1.0 * texture2D(src, uv + vec2(-d.x,  -d.y)).xyz +
            -2.0 * texture2D(src, uv + vec2(-d.x,   0.0)).xyz +
            -1.0 * texture2D(src, uv + vec2(-d.x,   d.y)).xyz +
            +1.0 * texture2D(src, uv + vec2( d.x,  -d.y)).xyz +
            +2.0 * texture2D(src, uv + vec2( d.x,   0.0)).xyz +
            +1.0 * texture2D(src, uv + vec2( d.x,   d.y)).xyz
           ) / 4.0;

  vec3 v = (
            -1.0 * texture2D(src, uv + vec2(-d.x,  -d.y)).xyz +
            -2.0 * texture2D(src, uv + vec2( 0.0,  -d.y)).xyz +
            -1.0 * texture2D(src, uv + vec2( d.x,  -d.y)).xyz +
            +1.0 * texture2D(src, uv + vec2(-d.x,   d.y)).xyz +
            +2.0 * texture2D(src, uv + vec2( 0.0,   d.y)).xyz +
            +1.0 * texture2D(src, uv + vec2( d.x,   d.y)).xyz
           ) / 4.0;

  gl_FragColor = vec4(dot(u, u), dot(v, v), dot(u, v), 1.0);
}
```

Listing 1.3. Fragment shader for calculating the structure tensor.

1.4.2   Filtering Process

The filtering is performed using the ideas from the previous section, but with redefined weighting functions.

We begin with calculating the bounding rectangle of an ellipse. An axis-aligned ellipse with major axis a and minor axis b is defined by

$$\frac{x^2}{a^2} + \frac{y^2}{b^2} = 1.$$

By rotating x and y by an angle φ we get the equation of a rotated ellipse:

$$\frac{(x\cos\varphi - y\sin\varphi)^2}{a^2} + \frac{(x\sin\varphi + y\cos\varphi)^2}{b^2} = 1.$$

This is a quadratic polynomial in two variables and by expanding and collecting terms it can be rewritten in normalized form:

$$P(x,y) = Ax^2 + By^2 + Cx + Dy + Exy + F = 0, \tag{1.4}$$

```
uniform sampler2D src;

void main (void) {
  vec2 uv = gl_FragCoord.xy / textureSize2D(src, 0);
  vec3 g = texture2D(src, uv).xyz;

  float lambda1 = 0.5 * (g.y + g.x +
      sqrt(g.y*g.y - 2.0*g.x*g.y + g.x*g.x + 4.0*g.z*g.z));
  float lambda2 = 0.5 * (g.y + g.x -
      sqrt(g.y*g.y - 2.0*g.x*g.y + g.x*g.x + 4.0*g.z*g.z));

  vec2 v = vec2(lambda1 - g.x, -g.z);
  vec2 t;
  if (length(v) > 0.0) {
    t = normalize(v);
  } else {
    t = vec2(0.0, 1.0);
  }

  float phi = atan(t.y, t.x);

  float A = (lambda1 + lambda2 > 0.0)?
    (lambda1 - lambda2) / (lambda1 + lambda2) : 0.0;

  gl_FragColor = vec4(t, phi, A);
}
```

Listing 1.4. Fragment shader for calculating the local orientation and anisotropy.

with

$$
\begin{aligned}
A &= a^2 \sin^2 \varphi + b^2 \cos^2 \varphi, \\
B &= a^2 \cos^2 \varphi + b^2 \sin^2 \varphi, \\
C &= 0, \\
D &= 0, \\
E &= 2(a^2 - b^2) \sin \varphi \cos \varphi, \\
F &= -a^2 b^2.
\end{aligned}
$$

The horizontal extrema are located where the partial derivative in the y-direction vanishes:

$$
\frac{\partial P}{\partial y} = 2By + Ex = 0 \quad \Leftrightarrow \quad y = \frac{-Ex}{2B}.
$$

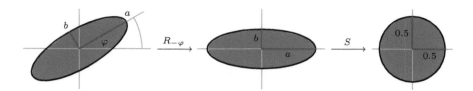

Figure 1.11. The mapping $SR_{-\varphi}$ defines a linear coordinate transform that maps an ellipse defined by major axis a, minor axis b and angle φ to a disc with radius 0.5.

```
vec4 t = texture2D(tfm, uv);
float a = radius * clamp((alpha + t.w) / alpha, 0.1, 2.0);
float b = radius * clamp(alpha / (alpha + t.w), 0.1, 2.0);

float cos_phi = cos(t.z);
float sin_phi = sin(t.z);

mat2 R = mat2(cos_phi, -sin_phi, sin_phi, cos_phi);
mat2 S = mat2(0.5/a, 0.0, 0.0, 0.5/b);
mat2 SR = S * R;

int max_x = int(sqrt(a*a * cos_phi*cos_phi +
                     b*b * sin_phi*sin_phi));
int max_y = int(sqrt(a*a * sin_phi*sin_phi +
                     b*b * cos_phi*cos_phi));

for (int j = -max_y; j <= max_y; ++j) {
  for (int i = -max_x; i <= max_x; ++i) {
    vec2 v = SR * vec2(i,j);
    if (dot(v,v) <= 0.25) {
      vec3 c = texture2D(src, uv + vec2(i,j) / src_size).rgb;
      for (int k = 0; k < N; ++k) {
        float w = texture2D(K0, vec2(0.5, 0.5) + v).x;

        m[k] += vec4(c * w, w);
        s[k] += c * c * w;

        v *= X;
      }
    }
  }
}.
```

Listing 1.5. Fragment shader implementation of the variance computation of the anisotropic Kuwahara filter.

Substituting y into Equation (1.4) yields

$$\left(A - \frac{E^2}{4B}\right)x^2 + F = 0.$$

The horizontal extrema of the ellipse are therefore given by

$$x = \pm\sqrt{\frac{F}{\frac{E^2}{4B} - A}} = \pm\sqrt{a^2\cos^2\varphi + b^2\sin^2\varphi}.$$

A similar calculation gives the vertical extrema:

$$y = \pm\sqrt{a^2\sin^2\varphi + b^2\cos^2\varphi}.$$

Suppose $r > 0$ is the desired filter radius. Let φ be the local orientation and let A be the anisotropy as defined in the previous section. We use the method proposed in [Pham 06] to define an elliptical filter shape. To adjust the eccentricity depending on the amount of anisotropy, we set

$$a = \frac{\alpha + A}{\alpha}r \quad \text{and} \quad b = \frac{\alpha}{\alpha + A}r.$$

The parameter $\alpha > 0$ is a tuning parameter. For $\alpha \to \infty$ the major axis a and the minor axis b converge to 1. We use $\alpha = 1$ in all examples, which results in a maximum eccentricity of 4. The ellipse defined by a, b and φ has its major axis aligned to the local image orientation. It has high eccentricity in anisotropic regions and becomes a circle in isotropic regions.

Now let

$$S = \begin{pmatrix} \frac{1}{2a} & 0 \\ 0 & \frac{1}{2b} \end{pmatrix},$$

then the mapping $SR_{-\varphi}$ maps points from the ellipse to a disc of radius 0.5 (Figure 1.11). Hence, the weighting functions over the ellipse can be defined by:

$$w_k(x,y) = K_0\left(\begin{pmatrix} 0.5 \\ 0.5 \end{pmatrix} + R_{-2\pi k/N}SR_{-\varphi}(x,y)\right).$$

The filter response is defined as in the case of the generalized Kuwahara filter by Equation (1.3).

The implementation of the anisotropic Kuwahara filter is very similar to the implementation of the generalized Kuwahara filter (Listing 1.2). Therefore, only the variance computation of the anisotropic Kuwahara filter is shown in Listing 1.5. In Listing 1.6 an optimized variance computation for $N = 8$ is shown.

```
{
  vec3 c = texture2D(src, uv).rgb;
  float w = texture2D(K0123, vec2(0.5, 0.5)).x;
  for (int k = 0; k < N; ++k) {
    m[k] += vec4(c * w, w);
    s[k] += c * c * w;
  }
}

for (int j = 0; j <= max_y; ++j) {
  for (int i = -max_x; i <= max_x; ++i) {

    if ((j !=0) || (i > 0)) {
      vec2 v = SR * vec2(i,j);

      if (dot(v,v) <= 0.25) {
        vec3 c0 = texture2D(src,uv + vec2(i,j)/src_size).rgb;
        vec3 c1 = texture2D(src,uv - vec2(i,j)/src_size).rgb;

        vec3 cc0 = c0 * c0;
        vec3 cc1 = c1 * c1;

        vec4 w0123 = texture2D(K0123, vec2(0.5, 0.5) + v);
        for (int k = 0; k < 4; ++k) {
          m[k] += vec4(c0 * w0123[k], w0123[k]);
          s[k] += cc0 * w0123[k];

          m[k+4] += vec4(c1 * w0123[k], w0123[k]);
          s[k+4] += cc1 * w0123[k];
        }

        vec4 w4567 = texture2D(K0123, vec2(0.5, 0.5) - v);
        for (int k = 0; k < 4; ++k) {
          m[k+4] += vec4(c0 * w4567[k], w4567[k]);
          s[k+4] += cc0 * w4567[k];

          m[k] += vec4(c1 * w4567[k], w4567[k]);
          s[k] += cc1 * w4567[k];
        }
      }
    }

  }
}
```

Listing 1.6. Fragment shader implementation of the variance computation of the anisotropic Kuwahara filter (optimized for $N = 8$).

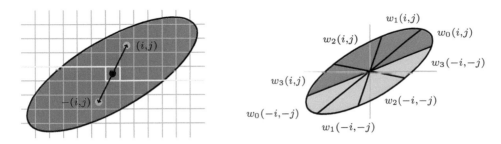

Figure 1.12. Symmetry about the origin of an ellipse (left). For $N = 8$ the values of the weighting functions can be fetched using two RGBA texture lookups (right).

In order to reduce the number of texture lookups, four weights are packed into a RGBA texture map. This texture map is constructed by sampling the weighting functions $w_0,...,w_3$ from section 1.3 as explained. Furthermore, the property of the ellipse being symmetric about the origin is used (Figure 1.12). Note that for $N = 8$ and $k = 0, \ldots, 3$ we have

$$w_{k+4}(x, y) = w_k(-x, -y).$$

1.5 Conclusion

In this chapter we have presented a GPU implementation of the anisotropic Kuwahara filter. Guided by the smoothed structure tensor, the anisotropic Kuwahara filter generates a feature-preserving, direction-enhancing look.

Unlike existing nonlinear smoothing filters, the anisotropic Kuwahara filter is robust against high-contrast noise and avoids overblurring in low-contrast areas, providing a consistent level of abstraction across the image. It also ensures outstanding temporal coherence when applied to video, even with per-frame filtering.

Acknowledgments

This work was supported by the German Research Foundation (DFG), Grant DO 697/5-1.

Original photographs from flickr.com kindly provided under Creative Commons license by Keven Law (Figures 1.3, 1.5, 1.8) and Tambako the Jaguar (Figure 1.1).

Bibliography

[Brox et al. 06] T. Brox, R. Boomgaard, F. Lauze, J. Weijer, J. Weickert, P. Mrázek, and P. Kornprobst. "Adaptive Structure Tensors and Their Applications." In *Visualization and Processing of Tensor Fields*, pp. 17–47. Springer, 2006.

[Comaniciu and Meer 02] D. Comaniciu and P. Meer. "Mean Shift: A Robust Approach Toward Feature Space Analysis." *IEEE Transactions on Pattern Analysis and Machine Intelligence* 24:5 (2002), 603–619.

[Kuwahara et al. 76] M. Kuwahara, K. Hachimura, S. Eiho, and M. Kinoshita. *Digital Processing of Biomedical Images*, pp. 187–203. Plenum Press, 1976.

[Kyprianidis and Döllner 08] J. E. Kyprianidis and J. Döllner. "Image Abstraction by Structure Adaptive Filtering." In *Proc. EG UK Theory and Practice of Computer Graphics*, pp. 51–58. Eurographics Association, 2008.

[Kyprianidis et al. 09] J. E. Kyprianidis, H. Kang, and J. Döllner. "Image and Video Abstraction by Anisotropic Kuwahara Filtering." *Computer Graphics Forum* 28:7. Special Issue on Pacific Graphics 2009.

[Papari et al. 07] G. Papari, N. Petkov, and P. Campisi. "Artistic Edge and Corner Enhancing Smoothing." *IEEE Transactions on Image Processing* 16:10 (2007), 2449–2462.

[Pham 06] T. Q. Pham. "Spatiotonal Adaptivity in Super-Resolution of Undersampled Image Sequences." Ph.D. thesis, Quantitative Imaging Group, Delft University of Technology, 2006.

[Tomasi and Manduchi 98] C. Tomasi and R. Manduchi. "Bilateral Filtering for Gray and Color Images." In *Proceedings International Conference on Computer Vision (ICCV)*, pp. 839–846, 1998.

[Yang et al. 96] G. Z. Yang, P. Burger, D. N. Firmin, and S. R. Underwood. "Structure Adaptive Anisotropic Image Filtering." *Image and Vision Computing* 14:2 (1996), 135–145.

Edge Antialiasing by
Post-Processing
Hugh Malan

2.1 Introduction

Antialiasing is critical for high quality rendering. For instance, high quality CG prioritizes antialiasing quality, and game "screenshots" produced for print and PR purposes are usually rendered with artificially high levels of super-sampling to improve image quality.

Hardware multi-sampled antialiasing (MSAA) [Kirkland 99] support is the standard way to implement antialiasing, but it is a very expensive way to achieve high quality antialiasing and offers little assistance for antialiasing deferred effects. This chapter introduces a new method for antialiasing edges by selective pixel blending. It requires a fraction of the space needed for MSAA, and is compatible with deferred effects.

2.1.1 Problems

Using deferred shading for shadows, localized lighting and decals is a very attractive option, but it will introduce aliasing problems if these effects are computed using a single depth or position value per pixel. For example, deferred effects that are partly occluded by geometry will introduce aliasing along the silhouette edge. Since deferred effects have a large per-sample cost, super-sampling them is often prohibitively expensive. Killzone 2 uses $2\times$ super-sampling [Valient 07]; many titles apply deferred effects with no super-sampling (e.g., many Unreal Engine 3 titles).

Hardware support for MSAA is now standard. Modern GPUs offer a variety of MSAA options such as quincunx [Kilgard 01, Young 07]. The downside to MSAA is that the frame buffer memory and bandwidth requirements scale in

Figure 2.1. Example image, antialiased using our method, with close-ups.

proportion to the number of samples, so high sample numbers are very costly. Recent graphics hardware can support up to 16×MSAA [NVIDIA 08] but 16× the frame buffer memory and fill rate is a very high price, implying a correspondingly high opportunity cost. The requirements also scale with the per-pixel size, so a multi-sampled fat frame buffer can be extraordinarily expensive. Tabula Rasa quoted a size of 50MB for a 1024 × 768 frame buffer with no super-sampling [Koonce 07]; Killzone 2's frame buffer is 1280 × 720 with 2×MSAA and requires 37MB [Valient 07]. So using MSAA to achieve high quality antialiasing is extremely expensive in terms of memory size and bandwidth.

On current console hardware, frame buffer size limitations mean that there is a substantial cost for implementing even 1280 × 720 at 2×MSAA, so many games run at a lower resolution (*Call of Duty* series) or with MSAA disabled (*Halo 3*) [Beyond3D 09].

This chapter describes a new approach that can efficiently provide high-quality edge antialiasing for real-time three-dimensional applications. It applies to deferred effects and allows MSAA to be disabled. The technique duplicates the subtle pixel-wide gradients on edges due to varying coverage that appear in high quality antialiased renderings. It requires no additional geometry or additional passes.

Our method is executed in two stages. First, the image is rendered without any kind of multisampling or super-sampling. As part of the render hints about proximity to the silhouette edge are written out to the frame buffer. A post-processing pass is then applied, which uses these hints to update the edge pixels to provide antialiasing. Applying the post-process after rendering deferred effects means they will receive edge antialiasing. Figure 2.1 shows the method in action.

The central component of this approach provides pixel shaders with an efficient method for computing the location of the nearest silhouette edge. This technique can also applied to shadow map magnification, and provides a method for upscaling that preserves sharp edges.

2.1.2 Related Work

One strategy for minimizing edge antialiasing problems with deferred effects is to use forward rendering with MSAA enabled to render the majority of the objects and lighting, and use the bare minimum set of deferred effects so the majority of edges will be antialiased.

In cases where deferred effects affect the majority of pixels, this strategy offers no advantage. [Shishkovtso 05] presents a method for selective edge blurring (employed in S.T.A.L.K.E.R.), where the depth and normal buffers are searched for discontinuities and the relevant pixels blurred. This method softens edges but leaves all other pixels untouched so the image as a whole is not softened.

However, without sub-pixel-accurate coverage information, high quality antialiasing effects are impossible. Along the edge of an object in a highly supersampled image, the pixels will be a combination of the background (occluded object) color and foreground (occluding object) color; the degree of blend between the two colors depends on how much the polygon covers the square corresponding to that pixel. Hence the requirement for coverage information.

DirectX 10.1 allows deferred effects to read from the individual samples of the multi-sampled depth buffer, so the code applying a deferred effect can detect edge pixels and enable super-sampling for those cases only [Huddy 08].

The solution outlined in the introduction requires the pixel shader to accurately calculate the location of the nearest silhouette edge. There are no good ways to efficiently find the mathematically correct answer; we take a different approach (i.e., cheat) to avoid this problem, and create robust silhouettes without the need for any new geometry.

A second problem is due to the hardware rasterizer. Given a triangle, rasterizers write to only the pixels whose centers are within that triangle. In the ideal antialiased image, any pixels that overlap the triangle will be affected by it. In Figure 2.2, three pixels that have their centers outside the triangle still overlap it. If we render them in the usual way, the three pixels will not be affected. In general, half the pixels affected by MSAA will have centers outside the triangle, and if they are ignored it will substantially degrade antialiasing quality.

In Section 2.2, we present a method that addresses both these problems, and in Section 2.3 we describe the post-process stage. After covering the role it provides, we work back to its data requirements, and then discuss how shaders

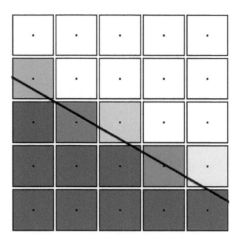

Figure 2.2. The diagonal black line marks the edge of a triangle. The area covered by each pixel is represented by squares, with black dots indicating their centers. They are shaded to indicate coverage: the darker the color, the greater the fraction of its area covered by the triangle. Several pixels have centers outside the triangle but still overlap it; they should be affected by the triangle but the rasterizer will not write to them.

can encode this information in the frame buffer. In Section 2.4 we list the known problems with the basic method, and provide some solutions. In Section 2.5 we cover implementation details.

2.2 Finding the Nearest Silhouette Edge

It is helpful to define some terms before describing the details of the solution. Let the *outward vector* of a vertex be the normalized, weighted average of the surface normals of all the triangles that meet at that point [Thürmer 98]. A *silhouette edge* is an edge shared by a back-facing and front-facing triangle.

The two problems described in the introduction were that the silhouette edge may be topologically distant from the current triangle, and that the rasterizer will not write to pixels that overlap the triangle, but have centers outside it.

Our solution to both these problems is to offset any vertex that has at least one back-facing triangle adjoining it outward, far enough to render at least an additional k-pixel border around the object. (Of course, the adjoining-back-face test result and offset vector must be the same for all coincident vertices to prevent the model splitting apart.)

Figure 2.3 shows how the vertex offset works in cross-section, with a one-pixel offset. This operation addresses both the problems described above. First, by

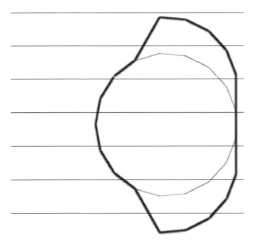

Figure 2.3. All vertices that adjoin a back-facing triangle are offset by one pixel. The regular horizontal lines indicate the view direction: the eye is some distance to the left, looking right. The original geometry is indicated by the thin black lines. After the vertices have been extruded, the geometry forms the shape indicated by the thick black lines.

offsetting vertices in this manner we render an additional set of pixels bordering the original geometry; if $k >= \sqrt{1/2}$ then the additional pixels will include all those that overlap the original geometry. Second, if we render the geometry with back-face culling enabled we can be confident that any rendered pixel closer than k pixels to the silhouette will be within a triangle with at least one vertex on the silhouette edge. To put it another way, the problem of finding the silhouette edge is avoided by explicitly forming the silhouette through this geometry change.

The per-vertex offset that meets these requirements could be found by finding the silhouette edges that meet at the vertex (which may be >2), express them in screen space, translate them outwards by k pixels, and find the appropriate intersection.

However, if the geometry can be assumed to never have creases sharper than 90 degrees, then simply offsetting by a distance of $k\sqrt{2}$ pixels is acceptable. In this case, the per-vertex offset may be found by projecting the outward vector defined above into screen space, setting $Z=0$ (to project to the screen plane), normalizing it, scaling it to account for screen resolution, and then scaling by the required pixel count of $k\sqrt{2}$. We will set $k >= 1$ for reasons described in the next section.

One extremely useful benefit of the explicitly formed silhouette is that it allows the test determining whether to offset the vertex to be inaccurate without the silhouette shape being damaged. In Figure 2.3, imagine that a vertex closer to the viewer incorrectly passed the adjoining-back-face test, or that the silhouette vertices incorrectly failed that test. In both cases, a slightly reduced silhouette is still present.

In comparison, offsetting only the vertices adjoining a silhouette edge is fragile: missing a single silhouette vertex will noticeably damage the silhouette shape.

The vertex program outputs the variable `silhouetteParameter`:   0 if the vertex has been offset, and 1 if it has not. If back-face culling is enabled, the only time the interpolated value will be other than 1 is if the pixel is within a triangle with at least one vertex on the silhouette edge.

The interpolated value of `silhouetteParameter` bears some resemblance to distance: it will be 0.0 on the silhouette edge and increases towards the interior. However, the interior vertex or vertices of the triangle may be just outside the border region or quite some distance away, so the distance from the border is not a function of `silhouetteParameter`.

However, it is possible to compute the partial derivatives of `silhouette Parameter` in screen space using the `ddx/ddy` or `dFdx/dFdy` instructions in DirectX and OpenGL, respectively. With this information we can estimate the number of pixels to the silhouette edge horizontally and vertically. If `ddx(silhouette Parameter)` and `ddy(silhouetteParameter)` are the screen-space partial derivatives of `silhouetteParameter` then the estimated number of pixels to the silhouette edge horizontally is:

$$\text{hdist} = -\text{silhouetteParameter}/\text{ddx(silhouetteParameter)}$$

and vertically is:

$$\text{vdist} = -\text{silhouetteParameter}/\text{ddy(silhouetteParameter)}.[1]$$

From these two values we can compute an approximation of the position of or vector to the nearest point on the silhouette edge, and write it to the frame buffer if required. At this point we will consider the post-process step, and return to the issue of what data should be written into the frame buffer later.

---

[1] Since `silhouetteParameter` will be interpolated across the triangle accounting for perspective correction, its value will not be a linear function of screen-space position and so using the formula above will not give a precisely correct result. Also, for triangles with only one vertex on the silhouette edge, the formula will imply that the silhouette edge is parallel to the line connecting the two non-silhouette vertices of the triangle, which can be a completely incorrect assumption. So this method will not provide the mathematically correct result, but it is adequate for our needs.

2.3   The Post-Process

The overall goal for this technique is for geometry edges to appear to be super-sampled. Pixels that overlap a silhouette edge should be a blend of the colors of the relevant objects, weighted by coverage.

For now, we will only consider the simplest case where a pixel has a single silhouette edge passing through it. Since we have rendered the frame buffer without any kind of super-sampling or multisampling, the color of a pixel is completely due to a single object: this will be called the *foreground color*. If the contributing triangle were not rendered, the pixel would be shaded differently; this new color is called the *background color*.

If we are restricting ourselves to a standard frame buffer holding only a single color per pixel, as opposed to some kind of deep frame buffer, there is no way to know the actual foreground and background color at a pixel. We can approximate the background color by sampling one of those pixels' neighbors. The further away the chosen neighbor is, the lower the correlation between the neighbor's color and actual background color.

From the method described in Section 2.2, for each pixel we have sub-pixel-accurate values for the number of horizontal and vertical pixels to the silhouette edge. With this information we can infer the location and direction of the (estimated) silhouette edge.[2]

If we are to restrict sampling to an immediate neighbor (N, NE, E, SE, etc.), the post-process can only affect pixels on the very border of the object (see Figure 2.4: the hatched pixels are the only ones that can be affected).

The relevant pixels are those for which the horizontal or vertical distance to the edge is less than one pixel, i.e., `min(abs(hdist), abs(vdist))`<1.0, if `hdist` and `vdist` are the horizontal and vertical distances defined above. Given this restriction, it is natural to let the blend factor between foreground and background colors be given by the same equation:

$$\texttt{blendfactor=min(abs(hdist), abs(vdist)).}$$

This choice means the minimum value for k is 1 in the vertex offset discussion in Section 2.2; values any greater than this will simply grow the object without affecting the edge quality.

Pixels approaching the edge will be progressively more affected by the background color; pixels whose centers are only just inside the triangle will have a color very close to the background color. As can be seen in the example images, the blur turns jagged stair-stepped edges into a series of smooth pixel-wide gradients.

---

[2]Actually we get the location of the edge produced by the vertex offset operation, which is k pixels outwards from the silhouette edge that would have been rendered with the original geometry.

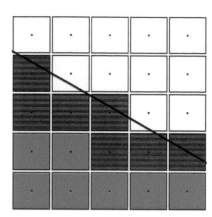

Figure 2.4.   Hatched squares correspond to pixels that have an immediate neighbor over the edge. This image is based on Figure 2.2; the black line indicates the new the triangle edge after the vertex offset operation.

Given a blend factor less than one, the next question is which neighbour pixel should be sampled to find the approximate background color (see Figure 2.4: there are many places where the only option is a diagonally adjacent neighbour. Therefore, one easy option is to choose the neighbour at (`sign(hdist)`, `sign(vdist)`). This will sample diagonally unless the edge is precisely parallel to the X or Y-axis).

In principle we could calculate the (estimated) location and direction of the silhouette edge for the original geometry, and proceed to calculate an estimate of the coverage value with an arbitrary pixel filter function, to use for blending the foreground and background color. We will ignore this for two reasons. First, the background color is being approximated by sampling one of its neighbors, and the quality of that approximation dramatically degrades with distance. Restricting the sample to an immediate neighbor is the safest option. Second, the post-process operation is speed-critical, so long calculations will directly impact frame rate.

Given `hdist` and `vdist`, pseudocode for the post-process step is as follows:

```
colbase=sourceImage[pixelPos.x, pixelPos.y];
colneb=sourceImage[pixelPos.x+sign(hdist),
                   pixelPos.y+sign(vdist)];
blendfactor=min(abs(hdist), abs(vdist));
colfinal=lerp(colneb, colbase, blendfactor);
```

The `lerp` will output `colneb` if `blendfactor=0`; it blends to `colbase` as blendfactor increases, and will implicitly clamp blendfactor values >1. Then `colfinal` is written out to the target image.

Now that the post-process requirements are known, we will move to the question of what is stored in the frame buffer. Since any additional per-pixel data will make proportionate demands on memory bandwidth, additional or higher bit-depth render targets are an expensive choice, so minimizing the size of the hint data stored in the frame buffer is extremely important.

The post-process is required to compute the sample offset and blend factor; it has no other need for `hdist` and `vdist`. If we restrict the sample offset to the four diagonal corners, then it can be stored with two bits. The blend factor can take any number of bits: for example two bits would mean four levels, which is inferior to 4×MSAA (which has five). For our implementation we chose six bits, allowing 64 different blend levels. With the two bits required to specify the sample offset we make full use of the 8-bit alpha channel.

This choice moves some additional work from the post-process to the shader: it must now also find which of the four diagonal neighbors is the appropriate choice, calculate the blend factor, and encode all that information in the alpha channel.

2.4 Refinements

The method described in Sections 2.2 and 2.3 correctly provides antialiasing in the majority of cases, but there are some situations where it fails. When the antialiasing method fails for an edge, the edge is treated incorrectly by the post-process pass—i.e., either it remains unaffected by the post-process when it should become antialiased or it becomes blurred when it should have been left as is. Super-sampling and MSAA will implicitly handle some situations for which edge blurring requires explicit support.

In this section we'll cover the list of problem cases, and describe their solutions.

Edges with no neighboring triangle ("open edges"). This class of edge should always be classed as a silhouette edge and receive edge blurring. Therefore the solution is to flag any vertices that are on an open edge so they automatically pass adjoining-back-face test. For these vertices the outward direction must be defined differently: each open edge meeting at the vertex in question contributes a vector at right angles to the open edge and triangle normal; the final outward direction should be the weighted average of those vectors.

Edges with discontinuous shading. This includes material boundaries, discontinuous normals, discontinuous shading parameters including discontinuous UVs. Edge-blur should be always enabled for this class of edge. If the adjoining-back-face test passes then operate as usual, but if it fails scale the blend value so the blend between foreground and background is 50% on the edge instead of 0%.

The reason is because the edge-blur will be applied to pixels on both sides of the edge. If side A is red and side B is blue, then the blur applied to the pixels on each side needs to provide a soft transition to a 50% combination of red and blue on the edge. In comparison, the behavior on a silhouette edge is for the blend factor to be 0% on the edge, so the background color dominates. If this were applied at the red-blue transition, then the pixels on side A would smoothly transition to blue, the color would abruptly change to red across the edge, and on side B the color would then smoothly transition back to blue.

Triangles where all three vertices pass the adjoining-back-face test. See Figure 2.5. Imagine a cube viewed down one axis so only one face is visible. In that situation all four vertices of that face would adjoin back-facing triangles; `silhouette Parameter` would be 0.0 everywhere and the derivative method's prediction for edge distance would fail. One solution to this problem is to subdivide the geometry so the faces with potential problems have a center vertex, but this is not always possible.

Pixel-sized triangles. In comparison to $n\times$MSAA we have only one sample per pixel instead of n, so the Nyquist limit scales correspondingly. Triangles at this scale will suffer from under-sampling.

Pixel-sized gaps. Due to the vertex offset described in Section 2.2, a thin gap between geometry (such as the gap between extended fingers) will close. Like pixel-scale triangles, a pixel-scale gap will also suffer from under-sampling problems.

Alpha blending. Alpha-blended billboard textures need no antialiasing if their shape is provided by alpha from a texture rather than geometry. Similarly, windows in a frame would have their edges antialiased by the opaque geometry they share vertices with. When rendering these cases, updates to the edge-blur hints in the frame buffer should be disabled, so edges seen through the window will still be softened by the post-process.

A second case is alpha-blended geometry that isn't bounded by an opaque edge, such as an object faded to 50% opacity or a glass tabletop. In these cases it would be best if the edge-blend hints would only be written to pixels at the very edge of the object, where they were required. If the transparent object writes hints everywhere, it will disable antialiasing on the edges of the objects seen through it. If the edge hints are stored in the alpha channel, this cannot be done efficiently on standard GPUs. One option when rendering constant-alpha objects is to set up the hint bit packing so the blend factor is packed into the most significant six bits, with the sample direction is packed into the low two bits. Render using a separate alpha channel blend function, with the blend function set to max; color is combined with a constant blend factor. Alternatively, disabling writes to the alpha channel when rendering the object and adds the hints by re-rendering it, writing only to the alpha channel and using `clip()` to disable updates to any pixels not at the edge.

Surfaces intersecting in the depth buffer. Our method does not provide antialiasing in this case.

2.5 GPU Implementation and Results

Each stage of the antialiasing process will be considered in turn.

2.5.1 Offset Vertices

The vertex program implements this operation. The outward vector is required, but since the main restriction is that it be the same for all coincident vertices, it is often possible to reuse the existing per-vertex normal. For shapes with discontinuous normals such as a cube, this is not possible. If the number of edges with discontinuous normals is low it may be cheaper to insert a quad for each such edge to join the discontinuous vertices together, rather than increasing vertex size by adding another channel.

Example code to adjust the final projected vertex position (hPos) in homogeneous space is as follows:

```
hPos.xy+=normalize(screenNormal.xy)*hPos.w*2.0*
          aaExtrudeDistPixel()/screenSizePixel();
```

- **screenNormal** is the vertex normal, projected into screen space.
- **aaExtrudeDistPixel()** returns "k," the extrusion distance in pixels, e.g., 1.5.
- **screenSizePixel()** returns the screen size, e.g., **float2**(1280, 720).

Implementing an exact adjoining-back-face test in the vertex program is complex and costly, especially for skinned characters. However, the silhouette construction is robust enough to survive an inexact test. Here are three basic options representing a trade-off between amount of vertex data, complexity, and accuracy:

```
dot(eye_vertex_vector, outward_vector)>=0
```

The most basic test, adequate for surfaces with low curvature.

```
dot(normalize(eye_vertex_vector), outward_vector)>threshold
```

This approximates the set of adjoining triangles with a cone. The **threshold** parameter is equal to **-cos(half_cone_angle)** and can be pre-computed and stored in the vertex stream. This test is more useful, but it fails at saddle points.

```
(dot(normalize(eye_vertex_vector), plane_normal[0])>0) ||
(dot(normalize(eye_vertex_vector), plane_normal[1])>0) ||
(dot(normalize(eye_vertex_vector), plane_normal[2])>0) ||
(dot(normalize(eye_vertex_vector), plane_normal[3])>0)
```

Figure 2.5. Triangles where all three vertices have passed the (low-fidelity) adjoining-back-face test have been colored white.

With each vertex, store four surface normals chosen from the triangles meeting at that vertex. This is the most accurate method but will require the most vertex data and program time.

When the test is inaccurate, the question is whether the silhouette is formed in front of or behind the ideal silhouette edge. If it is behind, then there is a danger that the vertices are not offset far enough to be visible over the silhouette edge provided by the non-offset geometry, which will be aliased. Increasing k to compensate may help—either globally, on a per-object basis, or even as a per-vertex setting. However, every unit that k is increased will noticeably grow the object onscreen so improving the quality of the test may well be a better option.

If the silhouette edge is in front, then there will be visible triangles for which all vertices passed the adjoining-back-face test and so `silhouetteParameter` will be constantly 0 on them. This case will be covered in the next section.

Of course, an inadequate adjoining-back-face test just means that an aliased edge will appear—perhaps not a show-stopping problem!

2.5.2 Sample Offset and Blend Values

The calculations follow the text very closely, as shown in Listing 2.1.

Some care must be taken to avoid quantization problems when the GPU writes the final floating-point color to the 8-bit per channel frame buffer. Because 0.0 maps to 0 and 1.0 maps to 255, the best solution is to encode the desired value as an integer in $[0, 255]$ and divide by 255 so the 8-bit quantization has no effect.

```
float derivX=dFdx(silhouetteParameter);
float derivY=dFdy(silhouetteParameter);
vec2 approxEdgeDist=vec2(
     -silhouetteParameter/derivX,
     -silhouetteParameter/derivY);
// hdist and vdist, packed into a vector
float coverage=min(abs(approxEdgeDist.x),
                   abs(approxEdgeDist.y));
vec2 postStep=vec2(
sign(approxEdgeDist.x), sign(approxEdgeDist.y));
// Encode the postprocess step and coverage,
// to be written out to
// the 8-bit alpha channel
float encodedPostStepX=(postStep.x>=0) ? 128 : 0;
float encodedPostStepY=(postStep.y>=0) ? 64 : 0;
float encodedValInt=encodedPostStepX + encodedPostStepY +
                    (saturate(coverage)*63);
finalColor.a=encodedValInt/255.0;
```

Listing 2.1. Pixel shader code given `silhouetteParameter`.

One change that slightly improves the quality is to pass the variable `screenNormal` described in Section 2.5.1 into the pixel shader and to use it to determine the post-process sample offset. The occasional pixel has problems with the **ddx/ddy** method, and this change improves them:

```
float2 postStep=float2(sign(screenNormal.x), sign(-screenNormal.y));
```

The -y accounts for the texture coordinates being vertically flipped in comparison to screen space.

It is possible for all three vertices of a triangle to pass the adjoining-back-face test. There are two main ways that this might happen. First, when the adjoining-back-face test is inaccurately greedy and passes vertices of a front facing triangle near the silhouette. Secondly, for a triangle in the interior of the object, where the test failed perhaps because of saddle points.

If all three vertices of a triangle pass the adjoining-back-face test, `silhouette Parameter` will be a constant 0, and so the derivative calculations fail. In this case, the best option is to set coverage to 0 and set the post-process sample offset based on `screenNormal` as described above.

This will erase one-pixel-wide triangles on silhouette edges due to adjoining-back-face test inaccuracies, which are the most common problem case. On large triangles all pixels will be shifted diagonally by one step, but this is unlikely to cause visible problems beyond a possible aliased edge.

```
float encodedAAVal=sourceColor.a*255;
vec3 unpackedAAVal=frac(float3(encodedAAVal/256, encodedAAVal/128,
                        encodedAAVal/64) );
vec2 postStep;
postStep.x=(unpackedAAVal.x>=0.5) ? +1.0 : -1.0;
postStep.y=(unpackedAAVal.y>=0.5) ? +1.0 : -1.0;
float coverage=unpackedAAVal.z;
```

Listing 2.2. Unpacking a number in floating point.

2.5.3 Blend Edge Pixels

Since we are working in floating-point rather than integers, unpacking the number is slightly more complex, as shown in Listing 2.2.

Then sample the texture at the requested offset, blend, and write out.

2.5.4 Implementation Costs

In likely order of cost, the requirements of the approach presented here are space for the additional (4–8) bits in the frame buffer, the additional post-process work, any additional vertex properties for the adjoining-back-face test, the additional pixel shader code, the additional vertex shader code, and the additional one or three interpolators. However, no changes to draw order, tessellation, or geometry are required: even a depth-prepass is supported.

2.6 Results

Interaction with a complex background is shown in Figure 2.6, including a 4×MSAA render for comparison. The magnified regions show the effect of sampling a neighboring pixel to approximate the background color: some lines in the background which approach the edge indirectly can be seen to be offset by one pixel in the blend region. This image was rendered using the four-plane adjoining-back-face test described in Section 2.5.1.

Skinned characters are much more difficult to support than static geometry. Saddle points are common, which means many triangles have all three vertices pass the adjoining-back-face test. Thin gaps (e.g., between fingers) will close up with every increase in k. Lastly, skinning complicates the adjoining-back-face test: implementing the four-plane test for a skinned character would be difficult, and would require quite a bit of extra vertex data.

For this reason, we used a simple and less accurate test for the skinned character shown in Figure 2.7. Here, we used the cone test described in 5.1b with a threshold value of -0.2 and k value of 1.5 pixels for all vertices. The cone test

Figure 2.6. Demonstration of interaction with a complex background. The left-hand image in each magnified section shows the 4×MSAA render; the right-hand image shows the edge-blur render. Interaction with straight lines in the background (top left). The post-process method provides more subtle sub-pixel detail than 4×MSAA (top right). The worst case situation for the post-process method—the diagonal sampling means the row of pixels in the blend area is noticeably shifted one step to the left (bottom right). Another example of strong parallel features, but since the lines approach the edge from roughly the same direction as the diagonal sample, no artifacts are visible (bottom left). As is apparent in the top left section, artifacts are much less noticeable without the regular parallel spacing.

Figure 2.7. Demonstration of the technique applied to a skinned character. A simpler and less exact adjoining-back-face test was used, meaning that a few edges did not become antialiased (see text for details).

is not exact and some silhouette edges don't receive the antialiasing blur. (All lighting including shadows and AO was baked into the textures for the character; the only change between poses is vertex position and normal.)

2.6.1 Performance

The most useful measure of cost is the increase in cycle count for the vertex and pixel shader, with the additional code required by our method. Timings are for an Xbox 360 at a screen resolution of 1280×720; cycle counts are comparable to DX9.

Vertex program.

- Cone test version (5.1b): 25 cycles per vertex.

- Four-plane test version (see 5.1c): 29 cycles per vertex.

Pixel shader.

- 14 cycles per pixel; $\sim$0.67ms to fill the screen.

Post-process.

- 0.33ms to resolve the rendered image to a texture.

- 0.60ms for the full-screen post-process. This time is constant, as it is independent of scene content.

2.7 Other Applications

2.7.1 Shadow Mapping

Enabling pixel shaders to estimate the silhouette edge location with sub-pixel precision opens up some interesting possibilities. One application is shadow maps: if hints about the location of the shadow edge are encoded as well as depth, the magnification code can use that information to provide a sharp edge with sub-pixel accuracy (see Figure 2.8).

One way to do this is for each pixel, write out the parameters of the equation expressing distance to the nearest edge as a function of onscreen position.

When sampling the shadow map, a custom magnification function is used instead of bilinear filtering. Given a position on the shadow map texture, the four surrounding texels are sampled. The distance-to-edge equation provided by each of these four texels is evaluated, and the depth value associated with the texel corresponding to the highest distance-to-edge value is used for the shadow test.

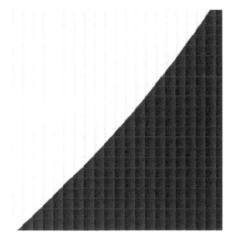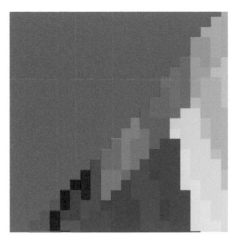

Figure 2.8. Example shadow map edge. A reasonably clean, antialiased edge is produced even though the triangles only cover a handful of pixels. The first image shows the resulting shadow map edge; the second image colors each pixel according to triangle index.

This means the shadow edge will run outside the group of texels that the shape rasterized to (without this property, clean intersections of silhouette edges are not possible).

The fragments of pixel shader code in Listing 2.3 implement this. Given silhouetteParameter, this code will encode the plane equation as a color to

```
float derivX=dFdx(silhouetteParameter);
float derivY=dFdy(silhouetteParameter);

vec2 vecToEncode=vec2(0.0, 0.0);
float encWeight=0.0;
if(silhouetteParameter<1.0)
{
  float d=sqrt((derivX*derivX)+(derivY*derivY))*1.0;
  vecToEncode.x=derivX/d;
  vecToEncode.y=derivY/d;
  encWeight=silhouetteParameter/d;
}
destColor.r=saturate(0.5 + vecToEncode.x*0.5);
destColor.g=saturate(0.5 + vecToEncode.y*0.5);
destColor.b=encWeight;
```

Listing 2.3. Sampling the shadow map.

```
// Sample shadow edge hints for the relevant four texels/points
vec4 colAA=texture2D(shadowEdgeHintMap, baseUV +
  (vec2(0,0)*singleUVStep) );
vec4 colBA=texture2D(shadowEdgeHintMap, baseUV +
  (vec2(1,0)*singleUVStep) );
vec4 colAB=texture2D(shadowEdgeHintMap, baseUV +
  (vec2(0,1)*singleUVStep) );
vec4 colBB=texture2D(shadowEdgeHintMap, baseUV +
  (vec2(1,1)*singleUVStep) );

// Sample shadowmap depths for the relevant four texels/points
float depthAA=texture2D(shadowDepthMap, baseUV +
  (vec2(0,0)*singleUVStep) ).r;
float depthBA=texture2D(shadowDepthMap, baseUV +
  (vec2(1,0)*singleUVStep) ).r;
float depthAB=texture2D(shadowDepthMap, baseUV +
  (vec2(0,1)*singleUVStep) ).r;
float depthBB=texture2D(shadowDepthMap, baseUV +
  (vec2(1,1)*singleUVStep) ).r;
// Calculate the distance-to-edge function for the four points
vec3 weightFuncAA=CalcWeightFunction(vec2(0,0), colAA);
vec3 weightFuncBA=CalcWeightFunction(vec2(1,0), colBA);
vec3 weightFuncAB=CalcWeightFunction(vec2(0,1), colAB);
vec3 weightFuncBB=CalcWeightFunction(vec2(1,1), colBB);

// Evaluate the distance-to-edge function for the four points
vec3 fracPosH=vec3(fracUV.x, fracUV.y, 1.0);
float weightAA=dot(weightFuncAA, fracPosH);
float weightBA=dot(weightFuncBA, fracPosH);
float weightAB=dot(weightFuncAB, fracPosH);
float weightBB=dot(weightFuncBB, fracPosH);

// Find the least distance-to-edge value, and use the
// corresponding depth for the shadow test.
float leastDistToEdge=-10.0;
float depthForTest=0.0;
if(weightAA>leastDistToEdge)
  { leastDistToEdge=weightAA; depthForTest=depthAA; }
if(weightBA>leastDistToEdge)
{ leastDistToEdge=weightBA; depthForTest=depthBA; }
if(weightAB>leastDistToEdge)
{ leastDistToEdge=weightAB; depthForTest=depthAB; }
if(weightBB>leastDistToEdge)
{ leastDistToEdge=weightBB; depthForTest=depthBB; }
// depthForTest contains the depth to be used for the shadowmap
// test.
```

Listing 2.4. Shadowmap magnification.

```
vec3 CalcWeightFunction(vec2 samplePt, vec3 sampleCol)
{
    vec2 unpackedDist=(sampleCol.rg-0.5)*2.0;
    float baseWeight=sampleCol.b;
    vec3 rc=0;
    rc.x=unpackedDist.x;
    rc.y=unpackedDist.y;
    rc.z=baseWeight;
    // Skew the function slightly to artificially increase the
    // distance-to-edge value as the queried point gets further
    // from the key corner. This provides a clearly defined
    // nearest corner in cases where the distance-to-edge value
    // is a constant 1, because there is no nearby edge.
    vec2 fallVec=vec2(1,1)-(samplePt*2);
    rc.xy+=fallVec*-0.02;
    rc.z-=(rc.x*samplePt.x)+(rc.y*samplePt.y);
    return rc;
}
```

Listing 2.5. Unpacking the parameters of the distance-to-edge equation.

be written out to a 32bpp RGBA frame buffer. Further packing is undoubtedly possible!

The next step is shadowmap magnification, which is shown in Listing 2.4. The colors of the four texels surrounding the sample point are colAA, colAB, colBA and colBB; depthAA, etc., are the four corresponding depths. baseUV holds the sample point UV rounded down to the nearest texel. fracUV contains the fractional part of the UV-coordinate, i.e., (0,0) is coincident with texel AA and (1,1) is coincident with texel BB.

The CalcWeightFunction() function (see Listing 2.5) unpacks the parameters of the distance-to-edge equation. It is evaluated by taking the dot product of the returned vector with a homogeneous two-dimensional coordinate. (For example, see weightAA in Listing 2.4.)

Alternatively, the shadow map test could be applied to the corner points (e.g., take the value 0 if shadowed, 1 if not) and the four resulting values blended to produce a softer edge. This can be extended to produce an antialiased shadow edge.

This method works well when the triangles cover a reasonably large area, but the edge quality breaks down with small, under-sampled triangles. (See Figure 2.9. The left-hand image shows the shape of the resulting edge; the texel size is indicated. For the right-hand image, the shadow map texels are colored according to triangle index. Despite the small triangles, a clean edge still resulted.)

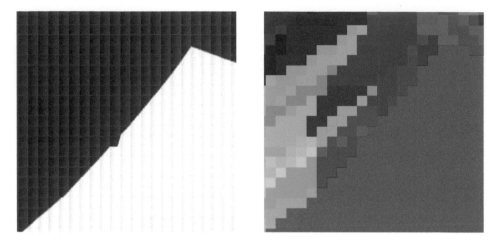

Figure 2.9. Extrapolation problem due to an under-sampled triangle.

2.7.2 Upscaling

One of the most visible problems with upscaling images using bilinear interpolation (or similar) is that the original resolution is betrayed by the steps along edges. If an edge in the original image has three steps, then it will still have three steps when up-scaled (there are other telltale signs of upscaling such as artifacts from bilinear filtering of high-contrast edges and under-sampling artifacts, which we'll ignore for now).

If we have access to sub-pixel accurate information about the edge, an up-scaler could use that information to deliver an edge that's pixel-accurate at the target resolution. The method described in 7.1 can be used to provide a sub-pixel accurate edge at the target resolution. The edge-blur method described can provide antialiasing; Figure 2.10 shows the result of a 2× up-scale demonstrating the technique in action.

Two possible uses for this idea are to render an image at (say) 720p, and then up-scale each frame to 1080p or, alternatively, to up-scale a low-res render target (e.g., for particles or transparencies) to the target frame buffer size. Since we are rendering to a smaller frame buffer, we save pixel shader time and bandwidth, but the low internal resolution does not reveal itself in the usual ways because the silhouette edges of the up-scaled result are still sharp.

One implementation of this idea suitable for small-scale factors is as follows. Each pixel of the source, low-res image has a color, distance to edge value, and partial derivatives of the distance-to-edge value. To find the color of a point on the destination image, begin by sampling the four containing samples in the

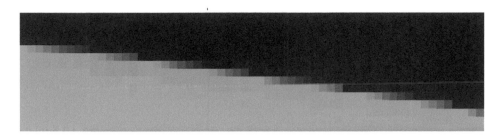

Figure 2.10. Close-up of a 2× up-scale using edge hints. The edge is pixel-accurate at the target resolution.

source image. Each of the four samples provides a distance-to-edge function. Depending on the distance-to-edge functions, one of two magnification modes will be used. If no silhouette edges run through the current quad, then simple bilinear interpolation will be used.

But if a silhouette edge runs through the current quad, then reproducing it in the destination (with antialiasing) requires more complex interpolation. Figure 2.11 shows an example situation.

For the situation in Figure 2.11, corners AA and BA are outside the silhouette, so they will hold the (default) function, which is a constant function returning the maximum value. Corners AB and BB are inside the silhouette and have a well-defined distance-to-edge function that will take the value 0 on the silhouette edge.

Corners AA/BA and AB/BB define distance-to-edge functions that are identical to the limit of precision. For reasons that will become clear shortly, we'll

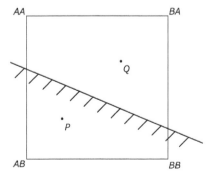

Figure 2.11. Upscaling when an edge passes through the quad. Points AA, AB, BA, and BB are the relevant four sample points in the source low-res image. Points P and Q are example points for consideration.

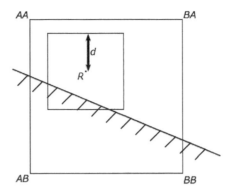

Figure 2.12. Calculation of blend value for antialiasing an edge during upscaling. When shading the point R, the smaller square represents the area covered by the destination pixel. The value d measures half the edge length.

adjust these functions slightly so the returned value gradually increases with distance from their base corner.

When evaluating the functions at a particular point in the square, one function will now unambiguously return the lowest non-negative value. Using the color associated with that corner is one basic way to up-scale: it will provide a variation on nearest-neighbor sampling, but the border between the colors on one side of the edge (AA/BA) and the other (AB/BB) will precisely follow the silhouette edge.

The next step is to extend this approach to provide antialiasing, by blending the colors on either side of the edge based on coverage.

The two requirements are to find the two colors to blend between, and to define the blend parameter.

The requirements for the blend parameter are very similar to those for the original edge-blur: the blend parameter indicates coverage so it must approximate the coverage value in a plausible way, and it needs to be cheap.

A reasonable value for the coverage/blend parameter can be derived from the distance-to-edge value in the same way as the edge-blur. Set up the distance-to-edge function so it is defined using the Manhattan metric, as before. Calculate the blend parameter by linearly remapping the distance-to-edge value from $[-d, +d]$ to $[0, 1]$, where d is half the size of the sample region (see Figure 2.12). Instead of searching for the lowest nonnegative distance-to-edge value, we now search for the lowest value greater than $-d$.

Finding the colors to blend requires picking colors from opposite sides of the edge. Take the first color to be the one described above (i.e., belonging to the corner whose function yielded the lowest value). Find the direction of the rate of

Figure 2.13. Demonstration of a 200% up-scale with edge hints.

greatest decrease of that function; round to +1 or -1, and step in that direction from the first corner. For point P in Figure 2.11, this would yield the colors from corners AB and BA, respectively.

This method may sound overly complex, but there are cases where other methods can break down, e.g., choosing the diagonally opposite corner can fail if the silhouette edge contains three corners.

This method is a very simple upscaling effect, so ugly artifacts start to appear if it is pushed too far, but it produces acceptable results for low scaling factors. This is enough to support the 150% up-scale from 720p to 1080p, for instance. Figure 2.13 shows an example image up-scaled by 200% using this technique.

While this method will preserve sharp edges, there are other standard up-scaling problems that are still relevant. Geometry under-sampling is a danger: in comparison to 4×MSAA, pixels might be four to eight times the area so the Nyquist limit is raised proportionally.

Also, since bilinear filtering is used for all pixel quads not straddling an edge, high-contrast features will lead to the usual artifacts. One possibility is to encode edge hints in the texture, transform the hint to screen space and write out to the frame buffer so a sharp border due to a texture is preserved by the up-scale, but this is far from trivial. Another option is to move high-frequency shading to the up-scale: encode UVs and other parameters in the "frame buffer," and during the up-scale extrapolate these parameters and calculated the final color procedurally.

The filtering will also tend to smooth out detail. One option is that during render to the low-res buffer, extrapolate the UVs, take four samples of a detail map (with one level of LOD bias), and pack their values into the buffer. During the up-scale, these values can be used to tweak the replicated color to add detail back. Since the source is an MIP-mapped texture this will not add noise.

The two previous approaches could be generalized and combined: shade four pixels at once, with the resulting four colors packed into a single (fat) pixel of the low-res target (this would provide something like a software version of MSAA). Performance gains are possible by calculating low-frequency effects once for all four pixels; high-frequency effects are calculated for each of the four pixels individually so detail is not lost.

In closing, this approach offers a third option for increasing resolution, between simply paying a proportionally higher price for more samples and suffering the normal upscaling artifacts. It is not cheap: it is quite possible that the additional render time required or other costs means it can not offer a net gain. Also, it will magnify any quality problems, so shader aliasing will be even more apparent. But in some contexts (e.g., little high-frequency detail and a high per-pixel cost), it can offer high resolution and antialiasing at a fraction of the cost of other options.

2.8 Conclusion

This chapter describes a method for antialiasing edges for real-time applications that also applies to deferred effects and avoids the need for a super-sampled/multi-sampled frame buffer. Applications to static geometry and skinned characters are shown, and the results are often comparable to high-sample MSAA.

Enabling pixel shaders to robustly find the nearest silhouette edge with sub-pixel precision opens up some interesting possibilities; the shadow map magnification and upscaling described here are only two.

Future work includes finding better approximations for the background color. One layer of depth peeling would be ideal, but since it requires a full re-render it may well be prohibitively costly. A cheaper, more specialized alternative related to the stencil-routed A-buffer described in [Myers 07] may well exist. This would also allow more sophisticated pixel filter functions than the one suggested in Section 2.3.

Future work would also require looking into other possibilities for the adjoining-back-face test. We only tried a few tests beyond the three described in Section 2.5. It would be useful to have more options, representing different trade-offs between accuracy and expense.

Bibliography

[Beyond3D 09] "List of Rendering Resolutions and Basics on Hardware Scaling, MSAA, Framebuffers." *Beyond3D*. Available at http://forum.beyond3d.com/showthread.php?t=46241, 14 Sept. 2009.

[Huddy 08] Richard Huddy. *DirectX 10.1*. Game Developer's Conference, 2008.

[Kilgard 01] Mark J. Kilgard. "OpenGL Extension Registry: NV_vertex_array_range." *OpenGL Extension Registry*. Available at http://oss.sgi.com/projects/ogl-sample/registry/NV/vertex_array_range.txt, April 2001.

[Kirkland 99] Dale Kirkland, Bill Armstrong, Michael Gold, Jon Leech, and Paula Womack. "GL_ARB_multisample." *OpenGL Extension Registry*. Available at http://www.opengl.org/registry/specs/ARB/multisample.txt, 1999.

[Koonce 07] Rusty Koonce. "Deferred Shading in Tabula Rasa." In *GPU Gems 3*, edited by Hubert Nguyen, pp. 429–457. Boston: Addison-Wesley, 2008.

[Myers 07] Kevin Myers and Louis Bavoil. 2007. "Stencil Routed A-Buffer." *ACM SIGGRAPH 2007 Sketches* (2007).

[NVIDIA 08] NVIDIA. *NVIDIA GeForce GTX 200 GPU Datasheet*. 2008.

[Shishkovtso 05] Oles Shishkovtso. "Deferred Rendering in S.T.A.L.K.E.R." In *GPU Gems 2*, edited by Matt Pharr and Randima Fernando. Boston: Addison-Wesley, 2005.

[Thürmer 98] Grit Thürmer and Charles A. Wüthrich. "Computing Vertex Normals from Polygonal Facets." *Journal of Graphics Tools* 3:1 (Mar. 1998), 43–46.

[Valient 07] Michal Valient. "Deferred Rendering in Killzone 2." Develop Conference, Brighton, UK, July 2007.

[Young 07] Peter Young. "CSAA (Coverage Sampling Anti-Aliasing)." Technical Report, NVIDIA Corporation, 2007.

3

Environment Mapping with Floyd-Steinberg Halftoning

László Szirmay-Kalos, László Szécsi, and Anton Penzov

3.1 Introduction

In many computer graphics applications we wish to augment virtual objects with images representing a real environment (sky, city, etc.). In order to provide the illusion that the virtual objects are parts of the real scene, the illumination of the environment should be taken into account when rendering the virtual objects [Debevec 98, Kollig and Keller 03]. Since the images representing the environment lack depth information, we usually assume that the illumination stored in these images comes from far surfaces. This means that the illumination of the environment is similar to directional lights, it has only directional characteristics, but its intensity is independent of the location of the illuminated point.

Environment mapping may be used to compute the reflected radiance of a *shaded point* $\vec{x}$ in *viewing direction* $\vec{\omega}$ as a directional integral

$$L(\vec{x},\vec{\omega}) = \int_{\Omega} L^{\mathrm{env}}(\vec{\omega}') f_r(\vec{\omega}',\vec{x},\vec{\omega}) \cos\theta'_{\vec{x}} V(\vec{x},\vec{\omega}') \mathrm{d}\omega',$$

where Ω is the set of all incident directions, $L^{\mathrm{env}}(\vec{\omega}')$ is the radiance of the environment map at *illumination direction* $\vec{\omega}'$, f_r is the BRDF, $\theta'_{\vec{x}}$ is the angle between illumination direction $\vec{\omega}'$ and the surface normal at $\vec{x}$, and $V(\vec{x},\vec{\omega}')$ is the indicator function checking whether environment illumination can take effect in shaded point $\vec{x}$ at direction $\vec{\omega}'$, i.e., no virtual object occludes the environment in this direction (Figure 3.1).

This integral is usually estimated by Monte Carlo quadrature, which generates M number of samples $\vec{\omega}'_1, \ldots, \vec{\omega}'_M$ with probability density $p(\vec{\omega}')$ and computes

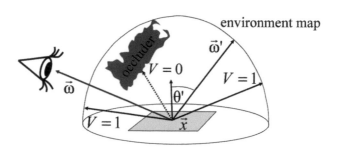

Figure 3.1. The concept of environment mapping stored in a cube map.

the estimate as an average:

$$L(\vec{x}, \vec{\omega}) \approx \frac{1}{M} \sum_{i=1}^{M} \frac{L^{\mathrm{env}}(\vec{\omega}_i') f_r(\vec{\omega}_i', \vec{x}, \vec{\omega}) \cos \theta_{\vec{x},i}' V(\vec{x}, \vec{\omega}_i')}{p(\vec{\omega}_i)}.$$

The most time consuming part of the evaluation of a sample is the computation of visibility factor V, i.e., the determination whether or not the environment is occluded. Real-time environment mapping algorithms usually ignore this factor and consequently the shadowing of environment lighting. However, for rendering photorealistic images, this simplification is unacceptable. Thus in this chapter we examine environment mapping approaches that correctly evaluate the occlusion of the illuminating environment.

The calculation of the visibility factor requires tracing a ray originating at shaded point $\vec{x}$ and having direction $\vec{\omega}_i'$. In order to improve the speed of environment mapping with shadow computation, the number of samples—that is, the number of traced rays—should be minimized.

For a given number of samples, the error of the quadrature depends on two factors:

1. Importance sampling. How well does density p mimic the integrand?

2. Stratification. How well does the empirical distribution of the finite number of samples follow the theoretical distribution defined by p?

This means that we should do a good job in both mimicking the integrand with the sample density and producing well stratified samples.

3.2   Parametrization of the Environment Map

The environment illumination is defined by a texture map $T(u, v)$ addressed by texture coordinates $u, v \in [0, 1]$. Thus we need a mapping or a parametrization that defines the correspondence between a texture coordinate pair and illuminating direction $\vec{\omega}'$.

A possible parametrization expresses direction $\vec{\omega}'$ by spherical angles θ', ϕ', where $\phi' \in [0, 2\pi]$ and $\theta' \in [0, \pi/2]$ in the case of hemispherical lighting and $\theta' \in [0, \pi]$ in the case of spherical lighting. Then texture coordinates (u, v) are scaled from the unit interval to these ranges. For example, in the case of spherical lighting, a direction is parameterized as

$$\vec{\omega}'(u, v) = (\cos 2\pi u \sin \pi v, \ \sin 2\pi u \sin \pi v, \ \cos \pi v),$$

where $u, v \in [0, 1]$.

A texture map is a two-dimensional image containing $R_u \times R_v$ texels where R_u and R_v are the horizontal and vertical resolutions, respectively. Note that the discussed parametrization is not uniform since different texels correspond to the same $\Delta u \Delta v = (1/R_u)(1/R_v)$ area in texture space, but different solid angles $\Delta \omega$ depending on texture coordinate v:

$$\Delta \omega = \sin \pi v \Delta u \Delta v = \frac{\sin \pi v}{R_u R_v}.$$

The integral of the reflected radiance can also be evaluated in texture space:

$$L(\vec{x}, \vec{\omega}) = \int\limits_{u=0}^{1} \int\limits_{v=0}^{1} E(u, v) R(u, v, \vec{x}, \omega) \mathbf{V}(u, v, \vec{x}) \mathrm{d}v \mathrm{d}v \approx$$

$$\frac{1}{R_u R_v} \sum_{i=1}^{R_u} \sum_{j=1}^{R_v} E\left(\frac{i}{R_u}, \frac{j}{R_v}\right) R\left(\frac{i}{R_u}, \frac{j}{R_v}, \vec{x}, \vec{\omega}\right) \mathbf{V}\left(\frac{i}{R_u}, \frac{j}{R_v}, \vec{x}\right),$$

where we used the following shorthand notations for the three main factors of the integrand:

$$E(u, v) = L^{\mathrm{env}}(\vec{\omega}'(u, v)) \sin \pi v = T(u, v) \sin \pi v$$

is the intensity of the *environment lighting* taking into account the distortion of the parametrization,

$$R(u, v, \vec{x}, \omega) = f_r(\vec{\omega}'(u, v), \vec{x}, \vec{\omega}) \cos \theta'_{\vec{x}}(u, v)$$

is the *reflection factor*, and

$$\mathbf{V}(u, v, \vec{x}) = V(\vec{x}, \vec{\omega}'(u, v))$$

is the *visibility factor*.

The evaluation of the reflected radiance by adding the contribution of all texels would be too time consuming. Therefore, we apply Monte Carlo methods, which approximate it from just a few sample directions, i.e., a few texels.

3.3   Importance Sampling

Monte Carlo methods use a probability density to select the sample points. According to the concept of importance sampling, we should find a density p that mimics the product form integrand. To define an appropriate density, we usually execute the following three main steps:

1. First we decide which factors of the product form integrand will be mimicked and find a scalar approximation of the usually vector valued integrand factor. In our case, environment lighting E and reflection factor R are vector valued since they assign different values for the wavelengths of the red, green, and blue light. Spectrum L can be converted to a scalar by obtaining the *luminance* of the spectrum $\mathbf{L}(L)$, which is a weighted sum of the red, green, and blue intensities. The resulting scalar approximation of the integrand is called the *importance function* and is denoted by I. Note that as the environment illumination is defined by a texture, the importance function is also represented by a two-dimensional image. When we want to emphasize this property, we refer to the importance function as the *importance map*.

   There are several options to define the importance function, as there are different alternatives of selecting those factors of the integrand that are mimicked. The simplest way is *BRDF sampling*, which mimics the luminance of the reflection factor. *Light-source sampling*, on the other hand, sets the importance function to be the luminance of the environment lighting. Finally, *product sampling* includes more than one factor of the integrand into the importance function. For example, the importance function can be the luminance of the product of the environment lighting and the reflection factor (double product sampling), or it can even incorporate a cheap visibility factor approximated by some simple proxy geometry included in the object (triple product sampling).

2. As the density should be normalized, the integral of the importance function needs to be computed for the whole domain. This computation can take advantage of the fact that the importance function is defined also as a two-dimensional array or a texture, similar to the texture map of the environment illumination:

$$\int_{u=0}^{1} \int_{v=0}^{1} I(u,v)\mathrm{d}v\mathrm{d}u \approx \frac{S}{R_u R_v},$$

   where

$$S = \sum_{u=1}^{R_u} \sum_{j=1}^{R_v} I\left(\frac{i}{R_u}, \frac{j}{R_v}\right)$$

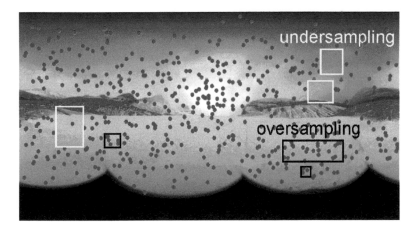

Figure 3.2. Environment map with random light-source sampling.

is the sum of all values in the importance map. Note that the importance function should be integrated as one step of the importance sampling. It means that the importance function must be much cheaper to evaluate and integrate than the original integrand.

3. Finally, the density is defined as the ratio of the importance function and the normalization constant:

$$p(u,v) = \frac{I(u,v)}{\int\limits_{u=0}^{1} \int\limits_{v=0}^{1} I(u,v)\mathrm{d}v\mathrm{d}u} = \frac{I(u,v)R_u R_v}{S}.$$

Having constructed the importance map and computed sum S, samples can be drawn with probability density p using the following simple method. We generate M statistically independent random numbers $r_1, \ldots, r_M$ that are uniformly distributed in the unit interval. Then for each random number, the two-dimensional array of the importance map is scanned, and the importance values are added together. This running sum is compared to $r_i S$. When the running sum gets larger, the scanning is stopped and the current texel (i.e., the direction corresponding to this texel) is considered as a sample. As can be easily shown, the process will select a texel with a probability proportional to its value.

Unfortunately, the application of statistically independent random samples provides poor results in many cases. To demonstrate the problem, we used light-source sampling to find directional samples on an environment map (Figure 3.2). The results are disappointing since making independent random texel selections, with probability in proportion to its luminance, does not guarantee that groups of samples will be well stratified. We still have large empty regions in important parts of the map (*undersampling*) and groups of samples needlessly concentrating to a small unimportant region (*oversampling*). We note that this problem has also been addressed by Kollig who proposed the relaxation of the samples [Kollig and Keller 03] and by Ostromoukhov who applied sophisticated tiling [Ostromoukhov et al. 04]. The method proposed in the next section provides similar results as these methods, but is much simpler and has practically no overhead with respect to the simple random approach.

3.4 Proposed Solution

The method proposed in this chapter has the goal of producing well stratified samples mimicking an *importance map*. It is effective, simple to implement, and is even faster than random sampling.

The proposed method is based on the recognition that importance sampling is equivalent to *digital halftoning* [Szirmay-Kalos et al. 09]. Halftoning is a technique used to render grayscale images on a black and white display (see Figure 3.3). The idea is to put more white points at brighter areas and fewer points at darker areas. The spatial density of white points in a region around a pixel is expected to be proportional to the gray level of that particular pixel. If we consider the gray level of the original image to be an importance function and the white pixels of the resulting image to be sample locations, then we can see that halftoning is equivalent to a deterministic importance sampling algorithm. The equivalence of importance sampling and halftoning stems from the fact that both of them are *frequency modulators* [Szirmay-Kalos and Szécsi 09]. The input of the frequency modulator is the upscal image or the importance map, respectively, and the output is a collection of discrete samples with a frequency specified by the input.

grayscale image   random halftoning   Floyd-Steinberg halftoning

Figure 3.3.   A grayscale image and its halftoned versions obtained with random halftoning and with the Floyd-Steinberg algorithm.

This equivalence holds for an arbitrary halftoning algorithm, including the random and ordered halftoning methods that add random noise or a periodic pattern to the original image before quantization, or, for example, error diffusion halftoning methods from which the Floyd-Steinberg algorithm is the most famous [Floyd and Steinberg 75]. Error diffusion halftoning provides better results than random or ordered halftoning because it does not simply make independent local decisions but gathers and distributes information to neighboring pixels as well. Because it takes gray levels in a neighborhood into account, the sample positions are stratified, making the resulting image smoother and reducing the noise compared to random or dithered approaches.

Because of these nice properties, we developed our sampler based on the Floyd-Steinberg method. Random dithering was implemented for comparison. We expected the same improvement in importance sampling as provided by the Floyd-Steinberg halftoning over random dithering.

3.4.1 Floyd-Steinberg Sampler

The sampling algorithm takes the importance map and computes the sum S of all texels. Then, the sampling is simply the execution of a Floyd-Steinberg halftoning on the map setting the threshold at $S/(2M)$ where M is the number of expected samples. In Figure 3.4 the threshold and the error are depicted by a red line and a white bar, respectively. The halftoning algorithm initializes an error value to 0 and scans the map row-by-row, changing the scanning order at the end of the rows. At each texel, the comparison of the error value to the threshold may have two outcomes. If the error is not greater than the threshold, then no sample is generated here (the texel becomes black) and the error is left unchanged. If the error is greater than the threshold, then this texel is a sample. The error value is decreased by S/M, i.e., we compute the negative complementer of the error represented by the black part of the bar in Figure 3.4.

In both cases, before stepping onto the next texel, the remaining error of the texel is distributed to its unvisited neighbors. The method continues similarly until all texels have been visited.

Listing 3.1 shows the implementation of this algorithm optimized to work as a geometry shader. Every time the shader is invoked, it processes the importance map of size `R.x` × `R.y`, the values of which are queried using the `getImportance` function. It emits 32 directional samples, with the probability of sample selection stored in the alpha channel. The function `getSampleDir` returns the direction associated with a texel of the importance map. We avoid maintaining an actual array of importance values by storing only the importance that has been carried to the next row. Variable `cPixel` contains the importance to be transferred to

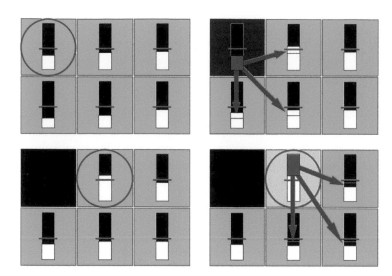

Figure 3.4. The Floyd-Steinberg sampling. The error (white bar) of the upper-left texel is smaller than the threshold (red line), so it is not selected (the texel will be black). Its error is distributed to the neighbors increasing their error levels. The next texel will have a larger error than the threshold, so it is selected (the texel will be white). The negative complementer error (black bar) is added to the neighbors, reducing their error value.

the next pixel, `cDiagonal` must be added to the pixel below the next, and `cRow` is an array, packed into `float4` vectors, that contains the importances to be added to pixels in the next row. Every row is processed in runs of four pixels, after which the four values gathered in variable `acc` can be packed into the `cRow` array. The size of `cRow` is `RX4`, which is the width of the importance map divided by four. Every time the importance map is read, the original importance value is loaded into variable `I`, and importance carried over from the neighbors is added to get the modified importance in variable `Ip`.

In addition to Floyd-Steinberg halftoning, the family of error diffusion methods has many other members that differ in the error distribution neighborhood and weights, as well as in the order of processing the texels [Kang 99]. These sophisticated techniques are also worth using as importance sampling methods. The weights need special care when the number of expected samples M is very small with respect to the number of texels. Multidimensional error diffusion methods perform well when they are in a stationary state, but need to warm up, i.e., they start producing samples later than expected. If very few samples are generated with the method, this delay becomes noticeable. To solve this problem, the weight of the faster running coordinate should be increased. In the extreme case, the algorithm should act as a one-dimensional error diffusion filter.

```
[maxvertexcount(32)]
void gsSampler( inout PointStream<float4> samples ) {
  uint M = 32; float S = 0;
  [loop]for(uint v = 0; v < R.y; v++)
    [loop]for(uint u = 0; u < R.x; u++)
      S += getImportance(uint2(u, v));
  float threshold = S / 2 / M;
  float4 cRow[RX4]={{0,0,0,0},{0,0,0,0},{0,0,0,0},{0,0,0,0}};
  float cPixel = 0, cDiagonal = 0, acc[4];
  [loop]for(uint j = 0; j < R.y; j++)  {
    uint kper4 = 0;
    [loop]for(uint k = 0; k < R.x; k += 4) {
      for(uint xi = 0; xi < 4; xi++) {
          float I = getImportance(uint2(k+xi, j));
          float Ip = I + cRow[kper4][xi] + cPixel;
          if(Ip > threshold) {
            float3 dir = getSampleDir(uint2(k+xi, j));
            samples.Append( float4(dir, I / S) );
            Ip -= threshold * 2;
          }
          acc[xi] = Ip * 0.375 + cDiagonal;
          cPixel = Ip * 0.375;
          cDiagonal = Ip * 0.25;
      }
      cRow[kper4++] = float4(acc[0], acc[1], acc[2], acc[3]);
    }
    j++; kper4--;
    [loop]for(int k = R.x-5; k >= 0; k -= 4) {
      for(int xi = 3; xi >= 0; xi--) {
          float I = getImportance(uint2(k+xi, j));
          float Ip = I + cRow[kper4][xi] + cPixel;
          if(Ip > threshold ) {
            float3 dir = getSampleDir(uint2(k+xi, j));
            samples.Append( float4(dir, I / S) );
            Ip -= threshold * 2;
          }
          acc[xi] = Ip * 0.375 + cDiagonal;
          cPixel = Ip * 0.375;
          cDiagonal = Ip * 0.25;
      }
      cRow[kper4--] = float4(acc[0], acc[1], acc[2], acc[3]);
    }
  }
}
```

Listing 3.1. The Floyd-Steinberg sampler implemented as a geometry shader.

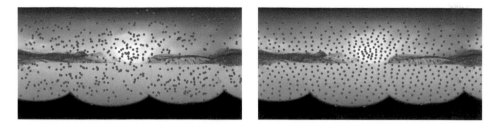

Figure 3.5. Sampling weighted environment maps with random sampling (left) and Floyd-Steinberg halftoning (right).

3.4.2　Application to Light-Source Sampling

In light-source sampling the importance function is based on the environment illumination and we also take into account that different texels correspond to different solid angles:

$$I(u, v) = \mathbf{L}(E(u, v)).$$

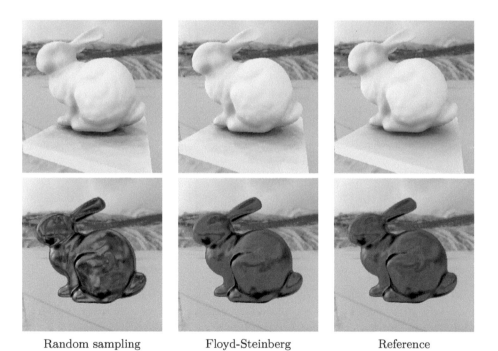

Random sampling　　　Floyd-Steinberg　　　Reference

Figure 3.6. Results of light-source sampling. Diffuse and specular bunnies illuminated by directional lights sampled randomly and with Floyd-Steinberg halftoning.

Ignoring the cosine weighted BRDF and the visibility degrades importance sampling. But since the importance function depends just on the illumination direction and is independent of the point being shaded, $\vec{x}$, sampling should be executed only once for all shaded points.

In this case, the proposed scheme is as simple as the Floyd-Steinberg halftoning of the environment map weighted by solid angle scaling $\sin \pi v$. Figures 3.5 and 3.6 compare the distribution of samples and the resulting images of the illuminated object for random sampling and for the Floyd-Steinberg sampler. As the Floyd-Steinberg sampler scans the map only once and obtains samples directly, it is not slower than random sampling. Sampling the 1024×512 resolution environment map of Figure 3.5 takes 47 msec on an NVIDIA GeForce 8800 GFX GPU.

3.4.3 Application to Product Sampling

Product sampling includes more than one factor of the integrand into the importance function. Note that the inclusion of all factors is not feasible since the computation of the importance must be cheaper than that of the integrand. In environment mapping, the expensive part is the visibility test, so we either ignore occlusions in the importance or replace it with some cheaper approximation. The importance function is defined as

$$I(u, v) = E(u, v) R(u, v, \vec{x}, \vec{\omega}) \tilde{\mathbf{V}}(u, v, \vec{x}).$$

where $\tilde{\mathbf{V}}$ is the approximation of the visibility factor. *Double product sampling* sets $\tilde{\mathbf{V}} = 1$ assuming that the environment is always visible when generating important directions. Alternatively, we can approximate visibility by computing intersections with a contained proxy geometry, for example, spheres inside the object. In this case, we talk about *triple product sampling*. We have to emphasize that the approximate visibility factor and the proxy geometry is used only in the definition of the importance map and for generating important directions. When the ray is traced, the original geometry is intersected, that is, the original visibility indicator is included into the integral quadrature. Triple product sampling helps to reduce the number of those rays that surely intersect some object, and thus their contribution is zero. Unfortunately, it is not always easy to find a simple proxy geometry that is inside the object. For example, in Figure 3.7 it is straightforward to put a sphere into the Ming head, but the definition of a proxy geometry for the wheel is difficult.

Unlike light-source sampling, now the importance function also depends on shaded point $\vec{x}$ and indirectly on the normal vector at $\vec{x}$. This means that we cannot process the environment map once globally for all shaded points, but the

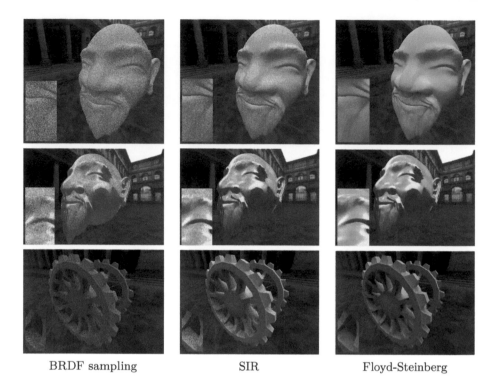

| | | |
| BRDF sampling | SIR | Floyd-Steinberg |

Figure 3.7. Double product sampling results. Note that the Floyd-Steinberg sampler eliminated the noise at fully visible surfaces both for the diffuse and specular cases. The lower row of images show a wheel having a lot of occlusions, which are not mimicked by the double product importance.

sampling process including the Floyd-Steinberg halftoning should be repeated for every single shaded point. Thus, while in light-source sampling the Floyd-Steinberg sampler has no overhead, product sampling pays off if ray tracing is more costly than the generation and processing of the importance map.

In order to test the approach, we have compared three techniques: BRDF sampling, random halftoning, which is similar to *sampling-importance resampling* (SIR) [Burke et al. 04, Talbot et al. 05] in the case of product sampling, and the new Floyd-Steinberg scheme. All three were implemented as GPU algorithms, which run on NVIDIA GeForce 8800 GFX graphics hardware. All methods traced $M = 32$ rays per pixel. Both sampling-importance resampling and the Floyd-Steinberg sampler obtained the real samples from 32×32 local importance maps generated separately for every shaded point $\vec{x}$. The results are shown by Figure 3.7. Note that the Floyd-Steinberg sampler completely eliminated the noise at fully visible surfaces, and some noise remained only at partially occluded regions.

3.5 Conclusion

The most important message of this chapter is that halftoning and importance sampling are equivalent, thus we can exploit the sophisticated halftoning algorithms in importance sampling. We investigated the application of the Floyd-Steinberg halftoning method in environment mapping and concluded that this approach produces samples with better distribution than random sampling. Thanks to this, the integrals evaluated with these samples are more accurate.

Bibliography

[Burke et al. 04] David Burke, Abhijeet Ghosh, and Wolfgang Heidrich. "Bidirectional Importance Sampling for Illumination from Environment Maps." In *ACM SIGGRAPH 2004 Sketches*, p. 112, 2004.

[Debevec 98] Paul Debevec. "Rendering Synthetic Objects Into Real Scenes: Bridging Traditional and Image-Based Graphics with Global Illumination and High Dynamic Range Photography." In *SIGGRAPH '98*, pp. 189–198, 1998.

[Floyd and Steinberg 75] Robert W. Floyd and Louis Steinberg. "An Adaptive Algorithm for Spatial Gray Scale." In *Society for Information Display 1975 Symposium Digest of Tecnical Papers*, p. 36, 1975.

[Kang 99] Henry R. Kang. *Digital Color Halftoning*. Bellingham, WA: SPIE Press, 1999.

[Kollig and Keller 03] Thomas Kollig and Alexander. Keller. "Efficient Illumination by High Dynamic Range Images." In *Eurographics Symposium on Rendering*, pp. 45–51, 2003.

[Ostromoukhov et al. 04] Victor Ostromoukhov, Charles Donohue, and Pierre-Marc Jodoin. "Fast Hierarchical Importance Sampling with Blue Noise Properties." *ACM Transactions on Graphics* 23:3 (2004), 488–498.

[Szirmay-Kalos and Szécsi 09] László Szirmay-Kalos and László Szécsi. "Deterministic Importance Sampling with Error Diffusion." *Computer Graphics Forum (EG Symposium on Rendering)* 28:4 (2009), 1056–1064.

[Szirmay-Kalos et al. 09] László Szirmay-Kalos, László Szécsi, and Anton Penzov. "Importance Sampling with Floyd-Steinberg Halftoning." In *Eurographics 09, Short Papers*, pp. 69–72, 2009.

[Talbot et al. 05] Justin Talbot, David Cline, and Parris K. Egbert. "Importance Resampling for Global Illumination." In *Rendering Techniques*, pp. 139–146, 2005.

4

Hierarchical Item Buffers for Granular Occlusion Culling
Thomas Engelhardt and Carsten Dachsbacher

4.1 Introduction

Culling algorithms are key to many efficient, interactive rendering techniques. Their common goal is to reduce workload from virtually all stages of the rendering pipeline. Although they have been studied by many researchers, thus spanning a large spectrum of variety and complexity, they often build upon the integral building block of visibility determination.

The most common algorithms employ frustum and portal culling in the application stage to exclude invisible geometry, often organized in a hierarchical data structure. More sophisticated algorithms precompute entire visibility sets in an expensive offline pre-process for efficient online visibility evaluation.

Recent advancements in the field of (occlusion) culling [Bittner et al. 04] employ hardware occlusion queries as a mechanism for efficient from-point visibility determination, provided by commodity graphics hardware. Geometry is rasterized against an existing depth buffer and pixels that pass the depth test are counted. The query result, however, has to be read back to the application and thus conservative visibility-based culling inherently synchronizes the otherwise asynchronous execution of CPU and GPU; a problem, the recently introduced occlusion predicates try to avoid.

Beyond that, GPUs exploit the built-in early-z optimization to autonomously discard pixels that fail the depth test before the pixel shader is executed. This optimization, however, becomes disabled in certain scenarios, e.g., in case that the pixel shader writes a depth value.

In [Engelhardt and Dachsbacher 09] we described a method that computes from point visibility in an output-sensitive way. It is designed to complement the early-z optimization and to extend the repertoire of existing GPU-based culling methods, in particular for rendering techniques that involve costly shaders. It is flexible in terms of adapting to varying user and shader demands by computing visibility of configurable granularity. That is, it is capable of computing visibility for different entities, i.e., individual primitives, batches of primitives or entire (batches of) objects. This is achieved by using a variant of an item buffer. Entities are assigned an identifier and rendered into the item buffer. Afterwards the occurrence of each entity in the item buffer is counted exploiting GPU-based scattering. Because the method executes entirely on the GPU, it is easy to implement and does not require any application feedback. This, for instance, enables visibility-based culling and LOD control in the geometry shader as well as in the upcoming tesselation shaders, and further enables culling in scenarios where the early-z optimization is disabled.

4.2   Hierarchical Item Buffers

The foundation of our method is the well-known item buffer [Weghorst et al. 84]. Similar to the original approach, we store a unique identifier (ID) for each rasterized entity that passed the depth test. An entity, for example, may be an individual triangle, a cluster of triangles, an individual instance within an instanced draw call, or in the simplest case, an object. Thus the type of an entity defines the granularity of the query. Afterwards, as illustrated in Figure 4.1 we employ a histogram algorithm to count the occurrence of each ID and thus compute an entity's visibility.

To compute the histogram, we use a scattering algorithm on the GPU similar to [Scheuermann and Hensley 07]. The item buffer is reinterpreted as a point list and the vertex shader computes a bin index from the ID. Each bin stores a counter and by rendering point primitives, we increment the counters in the

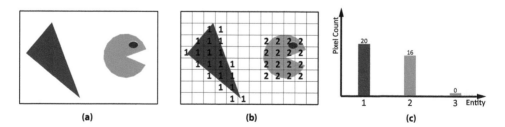

(a)   (b)   (c)

Figure 4.1. (a) Entities to determine visibility of; (b) the item buffer after rasterization; (c) histogram of the item buffer. No occurrences were counted for entity 3; hence it is invisible.

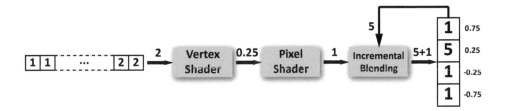

Figure 4.2. The histogram algorithm: a point with ID 2 is rendered and the vertex shader computes pixel address 0.25. Using additive blending, the value in the histogram bin is incremented.

histogram render target using additive blending (Figure 4.2). Afterwards an entity's visibility can be queried in any shader stage accessing its bin (texel) in the histogram texture.

4.2.1 ID Assignment

Obviously, the assignment of IDs to entities plays an integral part in the algorithm. In the simplest case a single ID can be assigned per object. Such an ID may be a user-specified attribute, but system generated semantics like the primitive or instance ID are also possible. However, more sophisticated assignment schemes can be used that enable visibility queries for subregions in screen-space. Therefore we subdivide the screen space into $2^t \times 2^t$ tiles and compute the final ID as follows:

$$ID = 2^{2t}ID_{\text{base}} + 2^t y_{\text{tile}} + x_{\text{tile}}.$$

Not only does such an assignment scheme allow querying the visibility of an entity in particular regions of the screen, but also enables queries in a hierarchical fashion building a quad-tree type structure. For instance, consider Figure 4.3(b). The

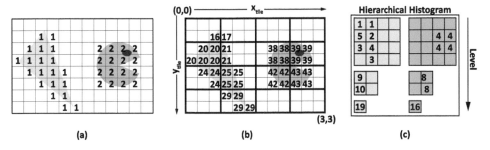

Figure 4.3. (a) The item buffer stores one base identifier per entity; (b) item buffer with 4×4 screen tiling; (c) histogram hierarchy obtained from (b).

visibility of the triangle in tiles $[0, 1] \times [2, 3]$ can be queried with a single access to the hierarchy(Figure 4.3(c)).

4.2.2   Direct3D 10 Implementation

To integrate the hierarchical item buffer into the Direct3D 10 rendering pipeline, the following steps have to be implemented: creating the item buffer and scattering.

Creating the item buffer. Creating the item buffer is performed in two steps. First we render all occluders into the depth buffer (see Listing 4.1). In a second pass we render all entities while leaving depth testing, as well as writing to the depth buffer enabled. The pixel shader then computes the entity's ID and, to decouple histogram coordinate computation from scattering, the according bin index, i.e., a texture coordinate within the histogram texture.

```
cbuffer cbHistogramDimensions
{
  float2 hDim;      // Width & height of histogram
  float2 tDim;      // Width & height of a tile in pixels
  float3 idScaling; // = float3(2^(2t), 2^t, 1)
};

struct PS_ID {
  float4 Position : SV_POSITION;
  float  BaseID    : TEXCOORD0;
};

float2 psRenderItemBuffer( in PS_ID vsIn ) : SV_TARGET0 {

  // Base ID and tile IDs
  float3 ID = float3( vsIn.BaseID,
    floor(vsIn.Position.xy) / tDim );

  // Composed ID
  float   itemID = dot( idScaling, ID );

  // Relative histogram texture coordinates [0,1]^2
  float tmp = itemID / hDim.x;
  float x   = frac( tmp );
  float y   = floor( tmp ) / hDim.y;

  // Relative viewport coordinates [-1;1]^2
  return (-1 + 2 * float2(x,y) + 1 / hDim);
}
```

Listing 4.1. HLSL pixel shader for rendering into an item buffer.

```
Texture2D<float2> tItemBuffer;

float4 vsScatter( in uint VertexID : SV_VERTEXID ) : SV_POSITION
[ uint w,h;
  tItemBuffer.GetDimensions( w, h );

  uint x = VertexID % w;
  uint y = VertexID / w;

  return float4( tItemBuffer.Load(int3(x,y,0)), 0, 1 );
}
```

Listing 4.2. HLSL vertex shader for scattering.

Scattering. Scattering is the second pass of the algorithm (see Listing 4.2). The histogram render target is bound to the output merger stage and the blending stage is configured to perform additive blending. The item buffer obtained in the previous pass is bound as an input resource to the vertex shader and a point list as large as the item buffer's pixel count is rendered. From the system generated vertex ID a lookup coordinate into the item buffer is computed to load the histogram bin's coordinate computed in the previous pass, which then is directly sent to the rasterization stage.

As a final and optional step, the natively supported mipmap generation scheme may be used to construct the hierarchy on the histogram. Please note that due to the inherent filtering in this creation scheme, the counters in the histogram bins have to be incremented by 2^{2t} in order to ensure correct results in the coarsest hierarchy level.

A potential performance bottleneck regarding scattering should be considered when implementing the algorithm. Scattering may trigger many successive increments by sending point primitives to the same bin and hence generates a lot of overdraw which degenerates the overall scattering performance. This is especially the case when screen tiling is kept low and the entity covers a large area in the item buffer.

Another cause for degraded performance are pixels that are not covered by an entity after they have been rasterized. Unfortunately, these pixels cannot be discarded before scattering, and reserving an additional bin to count the occurance of uncovered pixels may cause massive overdraw. Fortunately those pixels can be removed in the scattering process by initializing the item buffer with a bin index or histogram coordinate that does not fall into the histogram viewport. Hence we can rely on the rasterization stage to automatically cull those point primitives when scattered.

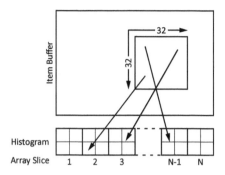

Figure 4.4. The compute shader operates on 32×32 blocks of the item buffer. For each ID in the item buffer, address (array slice, pixel coordinates) in the histogram is computed.

```
RWTexture2DArray<uint> Histogram : register( u0 );
Texture2D<uint> ItemBuffer       : register( t0 );

[numthreads(32,32,1)]
void CSMain(
  uint3 GID  : SV_GROUPID,
  uint3 DTID : SV_DISPATCHTHREADID,
  uint3 GTID : SV_GROUPTHREADID,
  uint  GI   : SV_GROUPINDEX )
{
  // Input dimensions
  uint w0,h0,s0;
  uint w1, h1;
  Histogram.GetDimensions( w0, h0, s0 );
  ItemBuffer.GetDimensions( w1, h1 );

  // xy pixel coordinate in the item buffer
  int2 pixelIndex = DTID.xy;

  // Entity ID
  uint entityID   = ItemBuffer[pixelIndex];

  // xy pixel coordinate in the histogram
  uint2 tileIndex = pixelIndex *
    uint2( w0, h0 ) / uint2( w1, h1 );

  // Interlocked increment
  InterlockedAdd( itemHistogram[int3(tileIndex,entityID)], 1 );
}
```

Listing 4.3. The scattering compute shader for generating the entity histogram.

4.2.3   Direct3D 11 Implementation

One of the new features of Direct3D 11 is the direct support for scattering in pixel and compute shaders. This greatly simplifies and extends the implementation of the hierarchical item buffer. Instead of exploiting the conventional graphics pipeline, a compute shader can be used to transform the item buffer into an entity histogram. As illustrated in Figure 4.4 our implementation of the compute shader operates on blocks of 32×32 item buffer pixels. Each pixel in the block is associated with a thread. Each thread reads the ID or histogram bin index from the item buffer and computes the target address, depending on the format or layout of the histogram texture. For simplicity we allocated a histogram texture array, where each array slice corresponds to one entity and each pixel in the slice corresponds to one screen tile. After the address of the histogram bin has been computed, an interlocked operation (as can be seen in Figure 4.3), is performed to increment the counter in the bin.

Rendering into an item buffer may limit certain applications since only one entity can appear in a pixel of the item buffer, i.e., mutual occlusion of entities has to be resolved in the item buffer creation pass. This limitation, inherent in our Direct3D 10 implementation, can be circumvented with Direct3D 11. Instead of rendering into an item buffer and scattering afterwards, the scattering can be directly exploited in the pixel shader to build the entity histogram. Care must be taken to ensure that the depth test against the previously rendered depth buffer is performed. By disabling depth writes, the early-z optimization ensures that an entity's visibility is correctly resolved before the pixel shader is executed.

4.3   Application

In the demo available in the web materials, we demonstrate the granularity and efficiency of our algorithm by means of a small example. We applied the item buffer visibility determination algorithm to speed up the shadow volume rendering technique for instanced shadow casters. Instancing greatly reduces the draw call overhead for many instances of the same object and shadow volumes are capable of producing highly accurate shadows, but are quite costly to render. Since the introduction of the geometry, shader shadow volumes can be created directly on the GPU. Hence this algorithm is now capable of handling dynamic scenes as gracefully as purely static ones. Unfortunately, the shadow volume extrusion can be quite costly, especially for many or complex objects. Besides that, the extruded shadow volumes have to be rasterized which consumes a lot of fill rate. Our solution is inspired by the algorithm described in [Lloyd et al. 04]. We refrain from extruding a shadow volume if the shadow caster lies within the shadow

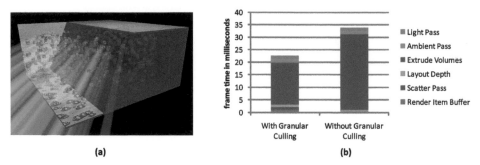

Figure 4.5. (a) Our application rendering 400 shadow casters. We do not extrude shadow volumes for casters contained in the shadow of the box. (b) Statistics for the frame seen in (a) obtained on a GeForce 8800 GTX. Creating a 512×512 item buffer and scattering into the histogram took about two milliseconds. Scattering alone took about one millisecond.

volume of another caster. This case is easily detected by applying a visibility pass from the light source's point of view.

In our example, shadow casters are rendered with instancing and the on-the-fly generated instance ID is used to identify each individual instance in the item buffer. The volume extrusion pass then queries the visibility directly on the GPU and only creates a shadow volume, if the instance is visible from the light source. For more details on the implementation, please refer to the source code available in the web materials.

4.4   Results

We have analyzed several aspects of our algorithm. Our results are restricted to Direct3D 10 level hardware, because the succeding generation of graphics cards is not yet available at the time this chapter is written. Figure 4.5 shows an in-depth analysis of the rendering time for a particular frame rendered on a Geforce 8800

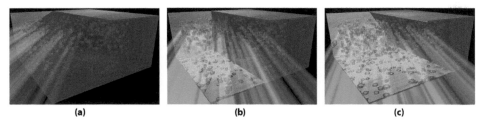

Figure 4.6. Three different stages of culling. From left to right, an increased number of shadow volumes are extruded.

Configuration	100 objects			250 objects			500 objects		
	A	B	C	A	B	C	A	B	C
NC+NI	85	85	85	36	36	36	14	14	14
NC+I	102	102	102	45	45	45	22	22	22
PC+NI	72	72	72	30	30	30	15	15	15
IB+I	188	125	107	93	60	52	51	32	27

Table 4.1. Rendering performance on a Geforce 8800 GTX. **NC:** No Culling, **NI:** No Instancing, **I:** Instancing, **PC:** Predicated Culling, **IB:** Item Buffer.

GTX gaphics card. The application renders 400 shadow casters with a single instanced draw call. As can be seen, the shadow volume extrusion pass takes a significant amount of the entire frame time. In this example, an item buffer of 512×512 pixels was used while the final image was rendered at a resolution of 1280×720 pixels. Both item buffer creation and scattering took about two milliseconds. Scattering alone took about one millisecond in this example. Please note, that the frame time for the scattering pass does not depend on the number of entities, but on the resolution of the item buffer.

Further, we compared our method to occlusion predicates. In this case, we cannot exploit instanced rendering because hardware occlusion queries operate on a per draw call granularity, i.e., visibility for individual entities, like individual instances, cannot be resolved. Thus each shadow caster is individually rendered and tested for visibility. In our predicated render path, we create a Direct3D 10 query object for each caster at application startup, set the occlusion predication flag and use a depth buffer of 512×512 pixels in the visibility pass. As illustrated in Figure 4.6, we have measured rendering performance for an increasing amount of objects for which shadow volumes have to be extruded. Results are shown in Table 4.1 and Table 4.2. Like in the previous example the rendering resolution was 1280×720 pixels and the resolution of the item buffer was 512×512 pixels. For completeness we included performance measurements for scenarios that did not exploit any kind of culling.

Configuration	100 objects			250 objects			500 objects		
	A	B	C	A	B	C	A	B	C
NC+NI	153	153	153	66	65	65	26	28	32
NC+I	193	199	280	85	92	130	45	49	71
PC+NI	85	58	51	35	25	20	16	10	9
IB+I	405	263	326	244	146	177	137	79	99

Table 4.2. Rendering performance on a Radeon 4890. **NC:** No Culling, **NI:** No Instancing, **I:** Instancing, **PC:** Predicated Culling, **IB:** Item Buffer.

As can be seen, our culling approach outperformed all other rendering paths in the application by large margins. Due to the costly geometry shader, culling is quite beneficial and rendering performance increases significantly. Interestingly, occlusion-predicated rendering exposes rather subpar performance in our scenarios, even for a small number of objects.

4.5   Conclusion

We have presented a culling method that operates directly on the GPU, which is entirely transparent to the application and very simple to implement, especially on the next generation of hardware and graphics APIs. We have shown that with very little overhead, rendering time per frame can be reduced significantly, especially for costly shaders or costly rendering techniques. It is especially targeted at early shader stages like the geometry shader and we believe that its target applications are manifold. For example, [Engelhardt and Dachsbacher 09] have shown an application of this technique to accelerate per pixel displacement mapping, but it also opens the possibility for visibility-based LOD control and culling in tesselation shaders.

Bibliography

[Bittner et al. 04] Jiří Bittner, Michael Wimmer, Harald Piringer, and Werner Purgathofer. "Coherent Hierarchical Culling: Hardware Occlusion Queries Made Useful." *Computer Graphics Forum* 23:3 (2004), 615–624. Proceedings EUROGRAPHICS 2004.

[Engelhardt and Dachsbacher 09] Thomas Engelhardt and Carsten Dachsbacher. "Granular Visibility Queries on the GPU." In *I3D '09: Proceedings of the 2009 Symposium on Interactive 3D Graphics and Games*, pp. 161–167. New York: ACM, 2009.

[Lloyd et al. 04] Brandon Lloyd, Jeremy Wend, Naga K. Govindaraju, and Dinesh Manocha. "CC Shadow Volumes." In *Rendering Techniques*, pp. 197–206, 2004.

[Scheuermann and Hensley 07] Thorsten Scheuermann and Justin Hensley. "Efficient Histogram Generation Using Scattering on GPUs." In *I3D '07: Proceedings of the 2007 Symposium on Interactive 3D Graphics and Games*, pp. 33–37. New York: ACM, 2007.

[Weghorst et al. 84] Hank Weghorst, Gary Hooper, and Donald P. Greenberg. "Improved Computational Methods for Ray Tracing." *ACM Transactions on Graphics* 3:1 (1984), 52–69.

Realistic Depth of Field in Postproduction

David Illes and Peter Horvath

5.1 Introduction

Depth of field (DOF) is an effect, typical in photography, which results in regions of varying focus based on their distance from the camera. In computer-generated special effects, artists try to mimic the effects of DOF to produce more realistic images [Demers 04]. When integrating computer-generated effects, which are rendered in perfect focus, with real captured images, DOF must be applied during the compositing phase. Mixing real and synthetic images requires a realistic defocus effect that can mimic the behavior of the original camera.

In this chapter we present an interactive GPU-accelerated DOF implementation that extends the capabilities of the existing methods with automatic edge improvements and physically based parameters. Defocus effects are usually controlled by blur radius, but can also be driven by physically based properties. Our technique supports postproduction defocus on images and sequences using a grayscale depth map image and parameters like focal length, f-stop values, subject magnitude, camera distance, and the real depth of the image.

5.2 Depth-of-Field Equations

Realistic depth of field is necessary compositing live action and CGI images. The quality of the results can be enhanced if depth of field is configured using real-world camera parameters.

Replace the far distance by an arbitrary distance D, the blur disk diameter b at that distance is

$$b = \frac{fm_s}{N}\frac{D-s}{D},$$

where f is the focal length, m_s is the subject magnification, N is the f-stop number, and s is the focus distance. F-stop number can be calculated using the following formula:

$$N = 2^{i/2},$$

where $i = 1(f/1.4)$, $i = 2(f/2)$, $i = 3(f/2.8)$, etc.

On a real-world camera, the *f-number* is usually adjusted in discrete steps called *f-stops*. Each value is marked with its corresponding *f-number*, and represents a halving of the light intensity from the previous stop. This corresponds to a decrease of the pupil and aperture diameters by a factor of $\sqrt{2}$ or about 1.414.

When the background is at the far limit of DOF, the blur disk diameter is equal to the circle of confusion c, and the blur is just imperceptible. The *circle of confusion* (CoC) is an optical spot caused by the effect of light rays from a lens not coming to a perfect focus when imaging a point source.

Based on the equations, the artist can set the camera *focal length, subject magnitude factor* and the *f-stop* value. An image sequence with depth maps typically does not contain real physical distance values. The user must provide the image range, which represents the foreground and background distance of the image, as well as the camera distance, which is the camera's distance from the image foreground (see Figure 5.1). The real physical distance between the camera and the focus point is computed as

$$s = d_{\text{camera}} + Im_r(Z_{\text{focus}}/Z_{\text{max}}),$$

where d_{camera} is the camera distance from the foreground, Im_r is the image range, Z_{focus} is the depth value of the focus point, Z_{max} is the maximum value of the Z-depth.

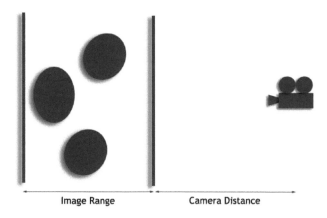

Image Range   Camera Distance

Figure 5.1. Camera position and image range.

Let x_d be the distance of the current pixel from the focus point. The distance is calculated based on the following equation:

$$x_d = Im_r |Z_{\text{focus}} - Z_{\text{current}}| / Z_{\text{max}}.$$

Using the above distances, the blur diameter b is defined as

$$b = \frac{fm_s}{N} \frac{x_d}{s}.$$

5.3 Camera Lens Simulation

Diaphragms are generally constructed with aperture blades that form an iris shape. Aperture shape (see Figure 5.2) affects the form of the light beams projected on the film. More blades result in more circular light beam shapes on the resulted image. Such aperture shapes can be constructed using curves or can be read as a custom bitmap image. A custom image aperture mask makes it possible to generate defocus effects based on real camera apertures. Instead of the advanced layered blurring in [Kraus and Strengert 07], our approach uses a local neighborhood search to approximate the final pixel color based on the depth properties of the image.

Our depth-of-field system uses several masks based on the depth value of the current pixel. For a seamless depth-of-field effect, the aperture kernel matrices need to have an odd width and height, and they must be interpolated. Smooth changes in depth of field require subpixel precision and floating-point values for the masks. The current kernel mask is calculated with the original adjacent kernels. For example if the new kernel size is 12.4×12.4 we generate the new mask from the 11×11 and from the 13×13 kernels with linear interpolation.

5.4 Exposure Simulation

During the exposure process, the film or the CCD unit records exposure values. The film is chemically processed and scanned, or the CCD matrix values are

Figure 5.2. Examples for the shape of the aperture blade.

read and converted to obtain a digital image. The final image I is transformed into pixel values without any additional physical properties. Exposure values are converted to pixel values using a non-linear mapping.

Also during the exposure process, each disk of light contributes to a neighborhood on the film. In theory, this results in a convolution of the pixel values similar to a Gaussian blur; however, simply performing a convolution on the pixel values would not generate the same visual result as a real world defocus.

We use the idea of [Cyril et al. 05] to simulate this phenomenon using an inverse mapping of the film. We also want to mix the effect of the contributing pixels in the exposure space.

5.4.1 Improvements by Local Neighborhood Blending

Current depth-of-field post processing implementations usually do not produce realistic results; edges are often blurred incorrectly, generating artifacts such as color bleeding, and darkened silhouettes. These artifacts result in images that are unrealistic. In the following sections we present a local neighborhood interpolation technique for eliminating these artifacts. Our approach uses an edge improvement algorithm for automatic and realistic depth-of-field calculation and is performed in three steps: pixel accumulation, pixel re-accumulation, and bloom.

Pixel Accumulation. The color of the current pixel is calculated from the color and luminance value of the adjacent pixels (Listing 5.1) based on the aperture mask (Figure 5.3).

The R,G,B, and luminance channels coming from the neighboring pixels are accumulated in different buffers. The number of neighbors which take part in the accumulation depends on the Z-depth. In an image where two objects with

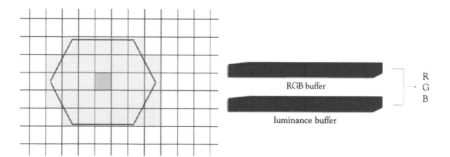

Figure 5.3. Marked pixels are processed during the accumulation phase. Pixel colors and luminance values are stored in the accumulation buffers. Final pixel is calculated based on the results of the two buffers.

```
for all neighboring pixels {
  // a.) Luminance:
  L = 0.3 * R + 0.59 * G + 0.11 * B;
  // b.) Multiply luminance with the aperture mask value
  multL = F(z) * L,
  // where F(z) scales the mask based on the pixel distance.
  // c.) Accumulate the resulting value with the RGB values.
  pixel->r += neighborColor->r * multL;
  pixel->g += neighborColor->g * multL;
  pixel->b += neighborColor->b * multL;
  // d.) Accumulate the luminance of the pixel.
  pixel->lum += multL;
}
// After accumulation, calculate the final color from
// the color and luminance buffers.
if (pixel->lum > 0) {
  pixel->r /= pixel->lum;
  pixel->g /= pixel->lum;
  pixel->b /= pixel->lum;
}
```

Listing 5.1. Pixel accumulation scheme.

different distances are close to each other the result can contain artifacts, since different mask sizes are used on the layers. Let us define an epsilon value as the minimum depth difference at which the two layers shall appear with different mask sizes, i.e., where there are edges in the image. Here the dominant pixel from the original image is always the one which is blurred the most. In order to get more realistic result, the sharper pixels have to be recalculated using the depth value associated with the more defocused pixel. The final color is a distance-based weighted average of the original color and the recalculated color. If the object in the background appears sharper, we ignore the pixels from the accumulation step which are outside a specified distance called samplingRadius.

Pixel Re-accumulation. The pixel recalculation phase is executed differently depending on where the focus point is. First case is when the focus point is between the foreground and the background. The other type is when the objects are all behind the focus point. In the first approach, if the foreground is more defocused than the background, then the pixels need to be recalculated with the kernel belonging to the foreground pixel weighted with the distance of the two pixels (Figure 5.4). Since the foreground pixel kernel is bigger, the values needed for recalculation *(depth, distance)* can be defined in the accumulation step of the foreground pixel (Listing 5.2). So the foreground recalculation can be processed only when all the pixel calculations are ready. Recalculation is based on the

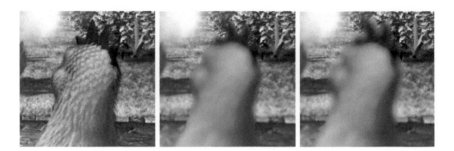

Figure 5.4. The figure shows the original rendered image, the image with defocus applied without the re-accumulation phase, and the effect of the re-accumulation step.

```
float dist = (abs(imgX - neighX)*abs(imgX - neighX)
+ abs(imgY - neighY)*abs(imgY - neighY));
float distScale = 1.0f - dist / zKernel->r;
if (distScale > recalcDist[neighborIndex])
  recalcDist[neighborIndex] = distScale;
if (zValue > recalcZValue[neighborIndex]) {
  recalcZDepth[neighborIndex] = zDepth;
  recalcZValue[neighborIndex] = zValue;
}
```

Listing 5.2. Collecting parameters of foreground re-accumulation.

previous calculation technique using the new calculated kernel, but all the adjacent pixels take part in the computation.

In the second approach the background recalculation is based on layers where the image is divided into N range, and the adjacent pixels are grouped by their depth value (Listing 5.3).

The current pixel is recalculated based on each dominant layer. A layer is dominant if its distance and the number of contained pixels is above a specified threshold (Listing 5.4).

```
int group = neighborPixel->group;
pixelCategoriesNum[group]++;
if (distScale > pixelCategoriesDist[group])
  pixelCategoriesDist[group] = distScale;
if (neighborPixel->zDepth < pixelCategoriesZDepth[group]) {
  pixelCategoriesZDepth[group] = neighborPixel->zDepth;
  pixelCategoriesZValue[group] = neighborPixel->zValue;
}
```

Listing 5.3. Collecting parameters of background re-accumulation.

```
  if (pixelCategoriesDist[i] > 0.05f
   && pixelCategoriesNum[i] > zKernel->size / 40) {
  reaccumulateBG(image,&kernel,pixelCategoriesZDepth[i],
    pixelCategoriesZValue[i],pixelCategoriesDist[i],
    pos,i);
  }
```

Listing 5.4. Dominant layer filtering.

```
for all pixels {
 for all neighbors {
  float multiplicator = (1.0f - distance / zKernel->r)
   *(recalcZDepth[pos]?recalcZDepth[pos]:
   imagePixels[pos].zDepth);
  if (multiplicator > 0)
  bloomValues[neighborIndex] += multiplicator;
  }
}
float bloomScale = bloomValues[pos]*bloomAmount/1000.0f;
newColor = bloomScale*white + (1.0f - bloomScale)*pixelColor;
```

Listing 5.5. Bloom effect.

The per-pixel-based recalculation can be done right after the calculation step. During the recalculation phase, only those pixels that are in the current layer or behind it are taken into account. Pixels that come from a layer closer to the camera are skipped.

Blooming. For more realistic highlights during the accumulation and reaccumulation steps, a *multiplicator* value is defined for the adjacent pixels based on the distance and the aperture kernel. Using the external bloom amount parameter, which controls the strength of the bloom effect, the current pixel color is scaled into white (Listing 5.5).

5.5 CUDA-Accelerated Computation

This depth-of-field approach has been implemented on the GPU using NVIDIA's CUDA API. With the CUDA architecture, computation-intensive parts of the program can be offloaded to the GPU. Highly parallelizable portions of our technique can be isolated into functions that are executed on the GPU. A given function can be executed many times, in parallel, as many threads. The resulting program is called a *kernel*. In our implementation each thread computes a single pixel.

```
// Parameters
CUDA_SAFE_CALL(cudaMalloc((void**)&paramsGPU,
sizeof(float) * 20));
CUDA_SAFE_CALL(cudaMemcpy(paramsGPU, params,
sizeof(float) * 20, cudaMemcpyHostToDevice));

CUDA_SAFE_CALL(cudaMalloc((void**)&imageGPU,
sizeof(float) * 4 * image.getSize()));
CUDA_SAFE_CALL(cudaMalloc((void**)&zMapGPU,
sizeof(float) * zMap.getSize()));
CUDA_SAFE_CALL(cudaMalloc((void**)&kernelsGPU,
sizeof(float) * kernelBufferSize));
CUDA_SAFE_CALL(cudaMalloc((void**)&outputGPU,
sizeof(float) * 4 * image.getSize()));
CUDA_SAFE_CALL(cudaMalloc((void**)&recalcDistGPU,
sizeof(float) * image.getSize()));
CUDA_SAFE_CALL(cudaMalloc((void**)&recalcZDepthGPU,
sizeof(float) * image.getSize()));
CUDA_SAFE_CALL(cudaMalloc((void**)&bloomValuesGPU,
sizeof(float) * image.getSize()));

// Upload buffers to the GPU device.
CUDA_SAFE_CALL(cudaMemcpy(imageGPU, imageData,
sizeof(float) * 4 * image.getSize(), cudaMemcpyHostToDevice));
CUDA_SAFE_CALL(cudaMemcpy(zMapGPU, zMapData,
sizeof(float) * zMap.getSize(), cudaMemcpyHostToDevice));
CUDA_SAFE_CALL(cudaMemcpy(kernelsGPU, kernels,
sizeof(float) * kernelBufferSize, cudaMemcpyHostToDevice));
```

Listing 5.6. Allocating buffers and uploading data.

In the first step, the input data is offloaded to the GPU's global memory. The input data includes the source buffers with red, green, blue, and luminance values, and the Z-depth map with a scalar grayscale value (Listing 5.6).

Based on the depth, we place masks of every possible size above the pixels produced from the original kernel mask by linear transformation. The transformed main aperture kernels are precomputed by the CPU and are also offloaded to the device. The user parameters (like focal point, blur strength, edge improvements constans, threshold for highlighting pixels, amount of highlights etc.) are also collected and transferred.

Kernel interpolation is computed on the GPU (Listing 5.7) using the uploaded kernel matrices because interpolation is unique for all threads depending on the actual pixel parameters. Each thread calculates a pixel and accumulates the result of the defocus to the global buffer channels on the GPU. During accumulation the pixels which must take part in the additional recalculation step are marked. The information for recalculation is stored in different global buffers.

```
dim3 threadBlock(NUM_THREADS,NUM_THREADS);
int blockCount = (int)(numPixels /
(NUM_THREADS*NUM_THREADS)) + 1;
accumulateGPU<<<blockCount, threadBlock>>>(imageGPU,zMapGPU,
kernelsGPU,paramsGPU,outputGPU,
recalcDistGPU,recalcZDepthGPU);
```

Listing 5.7. Computation step.

```
float* resultData = new float[4*size];
CUDA_SAFE_CALL(cudaMemcpy(resultData, outputGPU,
 sizeof(float) * 4 * size, cudaMemcpyDeviceToHost));

for(int i=0;i<numPixels;i++) {
    int pos = pixels[i];
    int index = 4*i;
    imagePixels[pos].r = resultData[index];
    imagePixels[pos].g = resultData[index+1];
    imagePixels[pos].b = resultData[index+2];
    imagePixels[pos].lum = resultData[index+3];
}
```

Listing 5.8. Downloading results.

In the third stage, pixels requiring edge quality improvements are recalculated. Like the previous calculation, this process can be assigned to the GPU.

Finally, the calculated color and luminance values are downloaded (Listing 5.8) and the final image may be displayed on the screen or saved to a file.

5.6 Results

The technique has been implemented as a Spark plugin for Autodesk Flame 2009 (Figure 5.5). The spark extension has been successfully used in various commercial and short film projects.

In order to demonstrate the efficiency of our technique, we provide some performance results here (see Tables 5.1, 5.2, and 5.3). These results were measured on an AMD Athlon 6000+ (3GHz) workstation with 2 GB RAM and GeForce 9800 GT GPU.

The demo application can be initialized with two input clips (*image and depth map*). The DOF effect may be controlled interactively using the graphical user interface. Each parameter is animatable to allow artists to control DOF transi-

Figure 5.5. The rendered image and the image with defocus applied. (Image courtesy of GYAR Post Production.)

	CPU 100%	**GPU 100%**
Accumulation	13.469 sec	6.265 sec
Re-accumulation	2.969 sec	1.438 sec
Calculation	16.5 sec	7.776 sec

Table 5.1. Simulation speed using a 64×64 kernel.

tions. The focus may be changed by selecting a part of the image that should be fully in focus. The application is able to render the DOF effect using two modes: *artist* and *physically based*. In the artist mode, the amount of defocus is set by adjusting the kernel size. In the physically-based mode, real-world properties and camera parameters can be defined for the defocus effect. In this mode the amount of blur is computed based on the camera parameters.

Post-processing solutions for DOF are only approximations of the distributed ray tracing technique described by [Cook et al. 84]. These approximations are imperfect because there is typically insufficient information about partially occluded scene elements at post-processing time. Therefore, the proposed approach may be used to mimic real-world depth of field with some limitations.

Because the single input image (with depth map) does not contain information about transparent objects and disoccluded geometries, some artifacts may result.

	CPU 60%	**GPU 60%**
Accumulation	4.984 sec	2.468 sec
Re-accumulation	0.579 sec	0.469 sec
Calculation	5.625 sec	3.063 sec

Table 5.2. Simulation speed using a 64×64 kernel resized to 60%.

	CPU 20%	GPU 20%
Accumulation	0.766 sec	0.328 sec
Re-accumulation	0.015 sec	0.079 sec
Calculation	0.844 sec	0.531 sec

Table 5.3. Simulation speed using a 64×64 kernel resized to 20%.

A possible extension to our post-processing technique might be to use multiple images per-frame as suggested by [Kass et al. 06]. Using this extension, the input scene is rendered into separate foreground and background layers that are defocused into a single output image. Another possible algorithm is to render deep images (similar to deep shadows [Lokovic and Veach 00]) with multiple color and depth values.

The disadvantage of our algorithm is the usual $O(n^2)$ complexity of the defocus problem. With increasing kernel size and image size the computation can take minutes to complete. For this problem, [Kass et al. 06] suggested a diffusion based solution with linear complexity, but the aperture size is limited to a Gaussian one. Our implementation gives more control for the depth-of-field effect, and scalability is maintained by caching repeating kernel calculations together with proxy image calculation for faster feedback.

5.7 Conclusion

The additional edge quality improvements in our depth-of-field implementation result in more realistic and believable images. The disadvantage of the local neighborhood blending algorithm is the quadratic computational capacity, however this can be compensated by the GPU.

Bibliography

[Cook et al. 84] Robert L. Cook, Thomas Porter, and Loren Carpenter. "Distributed Ray Tracing." In *Proceedings of SIGGRAPH '84*, 26, 26, 1984.

[Cyril et al. 05] Pichard Cyril, Michelin Sylvain, and Tubach Olivier. "Photographic Depth of Field Blur Rendering." In *Proceedings of WSCG 2005*, 2005.

[Demers 04] Joe Demers. "Depth of Field: A Survey of Techniques." In *GPU Gems*, pp. 375–390. Boston: Addison-Wesley, 2004.

[Kass et al. 06] Michael Kass, Aaron Lefohn, and John Owen. "Interactive Depth of Field Using Simulated Diffusion on a GPU." *Technical Report*.

[Kraus and Strengert 07] M. Kraus and M. Strengert. "Depth-of-Field Rendering by Pyramidal Image Processing." In *Proceedings of Eurographics 2007*, pp. 584–599, 2007.

[Lokovic and Veach 00] Tom Lokovic and Eric Veach. "Deep Shadow Maps." In *Proceedings of SIGGRAPH 2000*, 2000.

6

Real-Time Screen Space Cloud Lighting
Kaori Kubota

6.1 Introduction

Clouds are an important visual element when creating realistic virtual environments. Without clouds, the scene would appear too simple and monotonous. However, rendering beautiful clouds in real time can be very challenging because clouds exhibit multiple scattering that is difficult to calculate while maintaining interactive frame rates. Unfortunately most games can not afford the computational cost of computing physically correct cloud lighting.

This chapter introduces an extremely simple screen space technique for rendering plausible clouds in real time. This technique has been implemented on the PLAYSTATION3 and was used in the game *Uncharted Waters Online*. This technique is not focused on strict physical accuracy but instead relies on recreating the empirical appearance of clouds. This technique is suitable for ground scenes where players stay on the ground and are only able to view the clouds from a distance.

Lighting is one of the most important aspects of creating beautiful and realistic clouds. When sun light passes through clouds, it is absorbed, scattered, and reflected by cloud particles. Figure 6.1 demonstrates a typical outdoor scene. As shown in the figure, when looking at clouds from the view point indicated in the diagram, the clouds nearest to the sun appear brightest. This phenomenon is due to the sun's light reaching the back portion of the cloud and then, through multiple scattering events, re-emerging on the front part of the cloud (nearest the viewer). This observation is a key part of the technique presented in this chapter. In order to recreate this visual cue, a simple point blur or directional blur in screen space is sufficient to mimic light scattering through clouds.

Figure 6.1. A typical outdoor scene. The clouds nearest the sun exhibit the most scattering and appear brightest.

6.2   Implementation

Our technique for rendering clouds is executed in three passes. First, cloud density is rendered to an off screen render target. Cloud density is a scalar value that can be painted by an artist. Next, the density map is blurred. Finally the blurred density map is used to render the clouds with the appearance of scattering.

6.2.1   Lighting

When light goes through clouds, it is attenuated and scattered by cloud particles. At a given point on the cloud, there is incoming light, which arrives directly from the sun, as well as scattered light, which has reached that point through one or more bounces. Some of the light that reaches a point on the cloud is absorbed and some is scattered deeper into the cloud before finally emerging on the other side (the side nearest the viewer). Lighting clouds involves computing the amount of light passing through the clouds along the lighting ray. [Mitchell 07] estimates the probability of occlusion of the light source at each pixel by summing samples along a ray from the viewer to the light source. We consider cloud particles as transparent occluders and take transparency into account.

During the lighting pass, we compute the amount of light that passes through cloud particles at each pixel on the cloud plane. The cloud plane will be described in Section 6.2.2. We use a density map which represents the density of clouds at each pixel. The density map rendered in the first pass is blurred toward the sun's position.

The sun's position is given by perspective-transforming the sun's light direction vector at each pixel. Note that the blur becomes directional if the light ray is perpendicular to the view ray, and the blur direction should be inverted when the sun is behind the view position. Refer to [Kozlov 04] for a detailed discussion of perspective-transforming a directional vector.

```
// Pixel shader input
struct SPSInput {
    float2 vUV        : TEXCOORD0;
    float3 vWorldDir  : TEXCOORD1;
    float2 vScreenPos : VPOS;
};
// Pixel shader
float4 main( SPSInput Input ) {
    // compute direction of blur.
    float2 vUVMove = Input.vScreenPos * SCALE + OFFSET;

    // Scale blur vector considering distance from camera.
    float3 vcDir = normalize( Input.vWorldDir );
    float  fDistance = GetDistanceFromDir( vcDir );
    vUVMove *= UV_SCALE / fDistance;

    // Limit blur vector length.
    float2 fRatio = abs( vUVMove / MAX_LENGTH );
    float fMaxLen = max( fRatio.x, fRatio.y );
    vUVMove *= fMaxLen > 1.0f ? 1.0f / fMaxLen : 1.0f;

    // Compute offset for weight.
    // FALLOFF must be negative so that far pixels affect less.
    float fExpScale = dot( vUVMove, vUVMove ) * FALLOFF;

    // Blur density toward the light.
    float fShadow = tex2D( sDensity, Input.vUV ).a;
    float fWeightSum = 1.0f;
    for ( int i = 1; i < FILTER_RADIUS; ++i ) {
      float fWeight = exp( fExpScale * i );
      fShadow +=
            fWeight * tex2D(sDensity, Input.vUV+vUVMove*i).a;
      fWeightSum += fWeight;
    }
    fShadow /= fWeightSum;

    // 0 means no shadow and 1 means all shadowed pixel.
    return fShadow;
}
```

Listing 6.1. A pixel shader code snippet; constants are capitalized. This shader can provide either parallel or point blurring by setting the **SCALE** and **OFFSET** constants appropriately.

There are several requirements of the blur. The blur weights fall off according to distance from the sun because particles at a far distance are affected less by in-scattering. Also, the blur length or strength should be tweaked according to distance in world space. Sample code is shown in Listing 6.1.

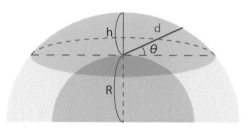

Figure 6.2. The earth and atmosphere. The deep blue regions is recognized as sky by a player.

6.2.2 Distance to the Sky and Clouds

We render sky as a screen quad in the final pass. In the pixel shader, the screen position is back projected to the world direction and is used to compute the distance light passes through the atmosphere. This distance is used to approximate the amount of scattering.

When the player stands on the ground, the atmospheric volume is represented as a spherical cap; you can visualize this as a piece of a sphere that is cut by a plane. Figure 6.2 demonstrates the shape of the volume. Clearly, when the sun is on the horizon, light must travel further to reach the viewer than when the sun is directly overhead. The distance light pass through the atmosphere d is

$$d(\theta) = -R\sin\theta + \sqrt{R^2\sin^2\theta + h^2 + 2h}.$$

Where R is the radius of the earth, h is the thickness of the atmosphere and θ is the vertical angle between a ground plane and the direction vector. We also compute the distance to the clouds using this equation with h' in the final pass (h' is the height of clouds and $h' < h$).

6.2.3 Scattering

In the final pass, sky, clouds and all other geometry are rendered with daylight scattering using [Hoffman and Preetham 02]. Here is the equation:

$$L(s,\theta) = e^{-s\beta_{ex}}L_0 + \left(\frac{\beta_{sc}(\theta)}{\beta_{ex}}E_{\text{sun}}\right)(1 - e^{-s\beta_{ex}}),$$

where s is the distance from the view position, β_{ex} is an extinction parameter, $\beta_{sc}(\theta)$ is in-scattering phase function, E_{sun} is the sun light, and L_0 is light from surfaces. For the sky, L_0 is zero. For the clouds, the blurred density map is used to compute L_0. We compute L_0 by scaling and adding an ambient term. The density map is also used as transparency.

To make the scene more natural, we extended the equation as follows:

$$L(s, \theta) = e^{-s\beta_{ex}} L_0 + \left(\frac{\beta_{sc}(\theta)}{\beta_{cx}} E_{\text{sun}} * \text{shadow} + C\right)(1 - e^{-s\beta_{ex}}),$$

where "shadow" is a shadow term. The shadow term represents the shadows cast by clouds. It is calculated in the second pass using a different falloff parameter and stored in another channel of the blurred map. Although we render a shadow map to cast shadows from clouds, there could be a lit part of terrain under dark clouds, which spoils the natural appearance. Therefore this shadow term is effective to darken the ground under clouds. The term C is a constant that can be used as a standard fog parameter which is useful for artists.

6.3   Results

Figure 6.3 contains screen shots of our technique. In the demo, the clouds are rendered as a uniform grid. A cloud texture includes four density textures in each channel. Each channel represents different layers of clouds and are blended in the pixel shader according to the weather in the first pass. It is also animated by scrolling the texture coordinates.

Figure 6.3. Screen shots that demonstrate our technique.

Figure 6.4. The density map (left) and result (right) without layering.

The size of render target used for blurring is a quarter of the screen resolution, which is sufficient because clouds tend to be somewhat nebulous and low frequency.

6.4   Extensions

Since lighting is performed as a two-dimensional blur, when the clouds become thick, clouds near the sun cast shadow to neighboring area. This phenomenon is acceptable in sunset or sunrise because it is happen in real environment. However, when the sun is above, clouds should not cast shadow to others otherwise it spoils lighting effect and results in poor toned and too darkened clouds.

To solve this, layering the density would be useful. When rendering to the density map, store neighboring clouds to different channels. Figure 6.4 and 6.5 render the same cloud density, but Figure 6.5 divides density as alternate stripes

Figure 6.5. The density map (left) and result (right) with layering.

and stores them to R and G channels, respectively. Blur is also applied to both channels, and these results are combined in the final pass. This approach is suitable for stratocumulus.

6.5 Conclusion

We discussed a technique for rendering a convincing sky in real time. Since the shape of clouds is decoupled from the lighting, procedural cloud generation and animation are possible.

We ignore certain physical properties of the atmosphere in order to create a more efficient technique. For example, no consideration for the density of the atmosphere is made. This property would be necessary in order to create realistic looking sunsets and sunrises. We also ignore the color of the light which goes into the clouds. In a scene with a sunset or sunrise, only the area close to the sun should be lit brightly and colorfully. It is necessary to take a more physically based approach to simulating the scattering between the sun and clouds to get more natural result.

Bibliography

[Hoffman and Preetham 02] Naty Hoffman and Arcot J Preetham. "Rendering Outdoor Light Scattering in Real Time." Available online (http://ati.amd .com/developer/dx9/ATI-LightScattering.pdf).

[Kozlov 04] Simon Kozlov. "Perspective Shadow Maps: Care and Feeding." In *GPU Gems*, edited by Randima Fernando. Boston: Addison-Wesley, 2004. Available online (http://http.developer.nvidia.com/GPUGems/ gpugems_ch14.html).

[Mitchell 07] Kenny Mitchell. "Volumetric Light Scattering as a Post-Process." In *GPU Gems 3*, edited by Hubert Nguyen. Boston: Addison-Wesley, 2007. Available online (http://http.developer.nvidia.com/GPUGems3/gpugems3_ ch13.html).

7

Screen-Space Subsurface Scattering
Jorge Jimenez and Diego Gutierrez

7.1 Introduction

Many materials exhibit a certain degree of translucency, by which light falling onto an object enters its body at one point, scatters within it, then exits the object at some other point. This process is known as *subsurface scattering.* We observe many translucent objects in our daily lives, such as skin, marble, paper, tree leaves, soap, candles, and fruit. In order to render these materials in a realistic way, we must recreate the effects of subsurface scattering in the rendering pipeline.

Skin is one of the most important materials that demonstrates a significant degree of subsurface scattering. Many video games are very character and story driven. These kinds of games seek to create believable, realistic characters so that the player becomes fully immersed in the game. Adding accurate subsurface scattering to human skin, especially on faces, can dramatically improve the overall impression of realism.

There has been an emerging trend towards applying computationally expensive three-dimensional methods (such as ambient occlusion or global illumination) in screen space. We present an algorithm capable of simulating subsurface scattering in screen space as a post-process (see Figure 7.1), which takes as inputs the depth-stencil and color buffer of a rendered frame.

In this chapter we will describe a very efficient screen-space implementation of subsurface scattering. We will measure the cost of our technique against other common screen-space effects such as depth of field or bloom, in order to motivate its implementation in current game engines. As we will see, our method maintains the quality of the best texture-space algorithms but scales better as the number of objects increases (see Figure 7.2).

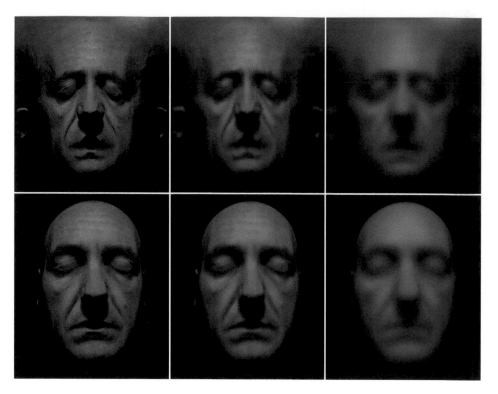

Figure 7.1. Blurring performed in texture space, as done by current real time subsurface scattering algorithms (top). Blurring done directly in screen space (bottom).

7.2   The Texture-Space Approach

7.2.1   Subsurface Scattering and Diffusion Profiles

Homogeneous subsurface scattering can be approximated by using one-dimensional functions called diffusion profiles. A diffusion profile defines how the light attenuates as it travels beneath the surface of an object, or in other words, it describes how light intensity ($R(r)$) decays as a function of the radial distance to the incidence point (r). As shown in Figure 7.3, a majority of the light intensity occurs close to the point of incidence, and quickly decays as it interacts with the inner structure of the object before escaping through the surface.

7.2.2   Irradiance Texture

Applying a diffusion profile implies calculating the irradiance at incident and adjacent points for each point of the surface, which leads to wasted calculations.

Figure 7.2. Examples of our screen-space approach. Unlike the texture-space approach, our method scales well with the number of objects in the scene (top). Rendering marble without taking subsurface scattering into account leads to a stone-like appearance (bottom left); our subsurface scattering technique is used to create a softer appearance, more indicative of subsurface scattering (bottom right).

In order to perform an efficient profile evaluation, an irradiance map—also known as light map—is created which stores the incoming light at each point of the surface, and serves as light *cache*, in the sense that it enables you to calculate the lighting at each point once but use that value many times. Figure 7.1 (top left) shows an example of an irradiance texture.

7.2.3 Gaussians and the Jittered Kernel

Once an irradiance map is calculated, applying a diffusion profile consists of no more than applying a two-dimensional convolution over this map. There are a few previous works that provide detailed insights into how to perform this convolution in an efficient way, all for the specific case of skin rendering.

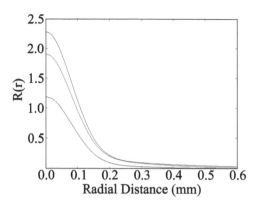

Figure 7.3. Diffusion profile of the three-layer skin model described in [d'Eon and Luebke 07].

The approach followed by d'Eon and Luebke [d'Eon and Luebke 07], consists of approximating this lengthy two-dimensional convolution by a sum of Gaussians, which can be separated into faster 1D convolutions. To summarize, rendering subsurface scattering using this sum-of-Gaussians consists of the following steps:

1. Render the irradiance map.

2. Blur the irradiance map with six Gaussians.

3. Render the scene, calculating a weighted sum of the six Gaussians, which will approximate the original diffusion profile.

While rendering an irradiance map (and in the following blurs), two optimizations that would otherwise be implicitly performed by the GPU are lost, namely backface culling and view frustum clipping. Jimenez and Gutierrez [Jimenez and Gutierrez 08] reintroduce those two optimizations in the rendering pipeline proposed in [d'Eon and Luebke 07]. They also perform an optimal, per-object modulation of the irradiance map size based on a simple, depth-based method.

Hable et al [Hable et al. 09], using a 13-sample jittered kernel, together with a small 512×512 irradiance map and a similar culling optimization, managed to improve the performance over the 6-Gaussian implementation [d'Eon and Luebke 07], at the cost of a loss of *fleshiness*, as the authors noticed.

7.2.4   Texture-Space Diffusion Problems

Current real-time subsurface scattering algorithms rely on texture-space diffusion, which has some intrinsic problems that can be easily solved by working in screen space instead. We outline the most important ones:

- It requires special measures to bring back typical GPU optimizations (back-face culling and viewport clipping), and to compute an irradiance map proportional to the size of the subject on the screen. In screen space, these optimizations are straightforward.

- Each subject to be rendered requires her own irradiance map (thus forcing as many render passes as subjects). In image space, *all subjects* of the same material are processed at the same time.

- Furthermore, rendering large amounts of objects with subsurface scattering is not efficient as either you have to use an irradiance map for each object, in order to be able to use instancing (which would be especially useful for rendering tree leaves for example), or you have to reuse the same irradiance map, and render each object sequentially.

- The irradiance map forces the transformation of the model vertices twice: during the irradiance map calculation, and to transform the final geometry at the end. In screen-space, only this second transformation is required.

- In texture space, for materials like skin that directly reflect a significant amount of light, lighting is usually calculated twice (once for the irradiance map and again for the sharpest of the Gaussian blurs since this Gaussian blur is usually replaced by the unblurred lighting in the final compositing pass). In screen-space, lighting must be calculated only once.

- Modern GPUs can perform an early-Z rejection operation to avoid overdraw and useless execution of pixel shaders on certain pixels. In texture space, it is unclear how to leverage this and optimize the convolution processes according to the final visibility in the image. In screen space, a depth pass can simply discard occluded fragments before sending them to the pixel shader.

- Adjacent points in three-dimensional world space may not be adjacent in texture space. Obviously this will introduce errors in texture-space diffusion that are naturally avoided in screen space. This implies that special care must be taken when preparing the UV map of the models, in order to reduce the number of seams as much as possible.

7.3 The Screen-Space Approach

7.3.1 The Big Picture

Our algorithm translates the evaluation of the diffusion approximation from texture- to screen-space. Instead of calculating an irradiance map and convolving

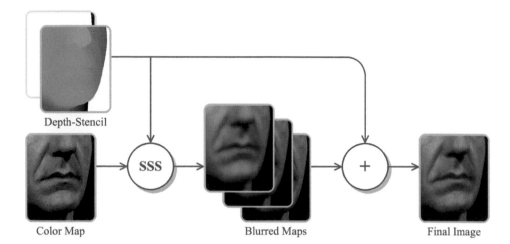

Figure 7.4. Conceptual interpretation of our algorithm (see text in the chapter for actual implementation details).

it with the diffusion profile, we apply the convolution directly to the final rendered image. Figure 7.4 shows an overview of our algorithm. As we have said, to perform this task in screen-space we need as input the depth-stencil and color buffer of a rendered frame.

As subsurface scattering should only be applied to the diffuse component of the lighting function, we could store the diffuse and specular components separately, for which we could use multiple render targets or the alpha channel of the main render target. However, we have found that applying subsurface scattering to both the diffuse and specular components of the lighting yields very appealing results, because a) the specular component is softened creating a more natural look, with less apparent aliasing artifacts, and b) it creates a nice bloom effect for the specular highlights.

In order to efficiently mask out pixels that do not need to be processed we use the stencil buffer. This vastly improves the performance when the object is far away from the camera, and thus occupies a small area in screen space. We also tried to use dynamic branching in our pixel shaders but we found the stencil method to be more efficient particularly when a large percentage of the screen must be rejected.

Our algorithm also requires linear depth information [Gillham 06] which we render into an additional render target. We use this depth together with the original depth-stencil map, which serves to perform the stenciling and to implement a depth-based Gaussians level of detail, as we will see in the next section. It is possible to access the depth buffer directly, but we are not able to simultaneously use the same depth buffer both as an input texture and as depth stencil buffer, so we must create a copy.

With the depth-stencil information as input, we apply the diffusion profile directly to the final rendered image, instead of applying it to a previously calculated irradiance map. For skin rendering, we use our own four-Gaussian fit of the three-layer skin model defined in [d'Eon and Luebke 07] (see Section 7.3.3 for details), and, as done in this work, perform each of them as two separated one-dimensional convolutions (horizontal and vertical blurs). The results obtained using our four-Gaussian fit are visually indistinguishable from the original six-Gaussian fit. For marble we calculated the profile using the parameters given by [Jensen et al. 01], for which we obtained a four-Gaussian fit (see [d'Eon and Luebke 07] for details on how to perform this fitting).

In screen space we need to take into account the following considerations:

- Pixels that are far from the camera need narrower kernel widths than pixels that are close to the camera.

- Pixels representing surfaces that are at steep angles with respect to the camera also need narrower kernels.

These considerations translate into the following *stretch factors*:

$$s_x = \frac{\text{ssslevel}}{d(x,y) + \text{correction} \cdot \min(abs(ddx(d(x,y), \text{maxdd}))},$$

$$s_y = \frac{\text{ssslevel}}{d(x,y) + \text{correction} \cdot \min(abs(ddy(d(x,y), \text{maxdd}))},$$

where $d(x,y)$ is the depth of the pixel in the depth map, "ssslevel" indicates the global subsurface scattering level in the image, "correction" modulates how this subsurface scattering varies with the depth gradient, and "maxdd" limits the effects of the derivative. This derivative limitation is required for very soft materials (like marble), as subtle artifacts may arise at depth discontinuities under very specific lighting conditions. These artifacts are caused by the huge derivatives found at those locations, that locally nullify the effect of subsurface scattering. The first and second terms in the denominators account for the first and second considerations listed above. This stretching is similar in spirit to the UV stretching performed in texture space algorithms.

The *stretch factors* are then multiplied by each Gaussian width in order to obtain the final kernel width:

$$\text{finalwidth}_x = s_x \cdot \text{width},$$
$$\text{finalwidth}_y = s_y \cdot \text{width}.$$

Figure 7.5. The influence of the ssslevel and correction parameters. Fixed correction = 800, maxdd = 0.001 and varying ssslevel of 0, 15.75 and 31.5, respectively (top). Note how the global level of subsurface scattering increases. Fixed ssslevel = 31.5, maxdd = 0.001 and varying correction of 0, 1200 and 4000, respectively (bottom). Note how the gray-to-black gradient on the nose gets readjusted according to the depth derivatives of the underlying geometry (the range of the correction parameter has been extended for visualization purposes; it usually is limited to [0..1200] because of the limited precision of the derivatives).

In the silhouette of the object, the derivatives will be very large, which means that the kernel will be very narrow, thus limiting the bleeding of background pixels into object's pixels. The value of ssslevel is influenced by the size of the object in three-dimensional space, the field-of-view used to render the scene and the viewport size (as these parameters determine the projected size of the object), whereas maxdd only depends on the size of the object. The images included in this chapter use fixed values of ssslevel = 31.5, correction = 800 and maxdd = 0.001; these values were chosen empirically for a head 1.0 units tall, a field-

```
float width;
float sssLevel, correction, maxdd;
float2 pixelSize;
Texture2D colorTex, depthTex;

float4 BlurPS(PassV2P input) : SV_TARGET {
  float w[7] = { 0.006, 0.061, 0.242, 0.382,
                 0.242, 0.061, 0.006 };

  float depth = depthTex.Sample(PointSampler,
                                input.texcoord).r;
  float2 s_x = sssLevel / (depth + correction *
                           min(abs(ddx(depth)), maxdd));
  float2 finalWidth = s_x * width * pixelSize *
                      float2(1.0, 0.0);

  float2 offset = input.texcoord - finalWidth;
  float4 color = float4(0.0, 0.0, 0.0, 1.0);
  for (int i = 0; i < 7; i++) {
    float3 tap = colorTex.Sample(LinearSampler, offset).rgb;
    color.rgb += w[i] * tap;
    offset += finalWidth / 3.0;
  }

  return color;
}
```

Listing 7.1. Pixel shader that performs the horizontal Gaussian blur.

of-view of 20°, and a viewport height of 720 pixels. Figure 7.5 illustrates the influence of ssslevel and correction in the final images.

Listing 7.1 shows the implementation of previous equation for the case of the horizontal blur. Our subsurface scattering approach just requires two short shaders, one for the horizontal blur and a similar one for the vertical blur.

Certain areas of the character, such as hair or beard, should be excluded from these calculations; we could therefore want to locally disable subsurface scattering in such places. For this purpose, we could use the alpha channel of the diffuse texture to modulate this local subsurface scattering level. We would need to store the alpha channel of this texture into the alpha channel of the main render target during the main render pass. Then, in our post-processing pass we would use the following modified stretch factors:

$$s_x' = s_x \cdot \text{diffuse}(x, y).a$$
$$s_y' = s_y \cdot \text{diffuse}(x, y).a$$

In the following, we describe the two key optimizations that our algorithm performs.

7.3.2   Depth-Based Gaussians Level of Detail

Performing the diffusion in screen space allows us to disable Gaussians on a per-pixel basis as we fly away from the model. Narrow Gaussians are going to have little effect on pixels far away from the camera, as most of the samples are going to land on the same pixel. We can exploit this to save computations.

For this purpose we use the following inequality, based on the final kernel width equation from the previous section, where we are making the assumption of camera facing polygons which have zero-valued derivatives:

$$\frac{\text{width} \cdot \text{ssslevel}}{d(x, y)} > 0.5.$$

If the width of the kernel for the current pixel is less than 0.5—that is, a half a pixel—all samples are going to land on the same pixel and thus we can skip blurring at this pixel (Figure 7.6, left).

We can use depth testing to efficiently implement this optimization. If we solve the previous inequality for $d(x, y)$:

$$2 \cdot \text{width} \cdot \text{ssslevel} > d(x, y),$$

then we just need to render the quad used to perform the convolution at a depth value of $2 \cdot$width$\cdot$ssslevel and configure the depth testing function to *greater than*. However, we have found that instead using a value of $0.5 \cdot$ width $\cdot$ ssslevel allows us to disable them much faster without any noticeable popping.

Though we have a copy of the depth-stencil buffer in linear space, the original depth-stencil buffer is kept in non-linear space for precision issues. This means that we have to transform the left side of previous inequality into the same non-linear space [Gillham 06], and clamp the resulting non-linear depth values to [0..1].

7.3.3   Alpha Blending Workflow

Using n Gaussians to approximate a diffusion profile means we need n render targets for irradiance storage. In order to keep the memory footprint as low as possible, we accumulate the sum of the Gaussians on the fly, eliminating the need to sum them in a final pass.

In order to accomplish this task, we require two additional render targets. The first render target is used to store the widest Gaussian calculated thus far (RT1) and the second for the usual render target ping ponging (RT2).

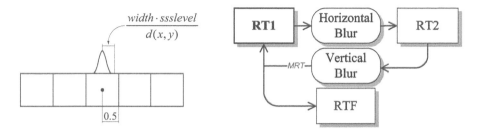

Figure 7.6. If a Gaussian is narrower than a pixel, the result of its application will be negligible (left). Alpha blending workflow used to enhance memory usage (right). Multiple Render Targets (MRT) is used to render to RT1 and RTF simultaneously.

Applying one of the Gaussians consists of two steps:

1. Perform the horizontal Gaussian blur into RT2.

2. Perform the vertical Gaussian blur by sampling from the horizontally blurred RT2 and outputting into both RT1 and RTF (the final render target) using multiple render targets. For RTF we use an alpha blending operation in order to mix the values accordingly. The exact weight required for the blending operation will be examined in the following paragraphs.

Figure 7.6 (right) shows the alpha blending workflow used by our algorithm. We need to sum the n Gaussians as follows:

$$R = \sum_{i=k}^{n} w_i G_i,$$

where w_i is the weight vector (different for each RGB channel) of each Gaussian G_i, and k is the first Gaussian that is wide enough to have a visible effect on the final image, as explained in the previous section.

As we may not calculate all Gaussians, we need to find a set of values w'_i that will produce a normalized result at each step i of the previous sum:

$$w'_i = \frac{w_i}{\sum_{j=1}^{i} w_i}.$$

Then we just need to configure alpha blending to use a blend factor as follows:

$$\text{color}_{\text{out}} = \text{color}_{\text{src}} \cdot \text{blendfactor} + \text{color}_{\text{dst}} \cdot (1 - \text{blendfactor}),$$

where blendfactor is assigned to w'_i. Listing 7.2 shows the FX syntax for the `BlendingState` that implements this equation.

```
BlendState BlendingAccum {
  BlendEnable[0] = FALSE;  // RT2
  BlendEnable[1] = TRUE;   // RTF
  SrcBlend = BLEND_FACTOR;
  DestBlend = INV_BLEND_FACTOR;
};
```

Listing 7.2. Blending state used to blend a Gaussian with the final render target.

Table 7.1 shows the original weights of our skin and marble four-Gaussian fits (w_i), alongside with the modified weights used by our screen-space approach (w_i').

In the case of skin, the first Gaussian is too narrow to be noticeable. Thus the original unblurred image is used instead, saving the calculation of one Gaussian. Note that the weight of the first Gaussian for both fits is 1.0; the reason for this is that the first Gaussian does not need to be mixed with the previously blended Gaussians.

Note that as we are performing each Gaussian on top of the previous one, we have to subtract the variance of the previous Gaussian to get the actual variance. For example, for the widest Gaussian of the skin fit, we would have $2.0062 - 0.2719 = 1.7343$. Also keep in mind that the `width` that should be passed to the shader shown in the Listing 7.1 is the standard deviation, thus in this case it would be $\sqrt{1.7343}$.

Skin	w_i			w_i'		
Variance	**R**	**G**	**B**	**R**	**G**	**B**
0.0064	0.2405	0.4474	0.6157	1.0	1.0	1.0
0.0516	0.1158	0.3661	0.3439	0.3251	0.45	0.3583
0.2719	0.1836	0.1864	0.0	0.34	0.1864	0.0
2.0062	0.46	0.0	0.0402	0.46	0.0	0.0402

Marble	w_i			w_i'		
Variance	**R**	**G**	**B**	**R**	**G**	**B**
0.0362	0.0544	0.1245	0.2177	1.0	1.0	1.0
0.1144	0.2436	0.2435	0.1890	0.8173	0.6616	0.4647
0.4555	0.3105	0.3158	0.3742	0.5101	0.4617	0.4791
3.4833	0.3913	0.3161	0.2189	0.3913	0.3161	0.2189

Table 7.1. Gaussian variances and original weights (w_i) of our Gaussian fits that approximate the three-layer skin and marble diffusion profiles, alongside with the modified weights used by our algorithm (w_i').

7.3.4 Antialiasing and Depth-Stencil

For efficiency reasons, when using MSAA we might want to use the resolved render targets (downsampled to MSAA 1x) for performing all the post-processing, in order to save memory bandwidth. However this implies that we cannot use the original MSAA stencil buffer to perform the depth-based blur modulation or the stenciling.

We explored two approaches to solve this problem:

1. Use dynamic branching to perform the stenciling by hand.

2. Downsample the depth-stencil buffer to be able to use hardware stenciling.

Both methods rely on generating multi-sample render targets containing depth and stencil values during the main pass, for which multiple render targets can be used.[1]

We found that in our implementation using hardware stenciling outperforms the dynamic branching method.

7.4 Model Preparation

When using models with hand painted normals (as opposed to scanned models) there are some considerations that must be taken into account. As noticed in [Hable et al. 09], most artists paint normals trying to match the soft aspect of subsurface scattering, without being able to use algorithms that simulate this effect. Thus they usually resort to make the normals much softer than they are physically. However, when using subsurface scattering for rendering, the best results will be obtained using bumpier normals, as subsurface scattering will be in charge of softening the illumination.

7.5 Discussion of Results

Table 7.2 shows the performance of our screen space algorithm (SS) in the case of skin rendering, against the texture space algorithm proposed by Hable et al [Hable et al. 09] (TS). We have chosen [Hable et al. 09] because it outperforms the original [d'Eon and Luebke 07] algorithm for skin rendering. For other materials, for which there is no clear way of applying the approach by Hable et al, we resort to comparisons with [d'Eon and Luebke 07], which is much more flexible.

For skin simulation, the distances we have chosen have the following meaning: near is a close-up of the head, usually found on in-game cut scenes; medium is

---

[1] When using DirectX 10.1 we can sample from the MSAA depth-stencil buffer directly, with no need to output depth and stencil values using multiple render targets.

Heads	TS	SS	Lights	TS	SS	Distance	TS	SS
1	102/72	137/73	2	102/72	137/73	Near	60/52	50/40
3	47/33	67/52	4	63/56	90/64	Medium	102/72	137/73
5	29/21	50/38	6	54/43	69/54	Far	120/82	220/91

Table 7.2. Performance measurements (fps) of our algorithm (SS), using both $1\times/8\times$ MSAA, in comparison with the texture space approach proposed in Hable et al. [Hable et al. 09] (TS). For each test we fixed the following parameters: the number of heads, the number of lights and the distance were set to 1, 2, and medium, respectively.

the distance typically found for characters of first-person shooters; at far distance the head covers very little screen area, and the effects of subsurface scattering are negligible. In the following text we will quote the performance for $1\times$MSAA (see Table 7.2 for a more detailed report). We can see how our algorithm scales better as we increase the number of heads (from 29 to 50 fps for 5 heads), as the number of lights increases (from 54 to 69 fps for six lights) and as we fly away from the model (from 120 to 220 fps for far distance). In the case of 10 heads, two lights and far distance, we obtain a speedup factor of $3.6\times$. We performed an additional test to explore the impact of the early-z optimization on both algorithms, which shows that when rendering five heads behind a plane that hides them from the camera, our screen space algorithm manages to perform at $2\times$ with respect to the texture-space approach. Similar speed-ups could be found when the objects fall outside of the viewport.

As we have discussed, there is no clear extension to Hable et al.'s algorithm that would allow for other translucent materials. We present an example of such materials by simulating marble (see Figure 7.2) and compare it with the approach of d'Eon et al. In this example, we achieve a speedup factor of up to $2.8\times$ when rendering five Apollo busts with two lights at medium distance.

In general, the best speed ups are found when there are many objects (or very large objects that would require huge irradiance textures) at very different distances (for example, when rendering tree leaves). In this kind of situation, no single irradiance map size would be a perfect fit.

In the image shown in Figure 7.2 (top), where subsurface scattering is dominating the scene, the costs of the bloom, depth-of-field, and subsurface scattering effects are 2.7ms, 5.8ms, and 14ms, respectively. On the other hand, in a more typical scene with three heads at medium distance, the costs are 2.7ms, 5.8ms, and 4.6ms.

Our performance measurements were taken using a shadow map resolution of 512×512, diffuse and normal maps with a resolution of 1024×1024. The human head and Apollo bust models have 3904 and 14623 triangles, respectively,

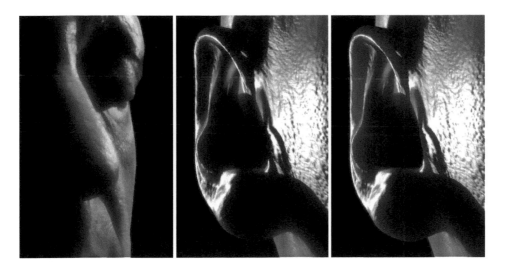

Figure 7.7. Screen space limitations and artifacts. Small haloes produced by incorrect diffusion from nose to cheek (left). Screen- vs. texture-space comparison where we can see how we cannot account for the diffusion produced in thin, high curvature features, as in screen space we do not have information from behind (Center and right).

both obtained from XYZRGB.[2] All renderings were performed on a machine equipped with a GeForce 8600M GS at a resolution of 1280×720. As recommended in [Gritz and d'Eon 07], we used sRGB render targets, which is crucial for multi-pass, physically based shaders like ours. For the specular highlights we used the Kelemen-Szirmay-Kalos approach [d'Eon and Luebke 07]. The rendered images shown in this chapter are filtered with a Gaussian bloom filter at the end of the rendering pipeline. Figure 7.2 (top) was rendered with an additional depth-of-field effect.

Quality-wise, the screen space approach manages to maintain the full *fleshiness* that the Hable et al. loses as result of using a small jittered kernel. Furthermore, it does not exhibit the stretching artifacts produced by texture space algorithms, especially by the Hable et al. approach [Hable et al. 09]. Finally, it is free from the seam problems imposed by the model's UV unwrapping (refer to the high resolution images available in the web materials for examples).

Our algorithm can introduce its own artifacts however. In certain camera and light conditions, small haloes may appear at depth discontinuities, as shown in Figure 7.7 (left). In this situation, light incorrectly scatters from the nose to the cheek. This artifact could be seen as the screen-space counterpart of both

---

[2]See http://www.xyzrgb.com/.

the stretching and seam problems of the texture-space approach. However, these haloes are low frequency artifacts and thus they generally do not hamper the soft appearance of translucent materials. Also, as shown in Figure 7.7 (middle and right), our algorithm is unable to reproduce the scattering produced in high-curvature, thin features like the ears or nose, as we do not have information from the back facing surfaces. In the case of skin, these issues do not seem to damage its general appearance, as has been proven by our previous work [Jimenez et al. 09]. In addition, the usage of very blurry profiles (like the one required for marble) can lead to aliasing problems, as the MSAA resolve is performed before applying subsurface scattering.

Another important difference is that our shader uses pre-scatter texturing (which means that we applied subsurface scattering after the full diffuse color is applied), in contrast with the Hable et al. approach [Hable et al. 09] that uses post-scatter texturing because the usage of a small irradiance map would excessively blur the high frequency details of the diffuse map. We believe that what looks best is a matter of subjective preference.

From an ease-of-use perspective, our algorithm offers various advantages. Being a post-process, integrating our technique into an existing pipeline will not require major changes. It is composed of two short shaders that can be encapsulated in a small class. Additionally, it does not require special UV unwrapping nor does it require dealing with seams, which can account for significant artist time. As we have described, there is no need to take care of special situations such as the objects being out of the viewport, or too far away from the camera, etc., as they are implicitly taken into account by the algorithm.

7.6   Conclusion

We have presented an efficient algorithm capable of rendering realistic subsurface scattering in screen space. This approach reduces buffer management and artist effort. It offers similar performance to the Hable et al. approach [Hable et al. 09] when the object is at moderate distances and scales better as the number of objects increases. Our method generalizes better to other materials. At close-ups it does lose some performance in exchange for quality, but it is able to maintain the *fleshiness* of the original d'Eon approach [d'Eon and Luebke 07]. However, in such close-ups, there is a good chance that the player will be focusing closely on the character's face, so we believe it is worth spending the extra resources in order to render the character's skin with the best quality possible. We believe that our subsurface scattering algorithm has a very simple implementation, has few requirements, and makes a nice balance between performance, generality, and quality.

7.7 Acknowledgments

We would like to thank Luisa García for her endless support, Christopher Oat for his very detailed review and XYZRGB Inc. for the high-quality head scans. This research has been partially funded by the Spanish Ministry of Science and Technology (TIN2007-63025) and the Gobierno de Aragón (OTRI 2009/0411). Jorge Jimenez was funded by a research grant from the Instituto de Investigación en Ingeniería de Aragón.

Bibliography

[d'Eon and Luebke 07] Eugene d'Eon and David Luebke. "Advanced Techniques for Realistic Real-Time Skin Rendering." In *GPU Gems 3*, edited by Hubert Nguyen, Chapter 14, pp. 293–347. Addison Wesley, 2007.

[Gillham 06] David Gillham. "Real-time Depth-of-Field Implemented with a Postprocessing-Only Technique." In *ShaderX5*, edited by Wolfgang Engel, Chapter 3.1, pp. 163–175. Charles River Media, 2006.

[Gritz and d'Eon 07] Larry Gritz and Eugene d'Eon. "The Importance of Being Linear." In *GPU Gems 3*, edited by Hubert Nguyen, Chapter 24, pp. 529–542. Addison Wesley, 2007.

[Hable et al. 09] John Hable, George Borshukov, and Jim Hejl. "Fast Skin Shading." In *ShaderX7*, edited by Wolfgang Engel, Chapter 2.4, pp. 161–173. Charles River Media, 2009.

[Jensen et al. 01] Henrik Wann Jensen, Steve Marschner, Marc Levoy, and Pat Hanrahan. "A Practical Model for Subsurface Light Transport." In *Proceedings of ACM SIGGRAPH 2001*, pp. 511–518, 2001.

[Jimenez and Gutierrez 08] Jorge Jimenez and Diego Gutierrez. "Faster Rendering of Human Skin." In *CEIG*, pp. 21–28, 2008.

[Jimenez et al. 09] Jorge Jimenez, Veronica Sundstedt, and Diego Gutierrez. "Screen-Space Perceptual Rendering of Human Skin." *ACM Transactions on Applied Perception*. (to appear).

8
The Skylanders SWAP Force Depth-of-Field Shader

Michael Bukowski, Padraic Hennessy, Brian Osman, and Morgan McGuire

8.1 Introduction

This chapter describes the depth-of-field (DoF) shader used in production at Vicarious Visions for the *Skylanders SWAP Force* game on multiple console platforms.

DoF is an important rendering effect. A real camera lens focuses on a single plane in the scene. Images of objects in that plane are perfectly sharp. Images of objects closer to or farther from the camera are blurry. Of course, most objects are typically outside the exact plane of focus. Photographers recognize that each point on an out-of-focus object blurs into the shape of the camera aperture, which is usually a disk, octagon, or hexagon. They call the bounding circle of a blurred point the *circle of confusion* (CoC) of that point. They say that an object is in focus (for a digital image) when the *radius* of the CoC is half a pixel or less. In that case, the object does not appear blurred because the blur falls below the image resolution. Photographers refer to the depth range over which the CoC radius is less than half a pixel as the *focus field*. They refer to the extent of this range as the *depth of field*. In computer graphics, that phrase is now associated with the effect of blurring images of objects outside of the field.

In a game, a DoF effect serves both gameplay and aesthetics. It allows the art director to control the player's attention by de-emphasizing background objects or those that are merely in the foreground to frame the shot. Rack-focus (Figure 8.1) in on a specific object can emphasize goals and powerups during gameplay without resorting to floating arrows or halos. In cut-scenes, DoF is a powerful cinematic tool. DoF also conceals many rendering limitations. Defocusing the background conceals aliasing and low level of detail. Defocusing the extreme foreground conceals texture magnification and tessellation limits.

Figure 8.1. Three frames from a cinematic "rack focus" transition designed to move the player's attention from the background to the extreme foreground. In each shot, the yellow dot shows the location of camera focus.

True DoF arises because each point on the camera lens has a slightly different viewpoint and the final image is a composite of images from all of them. Research papers have simulated this brute-force rendering of multiple viewpoints to an accumulation buffer, sampling viewpoints with distribution ray tracing [Cook et al. 84], and sampling with stochastic rasterization [McGuire et al. 10]. These methods are all too expensive to be practical today and are overkill for achieving a convincing effect. Since the goal is to blur parts of the image, we need not render a perfect result. It should be enough to selectively apply some post-processing blur filters to a typical frame. Like many other game engines, ours follows this approach. There's a good argument for this approximation over physically correct solutions: it is what Photoshop's Lens Blur and many film editing packages do. The DoF seen in advertisements and feature films is certainly of suffcient quality for game graphics.

We distinguish three depth ranges of interest: the *far field* in which objects are blurry because they are too far away, the *focus field* where objects are in focus, and the *near field* in which objects are blurry because they are too close to the camera.

A post-processing DoF shader is essentially a blur filter with a spatially varying kernel. The way that the kernel varies poses three challenges. First, unlike a typical Gaussian or box blur, DoF blur must respect depth edges. For example, the effect should not let a blurry distant object bleed over a nearer sharp object. We observe that it is most critical that the far-focus-near ordering of occlusion be preserved. However, incorrect blurring of images of neighboring objects *within* a field is often undetectable.

Second, when preventing bleeding, the effect must also not create sharp silhouettes on blurry objects in the near field. These sharp silhouettes are the primary visual artifact in previous methods.

Third, foreground objects have to be able to blur fairly far (up to 10% of the screen width) without compromising performance. The naïve approaches of scattering each pixel as a disk and the inverse of performing the equivalent gather operation are too slow—those methods require $O(r^2)$ operations for blur radius r and thrash the texture/L1 cache.

The DoF post-process in our engine is fast and produces good-quality near- and far-field blurring with little perceptible color bleeding. It reads a color buffer with a specially encoded alpha channel and produces a convincing DoF effect in three "full-screen" 2D passes over various size buffers. It uses 1.9 ms of GPU time running at 720p on the Xbox 360. On a PC it uses 1.0 ms of GPU time running at 1080p on a GeForce GTX 680.

We developed our DoF effect from Gillham's *ShaderX*[5] one [Gillham 07]. Like his and other similar techniques [Riguer et al. 03, Scheuermann 04, Hammon 07, Kaplanyan 10, Kasyan et al. 11], we work with low-resolution buffers when they are blurry and lerp between blurred and sharp versions of the screen. The elements of our improvements to previous methods are

- treating near field separately to produce blurry silhouettes on the near field,

- inpainting behind blurry near-field objects,

- a selective background blur kernel,

- using CoC instead of depth to resolve occlusion and blur simultaneously,

- processing multiple blurs in parallel with dual render targets.

8.2 Algorithm

Figure 8.3 shows the structure of our algorithm. The input is a color buffer with the (scaled and biased) *signed CoC radius* stored in the alpha channel. Two passes blur horizontally and then vertically in a typical separated blur pattern, and a final pass composites the blurred image over the sharp input. Each blur pass processes two textures: one that represents the focus and far field, and one that represents objects in the near field (with an alpha channel for coverage).

8.2.1 Input

The radius in the alpha channel of the color input buffer is signed, meaning that radius r at each pixel is on the range [−maximum blur, +maximum blur]. Farfield objects have a negative radius, near-field objects have a positive one, and $0.5 < r < 0.5$ in the focus field. Under a physically correct CoC model, this signed radius naturally arises. There, it models the fact that the silhouette of the aperture appears inverted in the far field. That inversion is irrelevant for the disc

Figure 8.2. Extreme near- and far-field defocus with smooth transitions rendered by our algorithm. Note the blurry silhouettes on near-field objects and detail inpainted behind them.

aperture that we model, but we depend on the signed radius for another reason. Signed radius decreases monotonically with depth, so if $r_A < r_B$, then point A is closer to the camera than point B. Thus the single signed radius value at each pixel avoids the need for separate values to encode the field, radius, and depth of a point.

Our demo supports two methods to compute the signed radius. The first is the physically correct model derived from Figure 8.4. Let a be the radius of the lens, $z_F < 0$ be the depth of the focus plane, and R be the world-space (versus screen-space) radius. By similar triangles, the screen-space radius r for a point at depth z is

$$\frac{R}{|z_F - z|} = \frac{a}{|z_F|}, \quad r \propto a\frac{|z_F - z|}{z_F \cdot z}.$$

The proportionality constant depends on screen resolution and field of view. Our art team felt that this physical model gave poor control over the specific kinds of shots that they were trying to direct. They preferred the second model, in which the artists manually place four planes (near-blurry, near-sharp, far-sharp, far-blurry). For the near- and far-blurry planes, the artists specify the CoC radius explicitly. At the near-sharp and far-sharp planes, the radius is $1/2$ pixel. The CoC at depths between the planes is then linearly interpolated. Depths closer than the near-blurry and farther than the far-blurry have radii clamped to the values at those planes.

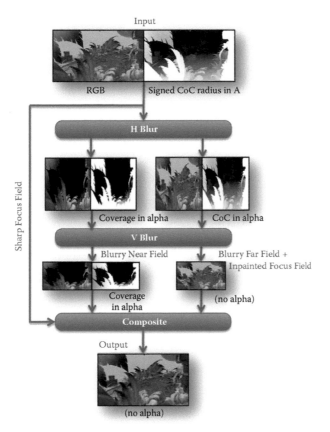

Figure 8.3. Diagram of shading passes with buffers shown. See the supplemental material for high-resolution images.

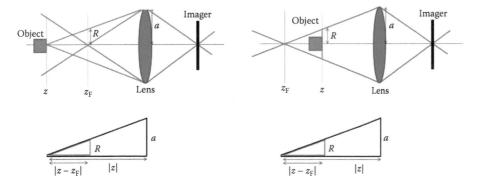

Figure 8.4. The geometry of lens blur. Left: the orange cube is in the far field and out of focus. Right: the orange cube in the near field and out of focus. The radius of the CoC (in camera space) is given by using similar triangles to find R in each case.

8.2.2   Blur Passes

The two blur passes are similar to one another. Each reads a fixed-length set of adjacent samples, either horizontal or vertical, and computes two weighted sums. The key outer loop section of the code is shown below.

```
// Accumulates the blurry image color
blurResult.rgb = float3(0.0f);
float blurWeightSum = 0.0f;

// Accumulates the near-field color and coverage
nearResult = float4(0.0f);
float nearWeightSum = 0.0f;

// Location of the central filter tap (i.e., "this" pixel's location)
// Account for the scaling down by 50% during blur
int2 A = int2(gl_FragCoord.xy) * (direction + ivec2(1));

float packedA = texelFetch(blurSourceBuffer, A, 0).a;
float r_A = (packedA * 2.0 - 1.0) * maxCoCRadiusPixels;

// Map large negative r_A to 0.0 and large positive r_A to 1.0
float nearFieldness_A = saturate(r_A * 4.0);

for (int delta = -maxCoCRadiusPixels; delta <= maxCoCRadiusPixels;
                                            ++delta) {

  // Tap location near A
  int2 B = A + (direction * delta);

  // Packed values
  float4 blurInput = texelFetch(blurSourceBuffer, clamp(B, int2(0),
                 textureSize(blurSourceBuffer, 0)
                  - int2(1)), 0);

  // Signed kernel radius at this tap, in pixels
  float r_B = (blurInput.a * 2.0 - 1.0) * float(maxCoCRadiusPixels);

  // [Compute blurry buffer]
  ...
  // [Compute near-field super blurry buffer and coverage]
  ....
}

blurResult.a = packedA;
blurResult.rgb /= blurWeightSum;
nearResult /= nearWeightSum;
```

The details of the two blur kernel sections follow. See also our demo source code, which contains extensive comments explaining optimizations and alternative implementations.

Let A be the center sample of the kernel and B be a nearby sample (note that $B = A$ is included in the set of samples that we consider). We compute the weight of sample B as follows.

```
If A is in the near field:
  // Inpaint behind A using some arbitrary constant weight k ≈ 1.
  w_B = k
else if B is not in the near field:
  // Obey occlusion; note that both r values are always negative in
  // this case.
  w_B = max(0, min(1, |r_A - r_B + 1.5|))· Gaussian (BA)
else:
  // Avoid divide-by-zero if every sample pair hits this case.
  w_B = ε
```

In practice, we smooth the transitions by implementing the branches with lerps. The relevant section of VVDoF_blur.glsl in our demo source code is

```
float weight = 0.0;

float wNormal =
    // Only consider mid- or background pixels (allows inpainting of the
    // near field).
    float(! inNearField(r_B)) *

    // Only blur B over A if B is closer to the viewer (allow 0.5 pixels
    // of slop and smooth the transition).
    saturate(abs(r_A) - abs(r_B) + 1.5) *

    // Stretch the Gaussian extent to the radius at pixel B.
    gaussian[clamp(int(float(abs(delta) * (GAUSSIAN_TAPS - 1)) /
        (0.001 + abs(r_B * 0.5))), 0, GAUSSIAN_TAPS)];

weight = lerp(wNormal, 1.0, nearFieldness_A);
// far- + mid-field output
blurWeightSum += weight;
blurResult.rgb += blurInput.rgb * weight;
```

We compute the coverage value (alpha) for the separate near-field buffer in the horizontal pass as

$$\alpha_B = \begin{cases} \min\left(1, \dfrac{r_B}{\text{maximum near-field blur}}\right)^4 & \text{if } |A - B| < r_B, \\ 0 & \text{otherwise;} \end{cases}$$

in code, this is somewhat more verbose:

```
float4 nearInput;
#if HORIZONTAL
    nearInput.a = float(abs(delta) <= r_B) *
        saturate(r_B * invNearBlurRadiusPixels * 4.0);
    nearInput.a *= nearInput.a; nearInput.a *= nearInput.a;

    // Compute premultiplied-alpha color.
    nearInput.rgb = blurInput.rgb * nearInput.a;
```

```
#else
    // On the second pass, use the already-available alpha values.
    nearInput = texelFetch(nearSourceBuffer, clamp(B, int2(0),
            textureSize(nearSourceBuffer, 0) - int2(1)), 0);
#endif

    weight = float(abs(delta) < nearBlurRadiusPixels);
    nearResult += nearInput * weight;
    nearWeightSum += weight;
}
```

We empirically tuned this coverage falloff curve to provide good coverage when
the near field is extremely blurry and to fade smoothly into the focus field. For
example, in Figure 8.5, the out-of-focus fence in the near field must have sufficient
coverage to smear white pixels over a large region, while we still want the transition of the ground plane into the focus field to look like gradual focusing and not
simply a lerp between separate blurry and sharp images. This is an extremely
hard case for a post-processing DoF algorithm that previous real-time methods
do not handle well.

The near-field buffer is written with premultiplied alpha values for the color
channel, and the color and alpha are both blurred during the subsequent vertical
pass.

8.2.3   Compositing

The compositing pass (shown below) reads the original input buffer along with the
low-resolution blurry near- and far-field buffers. It interpolates pixels between the

Figure 8.5. Input image with a chain-link fence very close to the camera (left), and
near field under extreme blur with inpainted details visible through the "solid" parts of
the fence and a smooth ground-plane transition between depth regions (right).

original input and the blurred, inpainted far-field buffer based on the CoC at each pixel. It then blends the near-field buffer over that result with premultiplied alpha blending. Near-field pixels exhibit inpainted detail from the far-field buffer and existing detail from the input buffer, both of which then receive the significantly blurred near-field content over them. Far-field pixels are blurry from the far-field image, the focus field is sharp and from the original image, and all transition regions are smooth because of the lerp.

```
uniform sampler2D packedBuffer;
uniform sampler2D blurBuffer;
uniform sampler2D nearBuffer;

out vec3 result;

const float coverageBoost = 1.5;

float grayscale(float3 c) {
  return (c.r + c.g + c.b) / 3.0;
}

void main() {
  int2 A = int2(gl_FragCoord.xy);

  float4 pack = texelFetch(packedBuffer, A, 0);
  float3 sharp = pack.rgb;
  float3 blurred = texture(blurBuffer,
            gl_FragCoord.xy / textureSize(packedBuffer, 0));
  float4 near = texture(nearBuffer,
            gl_FragCoord.xy / textureSize(packedBuffer, 0));

  // Normalize radius.
  float normRadius = (pack.a * 2.0 - 1.0);

  if (coverageBoost != 1.0) {\{}
    float a = saturate (coverageBoost * near.a);
    near.rgb = near.rgb * (a / max(near.a, 0.001f));
    near.a = a;
  }

  // Decrease sharp image's contribution rapidly in the near field.
  if (normRadius > 0.1) {\{}
      normRadius = min(normRadius * 1.5, 1.0);
  }

  result = lerp(sharp, blurred, abs(normRadius)) * (1.0 - near.a)
        + near.rgb;
}
```

The effect is extremely robust to camera and object movement and varying blur radii, independent of the scene. It should be tuned for two application-specific cases: transitions from mid to near depending on the field of view, and objects that don't write the depth buffer.

A compile-time constant, coverageBoost, allows increasing the partial coverage (alpha) of the near field to make it feel more substantial. This should always be greater than or equal to 1. If the near-field objects seem too transparent, then increase `coverageBoost`. If an obvious transition line is visible between the blurred near-field region and the sharp mid-field, then decrease the `coverageBoost`. Which of these cases an application is in largely depends on whether the field of view makes the ground plane visible within this transition region. For example, a first-person camera typically cannot see the ground plane in this region but a third-person camera often can. The third-person camera benefits from a smaller `coverageBoost` setting.

Because the effect assumes a single depth at each pixel in the input, we process particle systems separately by MIP-biasing their textures during a forward rendering pass rather than relying on the post-processing. For non-particle, translucent and reflective objects such as glass, we simply choose to use the depth of the translucent object or the background depending on the amount of translucency.

8.3   Conclusion

We knew that depth of field was an essential effect for the art direction of *Skylanders SWAP Force*, where the visuals resemble a CG animated film more than a traditional video game. By addressing the perception of the phenomenon of blurring instead of the underlying physics, we were able to achieve both high quality and high performance on a range of target platforms.

The primary limitations of previous real-time depth-of-field approaches are poor near-field blur and poor transitions between blurred and sharp regions. Figure 8.2 shows that even under a narrow depth of field, our effect overcomes both of those limitations. The interaction of depth of field with translucent surfaces remains problematic in the general case; however, we've described the forward-rendering techniques that we applied successfully to such surfaces in this specific game.

It is important for game graphics to serve game design for engagement as well as to please the eye. In this game, we've found depth of field to be a powerful tool for both gameplay and cinematic expression. Designers employ it for controlling attention and indicating gameplay elements as well as the artists using it to enhance visuals and mitigate certain artifacts. We hold this effect as an example of a technological advance serving to enhance all aspects of the player's experience.

Bibliography

[Cook et al. 84] Robert L. Cook, Thomas Porter, and Loren Carpenter. "Distributed Ray Tracing." In *SIGGRAPH '84: Proceedings of the 11th Annual Conference on Computer Graphics and Interactive Techniques*, pp. 137–145. New York: ACM, 1984.

[Gillham 07] David Gillham. "Real-Time Depth-of-Field Implemented with a Postprocessing-Only Technique. In *ShaderX⁵: Advanced Rendering Techniques*, edited by Wolfgang Engel, pp. 163–175. Boston: Charles River Media, 2007.

[Hammon 07] Earl Hammon, Jr. "Practical Post-Process Depth of Field." In *GPU Gems 3*, edited by Hubert Nguyen, Chapter 28. Upper Saddle River, NJ: Addison-Wesley, 2007.

[Kaplanyan 10] Anon Kaplanyan. "CryENGINE 3: Reaching the Speed of Light." Talk, SIGGRAPH 2010, Los Angeles, CA, July 28, 2010. (Available at http://www.crytek.com/sites/default/files/AdvRTRend_crytek_0.ppt.)

[Kasyan et al. 11] Nickolay Kasyan, Nicolas Schulz, and Tiago Sousa. "Secrets of CryENGINE 3 Graphics Technology." SIGGRAPH Course, Vancouver, Canada, August 8, 2011. (Available at http://www.crytek.com/sites/default/files/S2011_SecretsCryENGINE3Tech_0.ppt.)

[McGuire et al. 10] Morgan McGuire, Eric Enderton, Peter Shirley, and David Luebke. "Real-Time Stochastic Rasterization on Conventional GPU Architectures." In *Proceedings of the Converence on High Performance Graphics*, pp. 173–182. Aire-la-Ville, Switzerland: Eurographics, 2010.

[Riguer et al. 03] Guennadi Riguer, Natalya Tatarchuk, and John Isidoro. "Real-Time Depth-of-Field Simulation." In *ShaderX²: Shader Programming Tips and Tricks with DirectX 9.0*, edited by Wolfgang Engel, pp. 529–556. Plano, TX: Wordware Publishing, Inc., 2003

[Scheuermann 04] Thorsten Scheuermann. "Advanced Depth of Field." Presentation, Game Developers Conference 2004, San Francisco, CA, 2004. (Available at http://www.amddevcentral.com/media/gpu_assets/Scheuermann_DepthOfField.pdf.)

9

Simulating Partial Occlusion in Post-Processing Depth-of-Field Methods
David C. Schedl and Michael Wimmer

9.1 Introduction

This chapter describes a method for simulating depth of field (DoF). In particular, we investigate the so-called *partial occlusion* effect: objects near the camera blurred due to DoF are actually *semitransparent* and therefore result in partially visible background objects (Figure 9.1). This effect is strongly apparent in miniature and macro photography and in film making. Games and interactive applications are nowadays becoming more cinematic, including strong DoF effects, and therefore it is important to be able to convincingly approximate the partial-occlusion effect. We show how to do so in this chapter, with the proposed optimizations even in real time.

9.2 Depth of Field

Before we discuss the technique in detail, let us first revisit the theory. DoF is an effect caused by the fact that optical lenses in camera systems refract light rays onto the image sensor, but different light paths representing the same object point only converge exactly if the object is at the focus distance. For other distances, objects appear blurred. This imperfection is not reproduced by the standard pinhole camera model used in rendering and needs to be simulated. Object-space methods like ray tracing can do so at high quality but are too slow for interactive rates.

Faster methods are based on the idea of using rasterized images and simulating DoF via post-processing. The first to discuss such an approach were Potmesil and Chakravarty in 1981. Based on the parameters of an optical lens, the diameter of

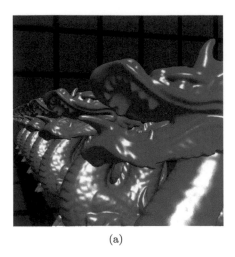
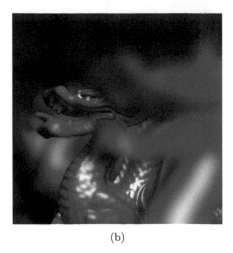

(a)   (b)

Figure 9.1. (a) A pinhole rendering resulting in a crisp image. (b) Simulating shallow DoF with the proposed method partly reveals occluded scene content. Note how the tongue of the dragon almost vanishes. This effect can be explained by partial occlusion.

the blurriness, the so-called *circle of confusion* (CoC) for an out-of-focus fragment at depth z can be calculated as

$$d_{\text{coc}}(z, f, N, z_{\text{focus}}) = \left| \frac{f^2(z - z_{\text{focus}})}{z\,N(z_{\text{focus}} - f)} \right|, \qquad (9.1)$$

where f is the focal length of the lens, N is the f-stop number, and z_{focus} is the distance to the focus plane [Potmesil and Chakravarty 81]. Note that Equation (9.1) is based on a thin lens model, which is sufficient for simulating DoF. To simulate DoF, each fragment in the rasterized image is blurred according to its CoC in a post-process.

However, if the blurriness of an out-of-focus object increases, fragments are strongly smeared and become transparent, thus revealing background information, as shown in Figure 9.1(b). Current rasterization renderings do not store occluded fragments, therefore it is not possible to accurately simulate this transparency. To do so, occluded information has to be either stored or interpolated. Most DoF methods that correctly simulate partial occlusion (such as [Lee et al. 10, Schedl and Wimmer 12]) store the scene content in depth layers. One way of assigning fragments into layers can be based on depth, which has the advantage that it is possible to uniformly blur each depth layer. Prominent artifacts in layered DoF methods are discretization artifacts: Layers are blurred and therefore object borders are smeared out. When this smeared-out layer is blended with the other layers, the smeared border region appears as a ringing artifact at object borders due to the reduced opacity [Barsky et al. 03].

One method to avoid that, from [Lee et al. 10], is to first render the scene content into layers and then use ray traversal to combine these layers, which is a costly operation but avoids the previously mentioned discretization artifacts and allows the simulation of additional lens effects (e.g., chromatic aberration and lens distortion).

9.3 Algorithm Overview

The approach presented in the following sections is a layered DoF method and is based on [Schedl and Wimmer 12]. We first decompose the scene into *depth layers*, where each layer contains pixels of a certain depth range. The resulting layers are then blurred with a filter that is sized according to the depth layer's CoC and then composited. This approach handles partial occlusion, because hidden objects are represented in more distant depth layers and contribute to the compositing.

In order to avoid rendering the scene K times, we use an A-buffer to generate *input buffers*. Note that each input buffer can contain fragments from the full depth range of the scene, while a depth layer is bound by its associated depth range. We then generate the depth layers by decomposing the input buffers into the depth ranges, which is much faster than rendering each depth layer separately.

To avoid discretization artifacts, we do not use hard boundaries for each depth layer, but a smooth transition between the layers, given by *matting functions*. Furthermore, we also show a method for efficiently computing both the blur and the layer composition in one step.

The algorithm consists of the following steps:

1. Render the scene into an A-buffer, containing the color and depth from front fragments and occluded fragments in an unsorted way. Sorting the fragments produces the input buffers I_0 to I_{M-1}.

2. Decompose the fragments of the input buffers into K depth layers L_0 to L_{K-1}, based on a matting function and the fragments' depth. Thus the rendered scene is now stored in a layered form, where each layer holds fragments of a certain depth range.

3. Blur every layer according to its CoC (computed by the layer's depth range) and alpha-blend them starting with the layer furthest away. We apply an optimization for this step where we blend and blur recursively: each layer L_k is blended onto the *composition buffers* I'_{front} (containing layers in front of the focus layer) or I'_{back} (holds layers behind the focus layer), where the composition buffers are blurred after each blending step. Finally the composition buffers are blended together.

We now describe the individual steps.

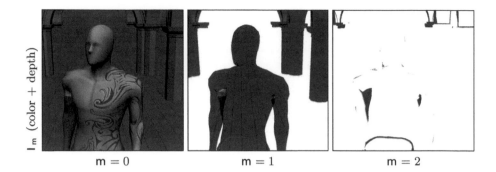

I_m (color + depth)

m = 0   m = 1   m = 2

Figure 9.2. The input buffers (color and depth) of the *Homunculus* scene, where m represents the mth fragment sorted by depth. The depth of the fragments is stored in the alpha channel, which is not represented in this figure. Note that white represents empty fragments and that there can be M input buffers.

9.4   Rendering

In [Schedl and Wimmer 12], rendering is done by the well-known depth-peeling technique, which needs to render the scene several times. Therefore, in our implementation we use an A-buffer [Carpenter 84] to avoid rerendering the scene. Our A-buffer consists of a 3D texture (A_0 to A_{M-1}) of depth M and a second texture for counting fragments, C. While the scene is rendered, each processed fragment increases the counting texture at the fragment's screen coordinate. Note that the increasing of the counter has to be atomic, which means that a value in the texture should not be altered in parallel. Based on the counter, the computed color of the fragment is written into the texture position A_c, where c is the value of the increased counter. Thus, all fragments processed by the graphics card are stored, in an unsorted way, in the 3D texture A. The counter is initially set to 0, therefore empty fragments have the counter value 0.

Next, all fragments in A are sorted by depth and written into the *input buffers* (I_0 to I_{M-1} for color and Z_0 to Z_{M-1} for depth), thus allowing up to M fragments per screen position, as shown in Figure 9.2. Note that only C fragments have to be sorted. Therefore the sorting effort depends on the scene complexity. We use the bubble sort algorithm to sort the fragments. Our implementation of the A-buffer is inspired by the implementation in [Crassin 10] and needs OpenGL 4.2 for atomic operations, and for image load and image store functionality. A pseudocode on how to render into an A-buffer is shown in Listing 9.1.

9.5   Scene Decomposition

The input buffers I_0 to I_{M-1} are decomposed into K *depth layers* L_0 to $L_{(K-1)}$. Only C fragments have to be matted, which reduces the matting costs for simpler

```
coherent uniform layout(size4x32) image2DArray abufferImg;
coherent uniform layout(size1x32) uimage2D abufferCounterImg

void main(void) {
  // atomic increment of the counter
  int c = int(imageAtomicInc(abufferCounterImg, coord.xy));

  vec4 val = ShadeFragment(); // compute shading color
  val.w = coord.z; // depth used for sorting

  // store fragment into A-buffer
  imageStore(abufferImg, ivec3(coord.xy, c), val);
}
```

Listing 9.1. Pseudocode for the fragment shader rendering fragments into the A-buffer. First the fragment counter C is increased to the value c. Then the shading color of the processed fragment is written into the 3D texture at position A_c.

scenes. For each depth layer, there are splitting depths (called *anchor points*) that specify which layer fragments will be sorted into. The decomposition is done by multiplying the fragments with a *matting function* (ω_k and $\dot\omega_k$), where the matting function differs for each depth layer L_k:

$$L_k = \Big(I_0 \cdot \omega_k(Z_0)\Big) \oplus \Big(I_1 \cdot \dot\omega_k(Z_1)\Big) \oplus \ldots \oplus \Big(I_{C-1} \cdot \dot\omega_k(Z_{C-1})\Big). \tag{9.2}$$

The notation $A \oplus B$ denotes alpha-blending of A over B. In Figure 9.3, a schematics of this algorithm is shown for an example layer L_k. Equation (9.2) is applied K times to produce K depth layers. (See Figure 9.5.)

9.5.1 Matting Functions

The matting function ω_k (Figure 9.4(a)) was introduced in [Kraus and Strengert 07] and guarantees a smooth transition of objects between layers. The special matting function $\dot\omega_k$ (Figure 9.4(b)) retains a hard cut at the back layer boundaries to avoid situations where background fragments would be blended over foreground layers. The formulas are

$$\omega_k(z) = \begin{cases} \dfrac{z_k - z}{z_k - z_{k+1}} & \text{for} \quad z_k < z < z_{k+1}, \\ \dot\omega_k(z) & \text{otherwise}, \end{cases} \tag{9.3}$$

and

$$\dot\omega_k(z) = \begin{cases} \dfrac{z - z_{k-2}}{z_{k-1} - z_{k-2}} & \text{for} \quad z_{k-2} < z < z_{k-1}, \\ 1 & \text{for} \quad z_{k-1} \leq z \leq z_k, \\ 0 & \text{otherwise}, \end{cases} \tag{9.4}$$

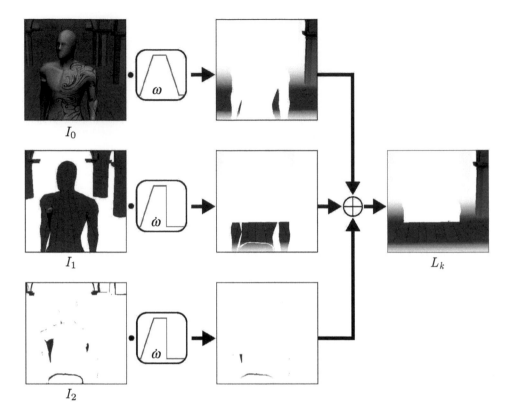

Figure 9.3. A flowchart showing how the input buffers get decomposed into a depth layer: First, the fragments in the input buffers get weighted by ω and $\dot{\omega}$. The resulting subdepth layers get alpha-blended to compose the depth layer L_k. The formula for this schematics can be found in Equation (9.2).

where z_{k-2} to z_{k+1} defines anchor points for the layer boundaries. Pseudocode for how to do matting in a fragment shader is shown in Listing 9.2.

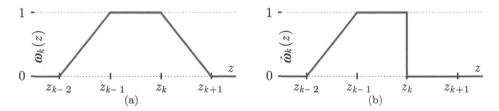

Figure 9.4. The matting functions (a) ω_k and (b) $\dot{\omega}_k$ with exemplary anchor points z_{k-2} to z_{k+1}.

```
uniform float anchor [4]; // anchor points array
// fragment counter and input buffer textures
uniform layout(size1x32) uimage2D abufferCounterImg;
uniform layout(size4x32) image2DArray inputBufferImg;

void main(void) {
  int C = int(imageLoad(abufferCounterImg, coord.xy).r);
  vec4 finalColor = vec4(0, 0, 0, 0);
  for(int c = 0; c < C; ++ c) {
    vec4 val = imageLoad(inputBufferImg, vec3(coord.xy, c));
    vec4 color = vec4(val.rgb ,1.0);
    float depth = val.z; // depth is stored in alpha channel

    // check if fragment is within z_{k-2} and z_{k+1},
    // or z_{k} if (c!=0)
    if(anchor [3] <= depth && depth < anchor [(c==0)?0:1]) {
      float w = 1.0; // weight
      // z_{k} < z
      if(anchor[1] < depth) {
        w = (anchor[0] - depth) / (anchor[0] - anchor[1]);
      }
      // z < z_{k-1}
      else if ( depth < anchor[2]) {
        w = (depth - anchor[3]) / (anchor[2] - anchor[3]);
      }

      // alpha blending
      finalColor += (1.0f - finalColor.a) * color * w;
} } }
```

Listing 9.2. Pseudocode for matting fragments into a depth layer with a shader (Equation (9.2)). The anchor points are computed on the CPU and handed in as a uniform array. Depending on which input buffer is processed, either ω or $\dot{\omega}$ is used.

9.5.2 Anchor Points

The layer matting relies on anchor points, which are spaced according to the filter size of the blurring method, similar to [Kraus and Strengert 07]. This means that the positions of the layer boundaries for a depth layer L_k are determined by the filter size (approximating d_k, the CoC for this layer) of the chosen blurring method. Since all fragments in the depth layer will be uniformly blurred, the anchor points should be evenly spaced with respect to the filter sizes. Therefore, we use the average CoC of a depth layer and its adjacent layer:

$$\bar{d}_k = \frac{d_k + d_{k+1}}{2}.$$

If we neglect the absolute value computation in Equation (9.1), we can invert the formula and calculate approximate depth values based on the filter size:

$$z_k = d_{\text{coc}}^{-1}(\bar{d}_k) = \frac{z_{\text{focus}} \cdot f^2}{f^2 + \bar{d}_k \cdot N \cdot (z_{\text{focus}} - f)}. \tag{9.5}$$

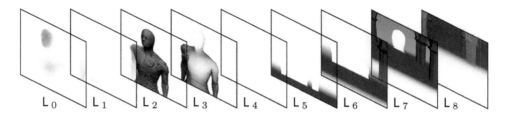

Figure 9.5. The depth layers produced after matting the input buffers.

Note that the CoCs (d_k) for depth layers located behind the focus plane ($k > k_{\text{focus}}$) will be negative and that Equation (9.5) is only applicable as long as

$$\bar{d}_{K-1} > \frac{f^2}{N \cdot (z_{\text{focus}} - f)}.$$

The anchor point furthest away from the camera, z_{K-1}, is limited by this constraint. Special care has to be taken when matting the foremost layer (L_0) and the back layer (L_{K-1}), shown in Figure 9.5, where all fragments with a depth smaller than the foremost anchor point (z_0) are matted into L_0 and fragments with depths beyond the back anchor point (z_{K-1}) are matted into L_{K-1}.

To simulate DoF, a sufficient number of depth layers spanning the whole depth range of the scene have to be generated.

Simply using the near and far clipping planes would produce empty depth layers, at the front and the back, if the rendered scene's depth range is smaller. Therefore, a better method is to use a dynamically adapted frustum, either by looking at bounding-box depth or by calculating a minimum-maximum mipmap on the framebuffer.

9.6 Blurring and Composition

Each depth layer L_k has a CoC d_k that determines the width of the blur filter. We use Gaussian filters, because they are separable, can be recursively applied, and produce smooth results. The mapping from CoC to the standard deviation σ of a Gaussian kernel H is chosen empirically as

$$d_{\text{pix}} = 4\sigma.$$

Note that d_{pix} is the d_{coc} in screen coordinates and has to be transformed into the world coordinate system.

One could convolve each layer separately, but this would require large and thus expensive filter widths farther away from the focus plane. Instead, we use a recursive filtering approach, where we start with the farthest layers and filter after each composition step. Thus, the further away from the focus plane a layer is, the more often it gets blurred.

```
GLuint pDepthLayer[K]; // storing the depth layers
GLuint bufferFront, bufferFocus, bufferBack; // composition b

// do front buffer compositing
bindAndClearFbo( bufforFront );
for( uint k = 0 ; k < kFocus ; ++ k ) {
  glBlendFunc( GL_ONE_MINUS_DST_ALPHA , GL_ONE );
  blendLayer( pDepthLayer[k] );
  blurBuffer( bufferFront, computeSigmaForLayer( k ) );
}

// do focus buffer compositing
bindAndClearFbo( bufferFocus );
blendLayer( pDepthLayer[kFocus] );

// do back buffer compositing
bindAndClearFbo( bufferBack );
for( uint k = K-1 ; k > kFocus ; -- k ) {
  glBlendFunc( GL_ONE, GL_ONE_MINUS_SRC_ALPHA );
  blendLayer( pDepthLayer[k] );
  blurBuffer( bufferBack, computeSigmaForLayer( k ) );
}
```

Listing 9.3. OpenGL pseudocode for blending and blurring the depth layers onto the composition buffers: front, focus, and back.

In particular, depth layers are blended onto one of three so-called *composition buffers* for the front, back, and focus parts of the scene. (I'_{front}, I'_{back}, and I'_{focus}). While the latter is only filled with the in-focus depth layer ($L_{k\text{focus}}$), the other depth layers are composed iteratively onto the front and back composition buffers, starting from the foremost and the furthest depth layer (L_0 and L_{K-1}), respectively. The two composition buffers have to be used because otherwise it is not possible to keep the correct depth ordering of the layers. Between each composition iteration, the composition buffers are blurred with a Gaussian filter $\hat{H}_k$, where the index k is the same as the recently composed depth layer L_k. Composition is done by alpha blending, where the front composition buffer is blended over the next depth layer and for the back composition buffer the depth layer is blended over the composition buffer ($I'_{\text{front}} \oplus L_k$ and $L_k \oplus I'_{\text{back}}$, respectively). Pseudocode for this operation is shown in Listing 9.3.

As desired, stronger blurs can be achieved with smaller filter kernel sizes. For example, a depth layer L_0 will be blurred $k_{\text{focus}} - 1$ times with the Gaussian kernels $\hat{H}_0$ to $\hat{H}_{k_{\text{focus}}-1}$. Blurring recursively has a similar result to blurring with a Gaussian kernel H_k, where the filter width (in σ) is the Euclidean distance of all applied recursive filter sizes:

$$\sigma_k = \sqrt{\sum_{i=k}^{k_{\text{focus}}} \hat{\sigma}_i^2}, \tag{9.6}$$

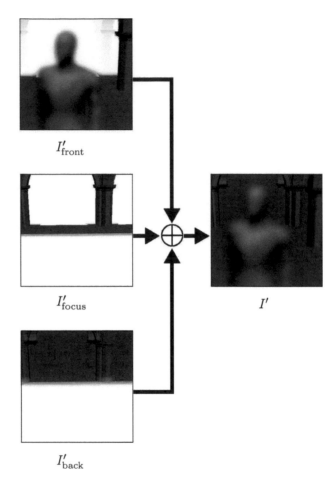

Figure 9.6. Final composition of the three composition buffers (front, focus, and back) as in Equation (9.7). The focus point is the pillar in the back, which is different to results shown in Figure 9.7.

where $\hat{\sigma}_{k\,\text{focus}} = 0$. In the previous example, this means that layer L_0 is as strongly blurred as it would have been if a bigger filter H_0 (σ_0 calculated by Equation (9.6)) has been used for blurring. Although the filtering results are not exactly the same, due to occlusions that are avoided if each layer is blurred separately, the results are sufficient for approximating DoF. In our implementation, we use a standard deviation of $\hat{\sigma}_k = |k - k_{\text{focus}}|$ for the recursive Gaussians, thus there are smaller kernel-size changes around the focal plane, which results in less visible grading.

The final composition I' is calculated by alpha-blending the composition buffers from front to back (Figure 9.6):

$$I' = I'_{\text{front}} \oplus I'_{\text{focus}} \oplus I'_{\text{back}}. \tag{9.7}$$

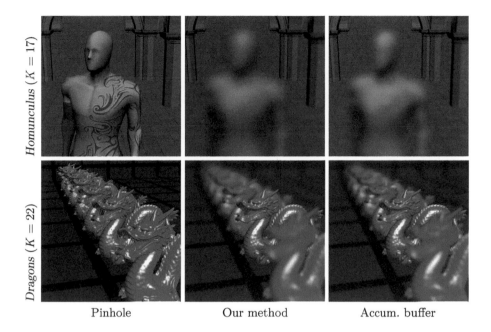

Figure 9.7. A pinhole rendering and DoF effects produced with our algorithm and the accumulation-buffer method (256 views). The first row shows the scene *Homunculus* (74,000 faces), and the second shows *Dragons* (6,000,000 faces). Renderings have the resolution $1{,}024 \times 1{,}024$, and 17 and 22 depth layers, respectively, have been used for our algorithm. The lens settings are $f = 0.1$, $N = 1.4$, and it is focused at the stone wall in the back ($z_{\text{focus}} = 18.5$) for *Homunculus* and at the foremost blue dragon ($z_{\text{focus}} = 3$) for *Dragons*.

9.6.1 Normalization

Due to the usage of matting functions ω and $\dot{\omega}$, resulting in expanded depth layers, and the usage of depth peeling, discretization artifacts as discussed in [Barsky et al. 03] are mostly avoided. However, in some circumstances (e.g., almost perpendicular planes), such artifacts may still appear, but they can be further minimized by normalizing the result (divide color by alpha). Note that for matting and blurring, premultiplied colors (color multiplied by alpha) are used.

9.7 Results

We show some results of the method, rendered on an Intel Core i7 920 CPU with a Geforce GTX 480 graphics card and implemented in GLSL. To avoid depth imprecisions when storing and sorting the fragments in the A-buffer, we

| | Our method | | Accum. buffer |
	A-buffer	Depth peeling	256 views
Homunculus $(K = 17)$	(3/6/36)45	(6/22/36)64	4,809
Dragons $(K = 22)$	(14/6/53)73	(114/28/52)194	4,163

Table 9.1. Performance comparisons, in ms, of our method using the A-buffer, with depth peeling (as in [Schedl and Wimmer 12]), and with the accumulation-buffer method for the scenes *Homunculus* (74k faces) and *Dragons* (6M faces). Renderings have the resolution 1024×1024 and $M = 8$. Note that the rendering times in brackets represent the costs for (scene rendering/matting/blurring).

use 32-bit float textures (GL_RGBA32F for color and depth and GL_R32F for the counter).

We compare our method to the accumulation buffer method and to an implementation of our method with depth peeling (as implemented in [Schedl and Wimmer 12]). The methods are applied to the scenes *Homunculus* (74,000 triangles) and *Dragons* (6,000,000 triangles), shown in Figure 9.7, next to a pinhole rendering of the scenes. In Table 9.1 the rendering times are shown. The retrieval of $M = 8$ hidden fragments is very costly with the previously used depth peeling, especially in complex scenes such as *Dragons*. Although simpler scenes (e.g., *Homunculus*) can be rendered several times with less impact, the latter might be less practical for applications with a constrained rendering budget. Our optimized A-buffer method also does more efficient layer matting, because with the counter texture we don't have to process empty input buffer fragments. The costs for blurring one depth layer are quite similar in both scenes.

The reference accumulation-buffer technique is implemented in OpenGL and uses a 32-bit-per-channel float texture for accumulation. The lens samples are positioned with a Gaussian distribution.

In [Schedl and Wimmer 12] we also compare our method to a ray-traversal technique, and we show that the rendering costs for [Lee et al. 10] are higher ($>$ $5\times$) at comparable settings. Note that for the scenes in [Schedl and Wimmer 12], only $M = 4$ input buffers are used, which is often sufficient.

9.8   Conclusion

We have shown an algorithm to render high-quality DoF effects, in particular including the partial occlusion effect. We use an A-buffer to avoid having to rerender the scene, which would be a costly operation. With recursive Gaussian filters, high-blur radii can be simulated efficiently, while previous methods produce sampling artifacts when too few rays are used. However, since blurring is the most costly operation, if higher frame rates are needed and visual quality can be sacrificed, faster methods (e.g., box and pyramid filters) can be used. With the usage of faster blurring methods, our method could be used in real-time applications such as games. Notice that altering the blurring method also changes the number of depth layers and the spacing between them. At the moment, our method produces practically artifact-free images at reasonable frame rates, making high-quality DoF with partial occlusion available for high-quality rendering applications at interactive rates. Furthermore, our method can be used to preview the impact of camera settings (i.e., focus and aperture) in scenes that later will be rendered with great computational costs, e.g., ray tracing.

The A-buffer uses the space of M screen-sized buffers on the GPU, although the A-buffer might not be filled completely. Therefore, one optimization to reduce memory demand is to use fragment-linked lists instead of an A-buffer (rendering costs might increase). To avoid allocating the A-buffer memory twice, we reuse the allocated A-buffer (unsorted fragments) for later storing the sorted input buffers.

Our implementation uses a texture for each depth layer simply for debugging reasons. However, memory consumption for depth layers can be easily reduced, if matting directly writes into the composition buffers.

9.9 Acknowledgments

Thanks to Juergen Koller for providing the Homunculus model. The Dragon and Sponza models are courtesy of Stanford Computer Graphics Laboratory and Marko Dabrovic.

Bibliography

[Barsky et al. 03] Brian A. Barsky, Daniel R. Tobias, Michael J. Horn, and Derrick P. Chu. "Investigating Occlusion and Discretization Problems in Image Space Blurring Techniques." In *First International Conference on Vision, Video, and Graphics*, pp. 97–102. Bath, UK: University of Bath, 2003.

[Carpenter 84] Loren Carpenter. "The A-buffer, an Antialiased Hidden Surface Method." *SIGGRAPH Computer Graphics* 18 (1984), 103–108.

[Crassin 10] Cyril Crassin. "Fast and Accurate Single-Pass A-Buffer Using OpenGL 4.0+." *Icare3D Blog*, http://blog.icare3d.org/2010/06/fast-and-accurate-single-pass-buffer.html, June 9, 2010.

[Kraus and Strengert 07] Martin Kraus and Magnus Strengert. "Depth-of-Field Rendering by Pyramidal Image Processing." *Computer Graphics Forum* 26:3 (2007), 645–654.

[Lee et al. 10] Sungkil Lee, Elmar Eisemann, and Hans-Peter Seidel. "Real-Time Lens Blur Effects and Focus Control." *ACM Transactions on Graphics* 29:4 (2010), 65:1–65:7.

[Potmesil and Chakravarty 81] Michael Potmesil and Indranil Chakravarty. "A Lens and Aperture Camera Model for Synthetic Image Generation." In *Proceedings of the 8th Annual Conference on Computer Graphics and Interactive Techniques*, SIGGRAPH '81, pp. 297–305. Dallas, TX: ACM, 1981.

[Schedl and Wimmer 12] David Schedl and Michael Wimmer. "A Layered Depth-of-Field Method for Solving Partial Occlusion." *Journal of WSCG* 20:3 (2012), 239–246.

10

Second-Depth Antialiasing
Emil Persson

10.1 Introduction and Previous Work

For nearly a decade multisampling was the one and only antialiasing solution for real-time rendering. For most of this time, multisampling was never challenged because it worked relatively well. As rendering technology has developed and engines become more advanced, multisampling has become an increasingly bigger stumbling block and maintenance problem when developing new rendering techniques. With the recent popularization of deferred shading, the memory inefficiency of multisample antialiasing (MSAA) has further been magnified to a point where it becomes impractical, in particular on current generation consoles, and the inherent weaknesses of this technique become much more apparent.

In recent years a number of interesting alternatives to multisampling has emerged. In 2009 morphological antialiasing (MLAA) [Reshetov 09] was introduced, starting off a wave of new techniques. The fundamental difference between MLAA and MSAA is that the former is entirely a post-process operation. This means that the algorithm is provided a finished rendered image, which it then analyzes and antialiases. This works by first detecting edges in the image (defined, for instance, by a certain difference in luminance between neighboring pixels) and then classifying those edges into a set of shapes. From these shapes it reconstructs what the original edge might have been and uses that to compute a coverage value used for blending with neighboring pixels. MLAA was initially a CPU-based technique for ray tracers but was later expanded to GPU implementations by others [Jimenez et al. 11]. At the point of this writing, several games have shipped with MLAA in some form as their antialiasing solution. Another very popular technique is fast approximate antialiasing (FXAA) [Lottes 11] that, due to its simple single-pass implementation with optimized targets for all important platforms, is a very convenient alternative.

The above and several other approaches can be described as post-process antialiasing techniques, because they require no particular knowledge about how the image was generated. Being decoupled from scene rendering is a great advantage, allowing for a more modular engine design. On the downside the heuristics on which these methods are based are not accurate and may fail or cause artifacts. There are also a number of analytical techniques emerging. These techniques do not try to recover information from buffers but instead take advantage of a priori knowledge of the scene. Examples of this include distance-to-edge antialiasing (DEAA) [Malan 10] and geometry buffer antialiasing (GBAA) [Persson 12]. By using available information about the underlying geometry, these methods can provide much more accurate results. The downside is that they require more engine support and consequently are not as modular and may require a greater amount of maintenance effort in an engine.

This chapter will introduce a semianalytical method that requires very little in terms of data from the game engine to do its job.

10.2   Algorithm

10.2.1   Overview

This technique uses the regular depth buffer and a buffer containing the second layer of depth. The former should already be available; however, the latter is not something an engine normally has and thus is something the engine will have to provide. Fortunately it is relatively straightforward to generate, and should the engine already be using a pre-Z pass, only a trivial change is required.

The underlying idea of this technique is to use the slope of depth to compute where the original edge is located. If we draw a line through the depth samples and find the intersection point, this is where the original edge was. This assumes that there is an adjacent triangle on the other side of an edge, which normally ought to be the case (with some exceptions). To understand how this works, we must first understand the basic properties of depth. If you already have a thorough understanding of depth, you may skip the next section.

10.2.2   Understanding depth

A depth buffer can contain a surprising amount of useful information. For instance, in deferred shading it is common to extract the world position for a pixel from a depth buffer value and its screen-space position alone. The depth buffer also has some interesting properties that are crucial for this technique. The key insight we need to bring before heading into the details of this technique is that a depth buffer is in fact linear.

It is commonly stated that Z is nonlinear. This claim is usually done in the context of Z-buffering and refers to the distribution of depth values in the depth buffer in regards to view distance. There is indeed a nonlinear distribution of depth values in depth buffers, at least with a perspective projection. In a traditional depth buffer ranging from 0 at the near plane to 1 at the far plane,

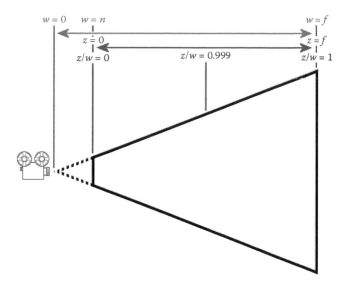

Figure 10.1. Distribution of z, w, and z/w. Both z and w are linear in view depth and differ only by a scale and bias; z/w is highly nonlinear.

the value 0.5 is absolutely not anywhere close to the middle of the frustum. It is in fact very close to the near plane. The vast majority of the values in the depth buffer will land somewhere very close to 1. The value in the middle of the frustum will be something like 0.999. This of course results in a significant loss of a precision, which is a problem. In the past the solution to this was a W-buffer, which some hardware supported, offering linear distribution of depth values. The difference between z and w is not that big, actually; z is essentially w with a slightly larger scale factor, and z starts at near plane whereas w starts at the eye position. So both z and w are linear, but it is z/w that is stored in a Z-buffer, which is not linearly distributed. Refer to Figure 10.1 for a visualization of z, w, and z/w.

While z/w has nonlinear distribution of values, it is on the other hand linear in the gradients pixel-to-pixel in screen space. If you have three neighboring pixels belonging to the same surface, or coplanar surfaces, you can expect the difference in depth values from the first pixel to the second to be equal to that of the second to the third pixel, ignoring precision issues of course. In other words, the screen-space gradients are constant. This is visualized in Figure 10.2.

Constant gradients are a highly desirable property for the hardware, because the z/w values can simply be computed at the triangle vertices and then linearly interpolated across the triangle. In addition to simplifying the rasterizer, this property also facilitates some newer hardware features such a Z-compression. In the relatively likely event that some screen-space tile—for instance, 8×8 pixels—

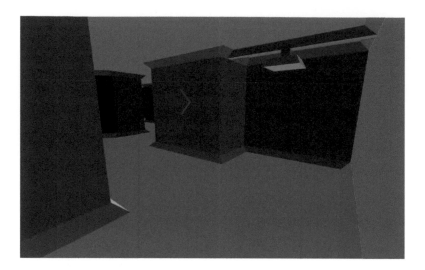

Figure 10.2. The screen-space linearity of z/w visualized by outputting the Z gradients. Notice the flat shading, indicating constant gradients within planar surfaces.

is completely covered by the same primitive, all of the entire tile's depth values can be encoded with three values, the two gradients and an offset, or essentially a plane equation. Assuming that the value is stored as three 32-bit floats,[1] this would represent a bandwidth reduction of no less than 95% for reading and writing depth.

The linearity in screen space is also a property that is very useful on the software side of things. It makes it easy to write an accurate edge-detection routine. Given that the gradients within a primitive are constant, if we detect that the depth delta to the left and to the right of a pixel is different, we know there is an edge there, and similarly in the vertical direction. We can also use this information to find where the original geometrical edge that generated the depth values is. This is the foundation upon which this technique is based.

10.2.3 Method

This technique extracts the original geometrical edges analytically from the depth buffer values. There are two types of edges that need to be handled separately, creases and silhouette edges. A *crease* is where a primitive meets an adjacent primitive—for instance, corners between walls—and a *silhouette edge* is where there is no adjacent primitive on the other side of the edge and instead you have

---

[1]The hardware is likely using a custom format that matches whatever precision the rasterizer has. The hardware also needs to allocate at least one bit to signal whether the tile is compressed or not.

```
bool edge_x = (abs(dx1 + dx2 - 2 * dc) > 0.00001 f * dc);
bool edge_y = (abs(dy1 + dy2 - 2 * dc) > 0.00001 f * dc);
```

Listing 10.1. Horizontal and vertical edge detection.

some sort of background there. The algorithm will first detect whether there is a discontinuity in the depth buffer. If not, we are in the middle of a primitive and no antialiasing is necessary. If a discontinuity is present, it will first attempt to resolve it as a crease. If that fails, it assumes it is dealing with a silhouette instead and resolves it as such.

Edge detection. Detecting a discontinuity in the depth buffer is fairly straightforward. For pixels from the same primitive we expect the delta to the left and to the right to be equal, or left + right − 2 × center = 0. Of course, due to limited precision and such, we need some sort of epsilon there. An epsilon relative to the center sample works quite well. Listing 10.1 has the edge detection part of the shader. Note that we are detecting both horizontal and vertical discontinuities here. To simplify understanding, for the rest of this chapter only the horizontal case will be covered, but the same operations are done in both directions. In the case that we detect a valid edge in both directions, we will decide with which direction to go depending on in which direction the edge is closer.

Creases. Once it has been established that we have an edge, we try to resolve it as a crease. If we have a crease, the original geometry would have the two primitives meet at some point. In Figure 10.3, the blue and green primitives meet at the purple dot. The red dots represent our depth buffer samples. Provided the constant gradients in the screen space, finding this edge point is simply about computing the intersection between the lines passing through the samples.

Figure 10.3. Finding the original geometric edge in the crease case.

```
  if (edge_x)
{
    float k0 = dx1 - dx0; // Left slope
    float k1 = dx3 - dx2; // Right slope
    float m0 = dx1 + k0; // Left offset
    float m1 = dx2 - k1; // Right offset
    offset.x = (m1 - m0) / (k0 - k1); // Intersection point

    is_silhouette = (abs(offset.x) > 1.0f);
    offset.x = (abs(offset.x) < 0.5f)? offset.x : 0.5f;
}
```

Listing 10.2. Computing horizontal crease intersection point.

In Listing 10.2 we are computing the intersection point horizontally. The math is relatively straightforward, and the resulting value is the coordinate relative to the center sample location. If the intersection point lands somewhere within a pixel in either direction, we have successfully resolved this as a crease. Otherwise, there is no valid intersection point here, indicating that we are dealing with a silhouette edge. If we have a valid crease, we only use it if the intersection point lands within half a pixel. This is because if the intersection point is further away, it is actually within the neighboring pixel's area, and it is that pixel that should do the blending.

Silhouette edges. So far we have only required a standard depth buffer. Unfortunately, when we have a silhouette edge, we do not have an adjacent primitive whose depth values can be used to derive the geometric edge. The background primitive has nothing in particular in common with the foreground primitive that we can take advantage of. In Figure 10.4, from the red dots alone, the only thing we can know is that there is a gap between the second and third sample, so the

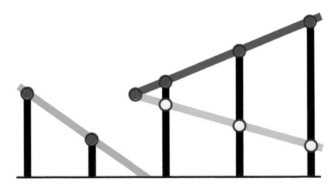

Figure 10.4. Finding the original geometric edge in the silhouette case.

```
if (edge_x)
{
  float k0 = sdx3 - sdx2; // Right second-depth slope
  float k1 = dx3 - dx2; // Right slope
  float k2 = sdx1 - sdx0; // Left second-depth slope
  float k3 = dx1 - dx0; // Left slope

  float m0 = sdx2 - k0; // Right second-depth offset
  float m1 = dx2 - k1; // Right offset
  float m2 = sdx1 + k2; // Left second-depth offset
  float m3 = dx1 + k3; // Left offset
  float offset0 = (m1 - m0) / (k0 - k1); // Right intersection
  float offset1 = (m3 - m2) / (k2 - k3); // Left intersection

  // Pick the closest intersection.
  offset.x = (abs(offset0) < abs(offset1))? offset0 : offset1;
  offset.x = (abs(offset.x) < 0.5f)? offset.x : 0.5f;
}
```

Listing 10.3. Computing horizontal silhouette intersection point.

edge is somewhere in between there, but there is no way for us to know how far that blue primitive stretches over the gap. What we really need here is the depths of the adjacent primitive in the mesh. For the silhouette case, the adjacent primitive will be behind the primitive and back-facing the viewer. We thus need a second layer of depth values for these hidden surfaces, hence the name of this technique: second-depth antialiasing. More on how we generate the second depth layer later in this chapter. Note though that for this to work we need closed geometry. If no back-face primitive exists, the edge will be left aliased.

Once you have a second layer of depth values, the silhouette case is quite similar to the crease case. However, we need to do a separate test to the left and to the right. Then we select whichever one happened to end up closer to the center pixel. Again, if the edge is determined to be within half a pixel from the center, we can use this edge distance information for blending. (See Listing 10.3.)

Once we have determined the distance to the edge, we need to do the final blending of the color buffer. The distance to the edge can be converted to the coverage of neighboring primitives on this pixel, which can be used for blending with the neighboring pixel. We either blend with a horizontal or vertical neighbor. This can be done in a single sample by simply using a linear texture filter and offsetting the texture coordinate appropriately [Persson 12]. The code for this is presented in Listing 10.4.

Generating second depths. A straightforward way to generate the second depth layer is to render the scene to a depth target with front-face culling. This is the equivalent of a pre-Z pass, except it is only used to generate the second depth texture. An additional geometric pass only for this may seem a bit excessive, though. A better approach is to use this pass instead of a traditional pre-Z pass,

```
// Convert distances to a texture coordinate shift for filtering.
if (abs(offset.x) > abs(offset.y))
{
  offset.x = 0;
  offset.y = ((offset.y >= 0)? 0.5f : -0.5f) - offset.y;
}
else
{
  offset.x = ((offset.x >= 0)? 0.5f : -0.5f) - offset.x;
  offset.y = 0;
}

return BackBuffer. Sample (Linear, TexCoord + offset * PixelSize);
```

Listing 10.4. Final blending.

where we generate this texture and get a full pre-Z at the same time. First we draw the scene to a depth buffer with front-face culling, then copy to the second depth texture, and then proceed with main scene rendering, using backface culling as usual. The second-depth values in the buffer will in general still be in front of whatever the frontmost surfaces cover, allowing nearly the same culling efficiency in theory. This is the approach the sample code is using by default.

There are two things to note about this approach. First, a second-depth pre-Z pass places the depth values further back than a tradition pre-Z pass. Hierarchical-Z (Hi-Z)) hardware usually stores a low-precision but conservative value of the most distant depth. For things that are very close to the back-face—for instance, things behind the wall that are standing next to the wall—there may be cases where the hardware is unable to cull those pixels because it cannot guarantee it is completely occluded with the low-precision Hi-Z value it has. In those cases a traditional pre-Z pass could be more effective, depending on the hardware. There are also cases where objects intersect, so that the back-facing depth values are actually behind the intersecting object's front faces. In those cases we do lose the Hi-Z culling. The second thing to note, though, is that a second-depth pre-Z pass is generally faster to render, which may or may not result in better performance overall. The reason it is faster is because plenty of geometry does not have anything behind it. The most distant surface never adds anything of value to a pre-Z pass, because there is nothing behind it to cull. For an indoor scene, such as the one in the sample application, the most distant surface is always front-facing. For outdoor scenes this is also the case if you consider the skybox to be a front-facing surface, which is reasonable. This means that if you render front-faces to pre-Z, you will also render walls that have nothing behind them to pre-Z, which is wasteful. On the other hand, realistically there will always be something behind the back-faces. For the kind of closed geometry in the sample application, this is a guarantee. For real game geometry there are exceptions, of course. Terrain is typically not closed geometry per se, i.e., there is no underside of it, so a second-depth pre-Z pass would not cull the skybox behind it if it was drawn immediately after the pre-Z pass. This is, of course, fixable in practice by drawing the terrain before the skybox in the main scene rendering. In that case a second-depth pre-Z pass would provide all the self-occlusion culling the terrain needs while not wasting any precious raster operations on filling large areas of the screen with essentially nothing but skybox behind it.

There are other conceivable approaches for generating a second depth buffer with the potential advantage of not requiring a pre-Z pass or second geometry pass at all. For instance, one method could be to use a geometry shader to send triangles to two different slices in a render target array depending on the facingness. One slice would contain the front-faces and the other the back-faces. Another approach could be to use a DX11-style linked list of fragments [Thibieroz 11]. If this is used for order-independent transparency, we could already have the second layer there ready for use. A full-screen pass could extract the first and second depths from the fragment list and write to a separate buffer. Neither of these methods has been applied to SDAA, so it is unclear if there are any potential issues or how they would compare performance-wise in real-world applications.

10.3 Results

Image quality. Second-depth antialiasing, like other analytical methods such as GBAA [Persson 12], has the advantage that the coverage value is derived analytically rather than reverse-engineered through a set of heuristics—and consequently is very accurately reproduced. This results in a very high-quality antialiasing regardless of edge orientation. However, it should be noted that SDAA is sensitive to depth-buffer precision. For hidden surface removal a 16-bit depth buffer is more than plenty for the simple scene in the accompanying code sample; however, it is insufficient to be useful for computing intersection points for SDAA. For this reason the demo is using the D32F format. However, it should be noted that a 24-bit depth buffer also works.

Figure 10.6 illustrates the antialiasing quality achieved with this method, compared to Figure 10.5 that has the original aliased image.

Figures 10.7 and 10.8 show a standard pixel-zoomed antialiasing comparison. Before applying SDAA we have the regular stair-stepped edge. After applying SDAA the edge is very smooth. Unlike MSAA and many other antialiasing techniques, the number of intermediate gradients is only limited by the precision of the underlying color format.

Performance. The full cost of this technique largely depends on the scene and the state of the engine prior to adding SDAA support. If there was previously no pre-Z pass, or only a partial one, the need for generating the second depth buffer may incur a sizeable overhead. The addition of a pre-Z pass may, of course,

Figure 10.5. Aliased scene before applying SDAA.   **Figure 10.6.** Scene antialiased with SDAA.

Figure 10.7. Zoomed pixels before SDAA.   **Figure 10.8.** Zoomed pixels after SDAA.

also improve performance. This is all very dependent on the application, so it is impossible to give a universal statement about performance. However, the sample application was profiled using GPU PerfStudio 2, from the default start position using an AMD Radeon HD5870 at a 1,920 × 1,080 resolution. The results are presented in Table 10.1.

The overhead of SDAA consists of the final resolve pass and the cost of copying the depth buffer after the pre-Z pass. The cost of the depth buffer copy is hard to do much about, but the resolve pass can be optimized. The main bottleneck in the standard DX10 implementation is texture fetches. GPU PerfStudio reports the texture unit being busy 97.5% of the time. Using `Gather()` in DX10.1, we can significantly reduce the number of fetches required, from 17 to 9. This brings the cost of the resolve pass down from 0.33 ms to 0.26 ms, and the total overhead of SDAA down from 0.51 ms to 0.43 ms. The texture unit is now 75% busy.

	DX10	DX10.1
SDAA off	1.736 ms	1.736 ms
SDAA on	2.255 ms	2.180 ms
Depth buffer copy	0.176 ms	0.176 ms
Resolve pass	0.335 ms	0.256 ms

Table 10.1. GPU times on an AMD HD5870 at 1,920 × 1,080.

10.4   Conclusion and Future Work

We have presented an effective analytical antialiasing technique offering high-quality edge antialiasing at a reasonable cost and relatively straightforward engine integration. However, there are several areas on which future work could improve.

The resolve pass is very texture fetch heavy. As shown by the profile and through the gains of DX10.1 optimization, this is a major bottleneck for this technique. Given that all samples are refetched for multiple neighboring pixels, this is a prime candidate for compute shader optimization, trading some increase in ALU for a significant reduction in texture fetches by sharing samples. It is likely that this would result in a moderate performance improvement over the DX10.1 results.

Better ways to generate the second-depth values would be desirable to avoid the need for a complete pre-Z pass. Alternatively, an approach worth studying is combining the crease solution from this technique with other methods for silhouette edges, such as, for instance, geometry post-process antialiasing (GPAA).[2] This would eliminate the need for the second depth buffer. Meanwhile the number of silhouette edges in a typical scene is relatively low, so the line rasterization overhead of GPAA should stay at a reasonable level.

This technique may lose its effectiveness when using very dense geometry where neighboring pixels typically come from different primitives. This is because the implementation presented in this chapter computes depth slopes from differences between neighboring depth values. A different approach might be to store gradients along with the depth values. This way the resolve shader would not require sampling any neighboring pixels and should be able to cope better with very dense geometry, at the expense of additional storage and output overhead. On the other hand, the resolve shader would likely run faster.

Bibliography

[Reshetov 09] Alexander Reshetov. "Morphological Antialiasing." Preprint, 2009. (Available at http://visual-computing.intel-research.net/publications/ papers/2009/mlaa/mlaa.pdf.)

[Jimenez et al. 11] Jorge Jimenez, Belen Masia, Jose I. Echevarria, Fernando Navarro, and Diego Gutierrez. "Practical Morphological Antialiasing." In *GPU Pro 2*, edited by Wolfgang Engel, pp. 95–114. Natick, MA: A K Peters, Ltd., 2011.

---

[2]GPAA works by drawing lines over the edges in the scene and filtering the pixels under the lines. The line equation is used to compute the distance from the pixel center to the line, and this is then converted to a coverage value for the neighboring surface. If the line is mostly horizontal, it will blend pixels with vertical neighbors and vice versa.

[Lottes 11] Timothy Lottes. "FXAA." White paper, NVIDIA, http://developer. download.nvidia.com/assets/gamedev/files/sdk/11/FXAA_WhitePaper. pdf, January 25, 2011.

[Malan 10] Hugh Malan. "Edge Anti-aliasing by Post-Processing." In *GPU Pro*, edited by Wolfgang Engel, pp. 265–290. Natick, MA: A K Peters, Ltd., 2010.

[Persson 12] Emil Persson. "Geometric Antialiasing Methods." In *GPU Pro 3*, edited by Wolfgang Engel, pp. 71–88. Boca Raton, FL: CRC Pres, 2012.

[Thibieroz 11] Nicolas Thibieroz. "Order-Independent Transparency Using Per-Pixel Linked Lists." In *GPU Pro 2*, edited by Wolfgang Engel, pp. 409–432. Natick, MA: A K Peters, Ltd., 2011.

Practical Framebuffer Compression

Pavlos Mavridis and Georgios Papaioannou

11.1 Introduction

In computer graphics, the creation of realistic images requires multiple samples per pixel, to avoid aliasing artifacts, and floating-point precision, in order to properly represent the high dynamic range (HDR) of the environmental lighting. Both of these requirements vastly increase the storage and bandwidth consumption of the framebuffer. In particular, using a multisample framebuffer with N samples per pixel requires N times more memory. On top of that, the usage of a 16-bit half-float storage format doubles the memory and bandwidth requirements when compared to the 8-bit fixed-point equivalent. As an example, a 1080p framebuffer using $8 \times$ MSAA requires 189 MB of memory when using half-float precision for the color and a 32-bit Z-buffer.

The total framebuffer memory can further increase when using algorithms that store multiple intermediate render buffers, such as deferred rendering or when simply rendering at very high resolutions in order to drive high-density displays, which is a rather recent trend in mobile and desktop computing. The same is also true when driving multiple displays from the same GPU, in order to create immersive setups. All of these factors vastly increase the consumed memory and put an enormous stress on the memory subsystem of the GPU.

This fact was recognized by the hardware manufacturers and most, if not all, of the shipping GPUs today include a form of lossless framebuffer compression. Although the details of these compression schemes are not publicly disclosed, based on the performance characteristics of the GPUs, it is rather safe to assume that these algorithms mostly exploit the fact that a fragment shader can be executed only once per covered primitive and the same color can be assigned to many subpixel samples. It is worth noting that according to the information theory, there is no lossless compression algorithm that can guarantee a fixed-rate encoding, which is needed in order to provide fast random access; therefore, these algorithms can only save bandwidth but not storage.

Figure 11.1. Using our method, color images can be rasterized directly using only two framebuffer channels: original uncompressed framebuffer stored using three color channels (left), and compressed framebuffer using two color channels in the YC_oC_g space (right). The compressed frame appears indistinguishable from the original one. Inset: Heat map visualizing the compression error (47.02 dB PSNR).

In this chapter we describe a practical lossy framebuffer compression scheme, based on chrominance subsampling, suitable for existing commodity GPUs and APIs. Using our method, a color image can be rasterized using only two frame-buffer channels, instead of three, thus reducing the storage and, more importantly, the bandwidth requirements of the rasterization process, a fundamental operation in computer graphics. This reduction in memory footprint can be valuable when implementing various rendering pipelines. Our method is compatible with both forward and deferred rendering, it does not affect the effectiveness of any lossless compression by the hardware, and it can be used with other lossy schemes, like the recently proposed surface-based antialiasing (SBAA) [Salvi and Vidimče 12], to further decrease the total storage and bandwidth consumption.

While our method is lossy, it does not result in any visible quality degradation of the final rendered image, as shown in Figure 11.1. Furthermore, our measurements in Section 11.7 indicate that in many cases it provides a rather impressive improvement on the GPU fill rate.

11.2   Color Space Conversion

The human visual system is more sensitive to spatial variations of luminance intensity than chrominance. This fact has been exploited by many image and video coding systems, such as JPEG and MPEG, in order to improve compression rates, without a perceptible loss of quality. This is usually achieved by representing the chrominance components of an image with lower spatial resolution than the luminance one, a process that is commonly referred as *chrominance subsampling*. This process forms the basis of our method.

The color of the rasterized fragments should first be decomposed into luminance and chrominance components. A lot of transforms have been proposed to perform this operation. The RGB to YC_oC_g transform, first introduced in h.264 compression [Malvar and Sullivan 03], has been shown to have better compression properties than other similar transforms, such as YC_bC_r. The actual transform is given by the following equation:

$$\begin{bmatrix} Y \\ C_o \\ C_g \end{bmatrix} = \begin{bmatrix} 1/4 & 1/2 & 1/4 \\ 1/2 & 0 & -1/2 \\ -1/4 & 1/2 & -1/4 \end{bmatrix} \begin{bmatrix} R \\ G \\ B \end{bmatrix}, \qquad (11.1)$$

while the original RGB data can be retrieved as

$$R = Y + C_o - C_g, \quad G = Y + C_g, \quad B = Y - C_o - C_g.$$

The chrominance values (C_oC_g) in the YC_oC_g color space can be negative. In particular, when the input RGB range is $[0\ 1]$ the output C_oC_g range is $[-0.5\ 0.5]$. Therefore, when rendering on unsigned 8-bit fixed-point render targets, a bias of 0.5 should be added to these values in order to keep them positive. This bias should be subtracted from the C_oC_g values before converting the compressed render target back to the RGB color space.

It is worth noting that, to avoid any rounding errors during this transform, the YC_oC_g components should be stored with two additional bits of precision compared to the RGB data. When the same precision is used for the YC_oC_g and RGB data, as in our case, we have measured that converting to YC_oC_g and back results in an average peak signal-to-noise ratio (PSNR) of 52.12 dB in the well-known Kodak lossless true color image suite. This loss of precision is insignificant for our purposes and cannot be perceived by the human visual system, but still, this measurement indicates the upper limit in the quality of our compression scheme.

11.3 Chrominance Multiplexing

One option to take advantage of chrominance subsampling is to downsample the render targets after the rendering process has been completed. The problem with this approach is that we can only take advantage of the bandwidth reduction during the subsequent post-processing operations, as described in [White and Barre-Brisebois 11], but not during the actual rasterization.

Instead, our method renders color images directly using two channels. The first channel stores the luminance of each pixel, while the second channel stores

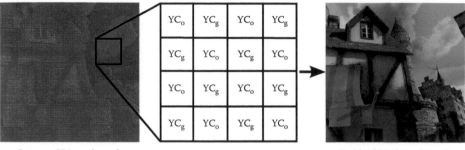

Compact FB/two channels   Resolved FB/three channels

Figure 11.2. Overview of our compact encoding format. The framebuffer is stored in two channels. The first channel stores the luminance of each pixel, while the second channel stores the chrominance interleaved in a checkerboard pattern. A simple and efficient image space reconstruction filter (Section 11.4) is used to uncompress and display the final framebuffer.

either the chroma orange (C_o) or the chroma green (C_g) of the input fragment, interleaved in a checkerboard pattern, as illustrated in Figure 11.2. This particular arrangement corresponds to a luminance-to-chrominance ratio of 2:1 and provides a 3:2 compression ratio, since two color channels are used instead of three. The same luminance-to-chrominance ratio is used by many video compression codecs and is referred as 4:2:2 in the literature, but the details on how the samples are produced and stored are different.

In order to create the compressed framebuffer on the GPU, applications can either request a render buffer with just two color channels, such as GL_RG16F or any similar format exposed by graphics APIs, or use a more traditional format with four color channels and use the free channels to store additional data. The latter case can be particularly useful in deferred rendering pipelines.

The fragments produced by the rasterization phase of the rendering pipeline should be directly emitted in the correct interleaved format. This can be easily done with the code snippet of Listing 11.1. In this code the fragment color is

```
// Convert the output color to YCoCg space.
vec3 YCoCg = RGB2YCoCg(finalColor.rgb);

// Store the YCo and YCg in a checkerboard pattern.
ivec2 crd = gl_FragCoord.xy;
bool isBlack = ((crd.x&1)==(crd.y&1));
finalColor.rg=(isBlack)? YCoCg.rg:YCoCg.rb;
```

Listing 11.1. Code snippet in GLSL to convert the output color in our compact interleaved format. The RGB2YCoCg function implements Equation (11.1).

first converted to the YC_oC_g color space and, depending on the coordinates of the destination pixel, the YC_o or YC_g channels are emitted to the framebuffer.

This approach can also provide some small additional benefits during the fragment shading, where the fragments can be converted to the two-channel interleaved format early in the shader code and then any further processing can be performed only on two channels, instead of three, in the YC_oC_g color space. The actual benefits depend on the exact shading algorithms used in the shader and the underlying GPU architecture (the mix of SIMD and scalar units).

The subsampling of chrominance in our method is performed with point sampling, without using any sophisticated down-sampling filters. In theory this can lead to aliasing of the chrominance components, since we have halved their sampling rate, but in practice we did not observe any severe aliasing issues.

11.4 Chrominance Reconstruction

When reading values of the compressed framebuffer, any missing chrominance information should be reconstructed from the neighboring pixels. The simplest way to do that is to copy the missing chrominance value with one from a neighboring pixel. This *nearest* filter can create some visible mosaic artifacts at the edges of polygons, where strong chrominance transitions occur, as shown in Figure 11.3. Using *bilinear* interpolation of the missing data from the four neighboring pixels mitigates these artifacts but does not completely remove them. Please note that these artifacts are not easily detectable by the human visual system in still im-

Figure 11.3. Quality comparison between the image space reconstruction filters. (a) Original uncompressed framebuffer, (b) nearest reconstruction (43.2 dB), (c) bilinear reconstruction (47.5 dB), (d) edge-directed reconstruction (48.2 dB). Please note that only the edge-directed filter avoids the mosaic artifacts at the edges.

```
//Return the missing chrominance (Co or Cg) of a pixel:
//a1-a4 are the four neighbors of the center pixel a0.
float filter(vec2 a0, vec2 a1, vec2 a2, vec2 a3, vec2 a4)
{
  vec4 lum = vec4(a1.x, a2.x, a3.x, a4.x);
  vec4 w = 1.0-step(THRESH, abs(lum - a0.x));
  float W = w.x + w.y + w.z + w.w;
  //Handle the special case where all the weights are zero.
  W = (W==0.0)? W : 1.0/W;
  return (w.x*a1.y+w.y*a2.y+w.z*a3.y+w.w*a4.y)*W;
}
```

Listing 11.2. GLSL implementation of the edge-directed reconstruction filter.

ages, since the luminance is always correct, but they can become more pronounced when motion is involved.

To eliminate these reconstruction artifacts, we have designed a simple and efficient *edge-directed* filter, where the weights of the four nearest chrominance samples are calculated based on the luminance gradient towards that sample. If the gradient has a value greater than a specific threshold, indicating an edge, then the corresponding chrominance sample has zero weight. Otherwise the weight is one. This is expressed compactly in the following equation:

$$C_0 = \sum_{i=1}^{4} w_i C_i, \qquad w_i = 1.0 - step(T - |L_i - L_0|), \qquad (11.2)$$

where C_i and L_i are respectively the chrominance (C_o or C_g) and luminance of pixel i. In our notation, zero denotes the center pixel, while the next four values denote the four neighbors. The step function returns one on positive values and zero otherwise. T is the gradient threshold. Our experiments with framebuffers from real games indicate that our algorithm is not very sensitive to this threshold, and values around $30/255$ give similar quality in terms of PSNR. However we have observed that this particular value ($30/255$) tends to minimize the maximum difference between the original and the compressed framebuffer.

The gradient can be computed as a simple horizontal and vertical difference of the luminance values, as shown in Listing 11.2. The strategy we follow when all the weights are zero, which happens when we cannot find a neighbor with similar luminance, is to set the chrominance to zero. Furthermore, to avoid handling a special case at the edges of the framebuffer, where only pixels inside the frame boundaries should be considered, we are using a "mirrored repeat" wrapping mode when sampling the framebuffer pixels, which is supported natively by the texture hardware. It is also worth noting that the implementation of this filter is using conditional assignments, which are significantly faster than branches on most GPU architectures.

Figure 11.4. Close-ups demonstrating the quality of our edge-directed reconstruction filter in low-dynamic-range sRGB input. As expected, the largest amount of error occurs on edges and areas with noisy content, but it is still low enough to not be visible to the human visual system. The error is measured as the absolute difference in the RGB colors between the original and the compressed data.

The quality of the framebuffer is very important, therefore the reconstruction should be robust enough to handle the most challenging cases, like high-frequency content and strong chrominance transitions, without introducing any visible artifacts. Figure 11.4 demonstrates that these challenging cases are handled without any visual artifacts by the edge-directed filter. High-dynamic-range (HDR) content provides some extra challenges to chroma subsampling schemes, since the HDR of the luminance tends to exaggerate any "chrominance leaking" on edges with high dynamic contrast. The edge-directed nature of the reconstruction in our method prevents the appearance of any chrominance leaks, even on edges with extremely high dynamic contrast, as the one shown in Figure 11.5. For the test in this figure we have integrated our technique to a well-known demo by Emil Persson, combining our compact format with multisample antialiasing (MSAA), HDR render targets, and proper tone mapping before the MSAA resolve.

To test the temporal stability of our method with moving scenes, we have conducted two experiments. In the first experiment we have used the demo of Figure 11.5 and moved the camera around. But since the content of a real game might be more demanding, we have also encoded a sequence of framebuffers from a real game with our method. In both tests our method appears to be temporally stable.

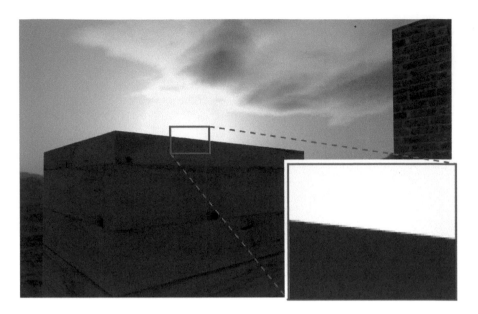

Figure 11.5. An edge with extremely high dynamic range contrast. Places like this naturally draw the attention of the human eye, thus the reconstruction filter needs to deliver best results. The edge-directed filter prevents any chrominance artifacts even in these challenging cases. This particular example combines our compact format with 8× MSAA, HDR render targets, and tone mapping.

11.4.1 Optimizations

A GLSL or HLSL implementation of our method has to perform five fetches, the actual pixel under consideration and four of its neighbors, in order to feed the edge-directed filter of Listing 11.2. Most of these fetches will come from the texture cache, which is very efficient in most GPUs, thus the overhead should be rather small on most architectures. It is worth noting that a GPGPU implementation can completely avoid the redundant fetches, by leveraging the local shared memory of the ALUs. Furthermore, newer architectures, like Nvidia's Kepler, provide intra-warp data exchange instructions, such as SHFL, that can be used to exchange data between threads in the same warp, without touching the shared memory. Nevertheless, since GPGPU capabilities are not available on all platforms, it is very interesting to investigate how the number of fetches can be reduced on a traditional shading language implementation. We focus here on the reduction of memory fetches, instead of ALU instructions, since for years the computational power of graphics hardware has grown at a faster rate than the available memory bandwidth [Owens 05], and this trend will likely continue in the future.

To this end, we can smartly use the built-in partial derivative instructions of the shading language. According to the OpenGL specification, the partial derivatives dFdx and dFdy are computed using local differencing, but the exact accuracy of computations is not specified. Using some carefully chosen test patterns, we have found that for each 2×2 block of pixels that is getting rasterized, the dFdx and dFdy instructions return the same value for pixel blocks of size 2×1 and 1×2, respectively. The same appears to be true for the ddx_fine and ddy_fine functions in HLSL. Assuming C is the chrominance (C_o or C_g) that is stored on each pixel, it is easy to see that we can effectively compute $[C_o C_g]$ with the following code snippet:

```
bool isBlack = ((crd.x&1)==(crd.y&1));
vec2 tmp = (isBlack)? vec2(C,0): vec2(0,C);
vec2 CoCg = abs(dFdx(tmp));
```

where crd are the integer coordinates of each pixel. In this case the missing chrominance has been copied from the horizontal neighbor, but the same principle can be applied in the vertical direction, using the dFdy instruction. Using this approach, we can read the missing chrominance from the two neighbors that fall in the same 2×2 rasterization block, without even touching the memory subsystem of the GPU, thus reducing the total fetches required to implement Equation (11.2) from five to three.

This reduction of fetches did not yield any measurable performance increase in our test cases. The results of course depend on the nature of each particular application and the underlying GPU architecture, therefore we still discuss this low-level optimization because it could be valuable in applications with different workloads or different GPU architectures. Another option is to feed Equation (11.2) with only the two neighbors that fall in the same 2×2 rasterization block, thus completely avoiding any redundant fetches. We have found, however, that the quality of this implementation is not always satisfactory, since in the worst case the required chrominance information will be located in the two missing neighbors.

11.5 Antialiasing

When rendering to a multisample framebuffer with our technique, each pixel will contain either multiple chroma orange (C_o) samples or multiple chroma green (C_g) samples, but never a mixture of both. Therefore, the framebuffer can be resolved as usual, before applying the demosaic filter of Section 11.4. The only restriction is that the reconstruction filter for the resolve should not be wider than one pixel, in order to avoid incorrectly mixing C_o and C_g samples. This means that a custom resolve pass should be used in case the automatic resolve operation of the hardware uses a wider filter. This is hardly objectionable, since custom resolve is also required in order to perform tone mapping on the samples before the resolve, as required for high-quality antialiasing. We should also note that if wider reconstruction filters are desirable, they can be used in the luminance channel only, which is perceptually the most important.

11.6 Blending

Since all operations in the RGB to YC_oC_g transform are linear, blending can be performed directly in the YC_oC_g color space. Therefore, our method directly supports hardware framebuffer blending, without any modification. This is particularly the case when rendering to floating-point render targets, but fixed-point rendering requires some attention.

When rendering to unsigned fixed-point render targets, as noted in Section 11.2, we have added a bias of 0.5 in the chrominance values, in order to keep them positive, since these buffers do not support signed values. This does not create any problems with traditional alpha blending, since the bias will always remain 0.5 and can be easily subtracted when converting back to RGB. Nevertheless, when using other blending modes, such as *additive blending*, the bias will be accumulated and will create clamping artifacts. Furthermore, when additive blending is used to accumulate N fragments, we should subtract $0.5N$ from the chrominance in the framebuffer, but in many cases N is either unknown or difficult to compute. One possible solution is to perform the blending operation inside the shader, in the correct $[-0.5, 0.5]$ range, by reading and writing to the same render target (using the `texture_barrier` extension), but this approach is limited to specific platforms and use cases. However, this limitation only concerns certain blending modes on unsigned 8-bit render targets. High-quality rendering usually requires HDR formats, which are trivially handled by our method.

11.7 Performance

Before providing any GPU measurements, it is worth investigating the theoretical gains from our method. For a visible fragment, the GPU has to read the old 32-bit depth value from the Z-buffer in order to perform the depth test, and then it has to write back the new depth and color information. When blending is enabled, the old color should also be fetched. Based on this theoretical analysis, we can calculate that, for a 16-bit half-float render target, our technique reduces the bandwidth consumption by 25% without blending and by 33% when blending is enabled. We should note that all our measurements and analysis include a depth buffer, since in practice rasterization without a Z-buffer is not very common.

To examine how these theoretical gains translate in practice, we have measured the fill rate during rasterization. The fill rate measures how fast the GPU

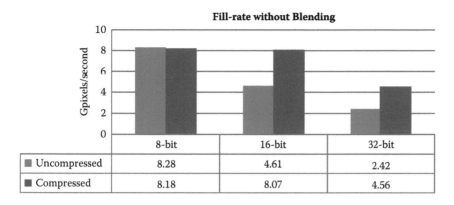

Fill-rate without Blending			
	8-bit	16-bit	32-bit
■ Uncompressed	8.28	4.61	2.42
■ Compressed	8.18	8.07	4.56

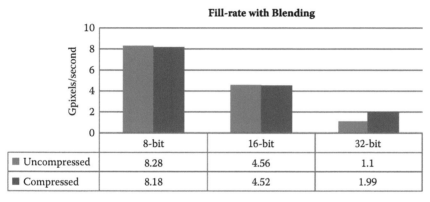

Fill-rate with Blending			
	8-bit	16-bit	32-bit
■ Uncompressed	8.28	4.56	1.1
■ Compressed	8.18	4.52	1.99

Figure 11.6. Fill-rate measurements (in gigapixels per second) when using the compressed framebuffer to perform forward rendering.

can rasterize pixels, and it is directly proportional to the available framebuffer bandwidth and the number of bits emitted for each pixel. Figure 11.6 shows the actual measurements on an Nvidia GTX 460 with 768 MB of memory (192-bit bus). The compressed framebuffer uses two output channels, while the uncompressed one uses four channels, since three-channel formats are not valid render targets due to memory alignment restrictions.

Our measurements indicate an impressive 75% fill-rate increase when rendering with half-float precision without blending, confirming our theoretical analysis. On the other hand, when blending is enabled on a half-float render target, we could not measure any gain, perhaps indicating some limitation in the flexibility of the render-output units in this specific GPU architecture. When using a 32-bit floating-point render target, our measurements demonstrate the expected increase in the fill rate when blending is both enabled and disabled, but this format is rarely used to store color information. In the 8-bit case we did not measure any

	8-bit	16-bit	32-bit
Uncompressed	0.55 ms	0.75 ms	1.01 ms
Compressed	0.56 ms	0.56 ms	0.78 ms
Speedup	0.98 ×	1.33 ×	1.29 ×

Table 11.1. The time in milliseconds for blitting a 720p render target to the GPU back buffer.

fill-rate increase, indicating that the 8-bit two-channel format (`GL_RG8`) is handled internally as a four-channel format (`GL_RGBA8`).

For the measurements above, we have used a typical fill-rate benchmark application that renders large visible quads on a render target. For the compressed case, the application also performs the compression and decompression of the render target. The results of course will be different on other GPU architectures, but generally we can expect that the performance increase due to the bandwidth reduction outweighs the small increase in the ALU instructions used to encode and decode the color. Although many applications are shader or geometry limited, an increase in the fill rate is always welcomed, especially when rendering particles and other fill-rate-intensive content.

Another operation worth investigating is the time it takes to uncompress and copy (blit) a compressed render buffer to the GPU back buffer. This operation is performed in our tests by rendering a full screen quad that uses the render buffer as a texture. When using a half-float format, resolving a compressed 720p render buffer takes 0.19 ms, which is 25% faster than the uncompressed case. Table 11.1 has the complete measurements for the other precisions too. As noted before, our desktop GPU does not internally support a two-channel 8-bit format, thus in this case our measuements show only the decompression overhead.

Of course, aside from any performance and bandwidth gains, the memory saved by our method can be used to improve other aspects of an application, such as the textures or the meshes. As an example, an uncompressed 1080p render target with 8× MSAA requires 189 MB of storage at 16-bit half-float precision, while with our method it requires only 126 MB. Both numbers include the Z-buffer storage.

11.8 Conclusion and Discussion

In this chapter we have presented a practical framebuffer compression scheme based on the principles of chrominance subsampling. Using our method, color images can be rasterized directly using only two framebuffer channels. The memory footprint of the framebuffer is reduced along with the consumed bandwidth, and as a consequence the fill rate of the GPU rasterizer is significantly increased.

Our solution is simple to implement and can work in commodity hardware, like game consoles. In particular, the memory architecture of the Xbox 360 game console provides a good example of the importance of our method in practice. The Xbox 360 provides 10 MB of extremely fast embedded memory (EDRAM) for the storage of the framebuffer. Every buffer used for rendering, including the intermediate buffers in deferred pipelines and the Z-buffer, should fit in this space. To this end, our technique can be valuable in order to fit more data in this fast memory. Bandwidth savings are also extremely important in mobile platforms, where memory accesses will drain the battery.

Our method was largely influenced by the way most digital cameras capture color images, where a mosaic of color filters is arranged in front of a single layer of monochromatic photo receptors, forming the so-called *Bayer pattern* [Bayer 76]. In fact, in our method we have also tried to use the Bayer pattern, instead of the pattern in Figure 11.2, something that would reduce the storage requirements down to a single channel, but in our experiments we were not satisfied by the robustness and the worst-case quality of this rather aggressive encoding format.

A rather obvious limitation of our method is that it can only be used to store intermediate results and not the final device framebuffer, because the hardware is not aware of our custom format. However, this does not limit the usefulness of our method, since most modern real-time rendering pipelines use many intermediate render buffers before writing to the back buffer.

In the supplemental material of this chapter, the interested reader can find a complete proof-of-concept implementation of our method in WebGL. Since the method consists of a few lines of code, it should be rather trivial to integrate it on any existing rendering pipeline.

11.9 Acknowledgments

We would like to thank Stephen Hill (Ubisoft Montreal) for his helpful and very insightful comments on the technique. Dimitrios Christopoulos (FHW) was kind enough to proofread our chapter and suggest various improvements. The Citadel dataset, used in many figures of this chapter, is from the publicly available Unreal Development Kit (UDK) from Epic Games. This work was not endorsed by Epic Games. We would also like to thank Emil Persson for providing the source of his HDR demo with a permissive license, allowing very quick testing for our method.

Bibliography

[Bayer 76] Bryce Bayer. "Color Imaging Array." United States Patent 3971065, 1976.

[Malvar and Sullivan 03] Henrique Malvar and Gary Sullivan. "YCoCg-R: A Color Space with RGB Reversibility and Low Dynamic Range." White paper, Joint Video Team (JVT) of ISO/IEC MPEG & ITU-T VCEG, Document No. JVTI014r3, 2003.

[Owens 05] John Owens. "Streaming Architectures and Technology Trends." In *GPU Gems 2: Programming Techniques, Tips, and Tricks for Real-Time Graphics*, edited by Matt Pharr, pp. 457–470. Reading, MA: Addison-Wesley, 2005.

[Salvi and Vidimče 12] Marco Salvi and Kiril Vidimče. "Surface Based Anti-Aliasing." In *Proccedings of the ACM SIGGRAPH Symposium on Interactive 3D Rendering and Games*, pp. 159–164. New York: ACM, 2012.

[White and Barre-Brisebois 11] John White and Colin Barre-Brisebois. "More Performance! Five Rendering Ideas from *Battlefield 3* and *Need For Speed: The Run*." SIGGRAPH Course: Advances in the Real-Time Rendering in Games, SIGGRAPH 2011, Vacouver, Canada, August 8, 2011.

Coherence-Enhancing Filtering on the GPU

Jan Eric Kyprianidis and Henry Kang

12.1 Introduction

Directional features and flow-like structures are pleasant, harmonic, or at least interesting to most humans [Weickert 99]. They are also a highly sought-after property in many of the traditional art forms, such as painting and illustration. Enhancing directional coherence in the image helps to clarify region boundaries and features. As exemplified by Expressionism, it also helps to evoke mood or ideas and even elicit emotional response from the viewer [Wikipedia 12]. Particular examples include the works of van Gogh and Munch, who have emphasized these features in their paintings. This chapter presents an image and video abstraction technique that places emphasis on enhancing the directional coherence of features. It builds upon the idea of combining diffusion with shock filtering for image abstraction, but is, in a sense, contrary to that of [Kang and Lee 08], which is outperformed in terms of speed, temporal coherence, and stability. Instead of simplifying the shape of the image features, the aim is to preserve the shape by using a curvature-preserving smoothing method that enhances coherence. More specifically, smoothing is performed in the direction of the smallest change (Figure 12.1(a)), and sharpening in the orthogonal direction (Figure 12.1(b)). Instead of modeling this process by a partial differential equation (PDE) and solving it, approximations that operate as local filters in a neighborhood of a pixel are used. Therefore, good abstraction results can be achieved in just a few iterations, making it possible to process images and video at real-time rates on a GPU. It also results in a much more stable algorithm that enables temporally-coherent video processing. Compared to conventional abstraction approaches, such as [Winnemöller et al. 06, Kyprianidis et al. 10], the presented method provides a good balance between the enhancement of directional features and the smoothing of isotropic regions. As shown in Figure 12.2, the technique preserves and enhances

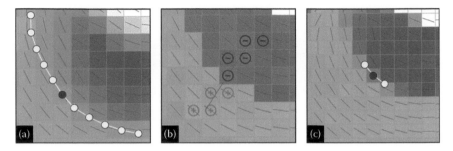

Figure 12.1. Illustration of the different key techniques employed in the presented algorithm. (a) Flow-guided smoothing for simplification and abstraction. (b) Shock filtering to preserve and enhance sharp edge transitions. (c) Edge smoothing for antialiasing.

directional features while increasing contrast, which helps to clarify boundaries and features. This chapter follows up on a technical paper [Kyprianidis and Kang 11] presented at Eurographics 2011 and provides an in-depth discussion of implementation details, including a few enhancements. For a discussion of related work and comparisons with other techniques, the interested reader is referred to the technical paper. The implementation is based on CUDA, and pitch linear memory is used for all image data. This has the advantage that image data is directly accessible on the device for reading and writing but can be bound to textures as well.

A schematic overview of the presented technique is shown in Figure 12.3. Input is given by a grayscale or color image (RGB color space is used for all examples). The algorithm runs iteratively and stops after a user-defined num-

Figure 12.2. Examples created by the technique described in this chapter.

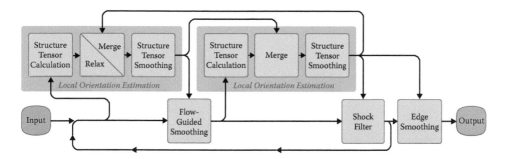

Figure 12.3. Schematic overview of the presented algorithm.

ber of iterations, controlling the strength of the abstraction. For each iteration, adaptive flow-guided smoothing (Figure 12.1(a)) and sharpening (Figure 12.1(b)) are performed. Both techniques require information about the local structure, which is obtained by an eigenvalue analysis of the smoothed structure tensor and computed twice for every iteration, once before the smoothing and again before the sharpening. With every iteration, the result becomes closer to a piecewise-constant image, with large smooth or even flat image regions where no distinguished orientation is defined. Since having valid orientations defined for these regions is important for the stability of the algorithm, the structure tensor from the previous calculation is used in this case. For the first calculation, where no result from a previous computation is available, a relaxation of the structure tensor is performed. As a final step, edges are smoothed by flow-guided smoothing with a small filter kernel (Figure 12.1(c)). In the following sections, the different stages of the algorithm are examined in detail.

12.2 Local Orientation Estimation

To guide the smoothing and shock-filtering operations, the dominant local orientation at each pixel must be estimated. For smooth grayscale images with nonvanishing derivative, a reasonable choice are the local orientations given by tangent spaces of the isophote curves (i.e., curves with constant gray value). Since for smooth images the gradient is perpendicular to the isophote curves, the local orientations can easily be derived from the gradient vectors by rotating them 90 degrees (Figure 12.4). Unfortunately, real images are seldom smooth, and computation of the gradient is highly sensitive to noise and other image artifacts. This is illustrated in Figure 12.5(a), where an image with single dominant orientation is shown. Since it is sufficiently smooth, all gradient vectors induce the same orientation. Adding a small amount of Gaussian noise, however, results in noisy gradients and a poor orientation estimation, as shown in Figure 12.4(b). A possible solution is to regularize the gradient computation by, for example,

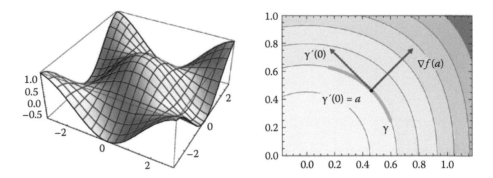

Figure 12.4. Plots of the function $f(x) = \cos(x_1)\cos(x_2)$. On the left, a 3D plot is shown. The contour plot on the right shows various level sets and illustrates that, for regular level sets, the gradient is orthogonal to the tangent of curves locally parameterizing the level set.

smoothing the image prior to derivative computation or using Gaussian derivatives. However, since such approaches also remove high-frequency anisotropic image structures, such as hair, they are generally not suitable for our purpose. Instead, averaged gradient vectors in the least-squares sense will be computed, leading to the structure tensor [Brox et al. 06]—a well-known tool in computer vision.

12.2.1   Smoothed Structure Tensor

For each point x of a grayscale image, let $g(x)$ be the gradient vector at x computed by convolving the image with a suitable derivative operator. As explained earlier, for typical images, these gradients are not sufficiently smooth for our purposes. Simply smoothing the gradient vectors is not an option, since gradient vectors have opposite signs in the neighborhood of extrema and would cancel each other out (Figure 12.5). Hence, a more sophisticated approach is required. For instance, one can seek a vector that approximates the gradient vectors in a neighborhood. To measure how well a unit vector v approximates a gradient vector $g(x)$, the scalar product $\langle g(x), v \rangle$ may be used, which can be interpreted as the length of the projection of $g(x)$ on v. By squaring the scalar product, the measure becomes independent of the sign of the gradient vectors. Moreover, multiplying with a spatially varying weight gives less influence to gradients that are farther away. Hence, the wanted unit vector is a vector whose sum of weighted scalar products is maximal:

$$v(x) = \arg\max_{\|v\|=1} \frac{1}{|G_\rho|} \cdot \sum_{y \in \mathcal{N}(x)} G_\rho(y-x)\langle g(y), v \rangle^2. \qquad (12.1)$$

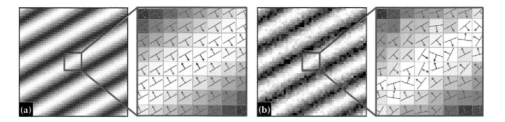

Figure 12.5. For smooth images with strong dominant local orientation, such as the one shown in (a), local orientation may be estimated using the gradient. However, if the image is corrupted by noise, as shown in (b), the gradients are noisy and require further processing. Notice that gradients in the neighborhood of extrema have opposite signs and would cancel each other out if processed with a smoothing filter.

For the spatial weight, a two-dimensional Gaussian function,

$$G_\rho(x) = \frac{1}{2\pi\rho^2} \exp\left(-\frac{\|x\|^2}{2\rho^2}\right),$$

with standard deviation ρ is used. The set $\mathcal{N}(x)$ refers to a local neighborhood of x with reasonable cutoff (e.g., with radius 3ρ), and $|G_\rho| = \sum_{y\in\mathcal{N}(x)} G_\rho(y-x)$ denotes the corresponding normalization term.

Equation (12.1) cannot be solved directly, but rewriting the scalar product $\langle g(y), v \rangle$ in matrix form as $g(y)^T v$ and utilizing the symmetry of the scalar product, yields

$$v(x) = \arg\max_{\|v\|=1} \frac{1}{|G_\rho|} \cdot \sum_{y\in\mathcal{N}(x)} G_\rho(y-x) v^T g(y) g(y)^T v.$$

Moreover, since v does not depend on y, it follows by linearity that

$$v(x) = \arg\max_{\|v\|=1} v^T J_\rho(x) v, \tag{12.2}$$

where

$$J_\rho(x) = \frac{1}{|G_\rho|} \cdot \sum_{y\in\mathcal{N}(x)} G_\rho(y-x) g(y) g(y)^T. \tag{12.3}$$

The outer product $g(x)g(x)^T$ is called the *structure tensor* at x, and $J_\rho(x)$ is called the *smoothed structure tensor* at x. Since it is a sum of outer products weighted by nonnegative coefficients, the smoothed structure tensor is a symmetric positive semidefinite 2×2 matrix. Therefore, from the Rayleigh-Ritz theorem [Horn and Johnson 85, Section 4.2], it follows that the solution of Equation (12.2) is given by the eigenvector associated with the major eigenvalue of $J_\rho(x)$. The eigenvalues are real, since $J_\rho(x)$ is symmetric, and nonnegative, since $J_\rho(x)$ is positive semidefinite. The major eigenvalue measures the squared rate of change in the direction of the major eigenvector. Its square root can thus be regarded as a generalized gradient strength. The minor eigenvalue, on the other hand, can be regarded as a measure for the error of the approximation.

Up to now, only the case of grayscale images has been considered. The most straightforward way to extend the previous discussion to color images is by solving Equation (12.1) jointly for all color channels, resulting in the following generalization of Equation (12.3):

$$J_\rho(x) = \frac{1}{|G_\rho|} \cdot \sum_{y \in \mathcal{N}(x)} G_\rho(y - x) \sum_{i=1}^{n} g^i(y)g^i(y)^T,$$

where n is the number of color channels (i.e., $n = 3$ for RGB images) and $g^i(y)$ denotes the gradient of the ith color channel. Another convenient way to express the sum of outer products is as the scalar product of the partial derivatives:

$$\sum_{i=1}^{n} g^i(y)g^i(y)^T = \begin{pmatrix} \sum_{i=1}^{n} \left(g_1^i\right)^2 & \sum_{i=1}^{n} g_1^i g_2^i \\ \sum_{i=1}^{n} g_1^i g_2^i & \sum_{i=1}^{n} \left(g_2^i\right)^2 \end{pmatrix} = \begin{pmatrix} \langle g_1, g_1 \rangle & \langle g_1, g_2 \rangle \\ \langle g_1, g_2 \rangle & \langle g_2, g_2 \rangle \end{pmatrix}.$$

12.2.2   Eigenanalysis of the Structure Tensor

In this section, the way in which the eigenvalues and eigenvectors of the structure tensor, or more generally of a symmetric positive semidefinite 2×2 matrix

$$J = \begin{pmatrix} E & F \\ F & G \end{pmatrix},$$

can be computed in a numerically stable way will be discussed. Although a straightforward implementation leads to reasonable results, a carefully crafted implementation, as shown in Listing 12.1, is able to achieve much better accuracy by taking care of the numerical subtleties of floating-point calculations [Goldberg 91].

Being positive semidefinite implies that $E, G \geq 0$ and $EG \geq F^2$. Hence, from $E + G = 0$, it follows that $F = 0$, which means that the matrix is zero. Let us now assume that $E + G > 0$. Computation of the eigenvalues requires solving the characteristic polynomial $\det(A - I\lambda) = 0$, which is a quadratic equation, and the solution can be obtained using the monic form of the popular quadratic formula:

$$\lambda_{1,2} = \frac{1}{2}(E + G \pm \sqrt{(E + G)^2 - 4(EG - F^2)}).$$

The quadratic formula is known to have numerical issues when implemented in a straightforward manner. The subtractions are problematic, as they may result

```
inline __host__ __device__
void solve_eig_psd( float E, float F, float G, float& lambda1,
                    float& lambda2, float2& ev )
{
    float B = (E + G) / 2;
    if (B > 0) {
        float D = (E - G) / 2;
        float FF = F*F;
        float R = sqrtf(D*D + FF);
        lambda1 = B + R;
        lambda2 = fmaxf(0, E*G - FF) / lambda1 ;

        if (R > 0) {
            if (D >= 0) {
                float nx = D + R;
                ev = make_float2(nx, F) * rsqrtf(nx*nx + FF);
            } else {
                float ny = -D + R;
                ev = make_float2(F, ny) * rsqrtf(FF + ny*ny);
            }
        } else {
            ev = make_float2(1, 0);
        }
    } else {
        lambda1 = lambda2 = 0;
        ev = make_float2(1, 0);
    }
}
```

Listing 12.1. Eigenanalysis of a symmetric positive semidefinite 2×2 matrix.

in loss of accuracy due to cancelation. In case of the major eigenvalue, only the subtractions under the square root are an issue, because of the assumption that $E + G > 0$. The subtractions are best implemented as $(E - G)^2$, since then catastrophic cancelation is avoided and replaced with benign cancelation [Goldberg 91]:

$$\lambda_1 = \frac{E + G}{2} + R, \qquad R = \sqrt{\left(\frac{E - G}{2}\right)^2 + F^2}.$$

For the computation of the minor eigenvalue, we have to take care of the subtraction in front of the square root. A common approach is to use the property that the product of the eigenvalues equals its determinant [Goldberg 91]:

$$\lambda_2 = \frac{\det(J)}{\lambda_1} = \frac{EG - F^2}{\lambda_1}.$$

Notice that $\lambda_1 > 0$, since we assumed $E + G > 0$. Because of rounding errors, $EG - F^2$ may become negative, and therefore it is advisable to compute $\max(0, EG - F^2)$.

Recall that a symmetric matrix has orthogonal eigenvectors. Therefore, it is sufficient to compute only one of the eigenvectors, since the other can be found by rotating the vector 90 degrees. Let us first assume that the eigenvalues are distinct, which can be easily verified by checking that the square root R is nonzero. Under this assumption, we have a well-defined major eigenvector, which can be found by solving the following linear system:

$$(A - \lambda_1 I)v = \begin{pmatrix} E - \lambda_1 & F \\ F & G - \lambda_1 \end{pmatrix} \begin{pmatrix} v_1 \\ v_2 \end{pmatrix} = 0.$$

By construction, $A - \lambda I$ is singular, and therefore the two equations are linearly dependent. Hence, a solution of one equation will also be a solution of the other, providing us with two alternatives to choose from:

$$\eta_1 = \begin{pmatrix} F \\ \lambda_1 - E \end{pmatrix} = \begin{pmatrix} F \\ -\frac{E-G}{2} + R \end{pmatrix}, \qquad \eta_2 = \begin{pmatrix} \lambda_1 - G \\ F \end{pmatrix} = \begin{pmatrix} \frac{E-G}{2} + R \\ F \end{pmatrix}.$$

By choosing η_1 if $E - G < 0$ and η_2 if $E - G \geq 0$, we can kill two birds with one stone. Firstly, subtractive cancelation is avoided, since the first term in the sum is positive. Secondly, if $F = 0$ and, correspondingly, $R = |E - G|/2$, then the computed vector is guaranteed to be nonzero. Finally, if the square root R is zero, we have a single eigenvalue with multiplicity two, and the eigenspace is two-dimensional.

A limitation of the discussed implementation is that computations of the form $\sqrt{a^2 + b^2}$ may underflow or overflow if not computed at higher precision. A common approach to avoid such issues is to exchange a and b if necessary, such that $|a| > |b|$, and compute $|a|\sqrt{1 + (b/a)^2}$.

12.2.3 Structure Tensor Relaxation

In low-contrast regions, the signal-to-noise ratio is low, making the gradient information unreliable. Accordingly, the estimated orientation is almost random and of little value. However, appropriate orientation information is critical for the presented algorithm. Therefore, in this section an approach for replacing unreliable structure tensors will be discussed. As explained earlier, the square root of the major eigenvalue is a generalization of the gradient magnitude and can thus be used to identify points with reliable structure tensors

$$\partial\Omega = \{ x \in \Omega \mid \sqrt{\lambda_1} > \tau_r \}, \tag{12.4}$$

where τ_r is a control parameter. The idea is now to look for a smooth function s that interpolates the structure tensors S defined on $\partial\Omega$. Such a function is given by the membrane that minimizes

$$\arg\min_s \int_\Omega |\nabla s|^2 dx \quad \text{with} \quad s|_{\partial\Omega} = S|_{\partial\Omega}.$$

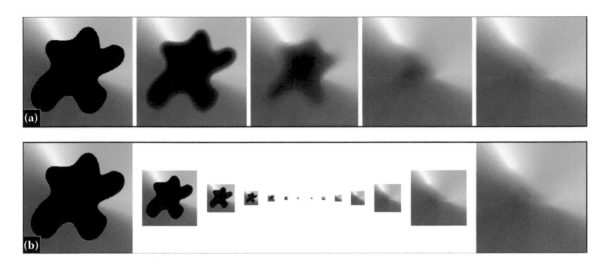

Figure 12.6. Solution of the Laplace equation. (a) Iterative solution using 100, 1,000, 5,000, and 50,000 Jacobi iterations. (b) Multiscale approach.

This problem is known to be equivalent to solving Laplace's equation $\Delta s = 0$ with the corresponding Dirichlet boundary condition $s|_{\partial\Omega} = S|_{\partial\Omega}$. Discretization of the Laplace operator yields a large sparse linear system of equations

$$\Delta s|_{i,j} \approx s_{i+1,j} + s_{i-1,j} + s_{i,j+1} + s_{i,j-1} - 4s_{i,j} = 0,$$

which may be solved using any technique for solving linear systems. One of the simplest approaches is to assume that in the ith equation only the ith parameter is unknown, leaving the other parameters fixed. Solving each of these equations independently and iterating the process converges to the solution and is known as the *Jacobi method*. More specifically, let $s_{i,j}^k$ denote the kth step's structure tensor at pixel (i, j); then a Jacobi relaxation step is given by

$$s_{i,j}^{k+1} = \begin{cases} s_{i,j}^k & \text{if } (i,j) \in \partial\Omega, \\ \dfrac{s_{i+1,j}^k + s_{i-1,j}^k + s_{i,j+1}^k + s_{i,j-1}^k}{4} & \text{otherwise.} \end{cases}$$

Since the computation involves a convex combination, the result is again a positive semidefinite matrix and, thus, is well-defined. Unfortunately, a very large number of iterations is typically required, which is demonstrated in Figure 12.6(a). Obtaining a sufficient approximation of the solution takes approximately 50,000 Jacobi iterations. Even on modern high-end GPUs, this takes several seconds to compute. The implementation of a Jacobi step is shown in Listing 12.2.

```
__global__ void jacobi_step( gpu_plm2<float4> dst ) {
    const int ix = blockDim.x * blockIdx.x + threadIdx.x;
    const int iy = blockDim.y * blockIdx.y + threadIdx.y;
    if (ix >= dst.w || iy >= dst.h) return;

    float4 st = tex2D (texST, ix, iy);
    if (st.w < 1) {
        st = make_float4((
                make_float3(tex2D(texST, ix+1, iy  )) +
                make_float3(tex2D(texST, ix-1, iy  )) +
                make_float3(tex2D(texST, ix,   iy+1)) +
                make_float3(tex2D(texST, ix,   iy-1))) / 4,
                0);
    }
    dst(ix, iy) = st;
}
```

Listing 12.2. Implementation of a Jacobi relaxation step.

Jacobi iterations are effective for removing high-frequency oscillations in the residual, but they perform rather poorly when the residual becomes smooth. Multigrid methods [Briggs et al. 00] address this issue by solving for the residual on a coarser level. A similar approach, which can be regarded as a simplified variant of a multigrid solver, where computation of the residual is avoided, is adopted here. As a first step, which structure tensors should be kept unmodified is determined using Equation (12.4). To this end, the fourth color channel is used, with one indicating a boundary pixel and zero used otherwise.

The reason why convergence of the Jacobi method is slow is illustrated in Figure 12.6(a). One Jacobi iteration computes the average of the neighboring pixels; consequently, it takes a large number of iterations until values on the boundary diffuse into the inner parts. Apparently, a simple way to speed up the diffusion is to compute it on a coarser grid. Since the transfer to a coarser grid can be repeated recursively, this yields a pyramid of images. Moving from a finer to a coarser level is referred to as *restriction*. The pixels on a coarser pyramid level are defined as the average of four pixels on the finer pyramid level, with nonboundary pixels being excluded (Figure 12.7(a)). The left of Figure 12.6(b) exemplifies the pyramid construction. Once the finest pyramid level is reached, the pyramid is processed in a coarse-to-fine manner. On each pyramid level, one to three Jacobi iterations are performed. Nonboundary pixels on the next-finer pyramid level are then replaced by sampling the result using bilinear interpolation. These operations are repeated until the finest pyramid level has been reached, as shown on the right of Figure 12.6(b). The implementations of the restriction and interpolation operations are shown in Listings 12.3 and 12.4.

Nevertheless, performing the relaxation for every computation of the structure tensor is expensive. Therefore, the relaxation is only performed for the first computation of the structure tensor. All subsequent computations substitute the structure tensor of the previous computation.

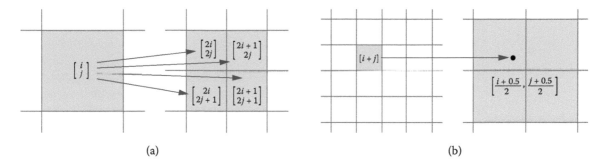

(a)   (b)

Figure 12.7. Illustration of the restriction and interpolation operations. (a) Restriction collapses four pixels into a single pixel by averaging those that are boundary pixels. (b) Interpolation is performed using bilinear interpolation.

```
__global__ void restrict ( const gpu_plm2<float4> st,
                           gpu_plm2<float4> dst)
{
    const int ix = blockDim.x * blockIdx.x + threadIdx.x;
    const int iy = blockDim.y * blockIdx.y + threadIdx.y;
    if (ix >= dst.w || iy >= dst.h) return;

    float4 sum = make_float4(0);
    float4 tmp;
    tmp = st (2*ix,   2*iy  ); if (tmp.w > 0) { sum += tmp; }
    tmp = st (2*ix+1, 2*iy  ); if (tmp.w > 0) { sum += tmp; }
    tmp = st (2*ix,   2*iy+1); if (tmp.w > 0) { sum += tmp; }
    tmp = st (2*ix+1, 2*iy+1); if (tmp.w > 0) { sum += tmp; }
    if (sum.w > 0) sum /= sum.w;
    dst(ix, iy) = sum;
}
```

Listing 12.3. Implementation of the restiction operation.

```
__global__ void interpolate( const gpu_plm2<float4> st_fine,
                             gpu_plm2<float4> dst)
{
    const int ix = blockDim.x * blockIdx.x + threadIdx.x;
    const int iy = blockDim.y * blockIdx.y + threadIdx.y;
    if (ix >= dst.w || iy >= dst.h) return;

    float4 st = st_fine(ix, iy);
    if (st.w < 1) {
        st = make_float4(make_float3(
                tex2D(texST, 0.5f * (ix + 0.5f),
                             0.5f * (iy + 0.5f) )), 0);
    }
    dst(ix, iy) = st;
}
```

Listing 12.4. Implementation of the interpolation operation.

12.3   Flow-Guided Smoothing

Let $v\colon \mathbb{R}^2 \to \mathbb{R}^2$ be a vector field, and let (a, b) be an open interval. A curve $\gamma\colon (a, b) \to \mathbb{R}^2$ satisfying $\gamma'(t) = v(\gamma(t))$ for all $t \in (a, b)$ is called an *integral curve* or *stream line* of the vector field v. Taken together, the minor eigenvectors of the smoothed structure tensors at each pixel define a vector field, which is smooth up to a change of sign and closely aligned to image features. The general idea behind the flow-guided smoothing is to perform a filtering operation by following the minor eigenvectors through tracing the corresponding stream line. In contrast to the isophote curves of the image, the stream lines defined by the smoothed structure tensor are much smoother, and smoothing along them results in a regularization of the geometry of the isophote curves. The next section discusses the computation of the stream lines. Then, filtering along them will be examined. Finally, how to adjust adaptively the length of the stream lines used for filtering will be discussed.

12.3.1   Streamline Integration

Formally, finding the stream line $\gamma\colon (a, b) \to \mathbb{R}$ passing through a point x_0 of a vector field v can be described as solving the system of ordinary differential equations $\gamma'(t) = v(\gamma(t))$, $t \in (a, b)$ with initial condition $\gamma(t_0) = x_0$ for $t_0 \in (a, b)$. Several numerical techniques are available to solve such a system. For the presented algorithm, the second-order Runge-Kutta method is used, since it is simple to implement, achieves high-quality results, and has reasonable computational complexity. For pedagogical reasons, the simpler first-order Euler integration method is explained first. Taking the initial condition as a starting point, both methods operate iteratively, adding a new point with every step. Since for the computation of the smoothing operation at a point, a stream line passing through it is required, the integration has to be performed in forward and backward directions, as shown in Figure 12.8.

If the considered vector field is given by the minor eigenvectors, special attention must be paid to their sign, since the structure tensor defines only orientation but no particular direction. This is due to the quadratic nature of the structure tensor. A straightforward way to define the sign of the minor eigenvectors is to

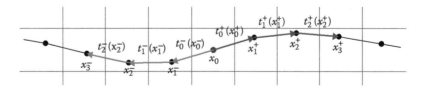

Figure 12.8.   Integration of a stream line passing through a point x_0 is performed iteratively in forward and backward directions.

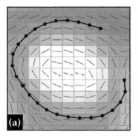 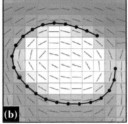 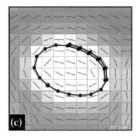 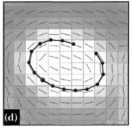

Figure 12.9. Illustrations of different stream line integration methods: (a) first-order Euler integration, (b) second-order Runge-Kutta, (c) second-order Runge-Kutta with fixed length, and (d) second-order Runge-Kutta with adaptive length.

choose the sign that minimizes the curvature of the stream line. This can be achieved by ensuring that the scalar product between the minor eigenvectors of the current and the previous steps is positive. More precisely, let x_0 be the current point, let $+$ and $-$ denote the forward and backward directions, respectively, and let $t_0^{\pm}(x_0) = \pm\xi(x_0)$; then, for $k \geq 0$, the next minor eigenvector is given by

$$t_{k+1}^{\pm}(x) = \text{sign}\left\langle t_k^{\pm}, \xi(x) \right\rangle \cdot \xi(x),$$

where $\xi(x)$ denotes the minor eigenvector at the point x, computed using Listing 12.1. Let $x_0^{\pm} = x_0$, then for $k \geq 0$, a step with step size h of the Euler method is given by

$$x_{k+1}^{\pm} = x_k^{\pm} + h t_k^{\pm}(x_k).$$

At least for long stream lines, which are required by the flow-guided smoothing, the Euler method is comparatively inaccurate. This is illustrated in Figure 12.9(a). The Euler integration method smooths pixels lying on adjacent isophote curves of the image. This corresponds to smoothing in the direction of the major eigenvector and a loss of information (Figure 12.10(a)). Therefore, instead of using the Euler integration method, the more precise second-order Runge-Kutta method is used, which traces stream lines at a higher accuracy (Figure 12.9(b)), reducing blurring across edges (Figure 12.10(c)). A step with step size h of the second-order Runge-Kutta method is given by

$$x_{k+1}^{\pm} = x_k^{\pm} + h t_k^{\pm}\left(x_k^{\pm} + \tfrac{h}{2} t_k^{\pm}(x_k)\right).$$

The second-order Runge-Kutta method requires values of the minor eigenvector for arbitrary positions. One option is to calculate these in one pass and then use nearest-neighbor sampling while tracing the stream lines. Bilinear interpolation of the eigenvectors is complicated, since opposite vectors may cancel each other out. A better approach is to sample the structure tensor directly using bilinear interpolation. This is more expensive, since the minor eigenvector has to be computed for every sample, but also provides clearly superior results.

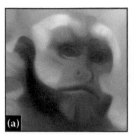   

Figure 12.10. Comparison of flow-guided smoothing using first-order Euler versus second-order Runge-Kutta stream line integration with and without shock filtering: (a) Euler, (b) Euler + shock filtering, (c) Runge-Kutta, and (d) Runge-Kutta + shock filtering.

12.3.2 Line Integral Convolution

Let $\gamma: (a, b) \to \mathbb{R}^2$ be a smooth curve, and let $f: \mathbb{R}^2 \to \mathbb{R}$ be a scalar field. Then the *line integral* of f along γ is defined by

$$\int_\gamma f \, ds = \int_a^b f(\gamma(t)) \|\gamma'(t)\| dt.$$

The factor $\|\gamma'(t)\|$ adjusts for the velocity of the curve's parameter and assures that the line integral is invariant under orientation-preserving reparameterizations. Based on this definition, the convolution of a scalar field with a one-dimensional function $g : \mathbb{R} \to \mathbb{R}$ along a curve can be defined:

$$(g *_\gamma f)(t_0) = \int_a^b g(t_0 - t) f(\gamma(t)) \|\gamma'(t)\| dt. \tag{12.5}$$

If g is normalized, that is, $\int_a^b g(t)dt = 1$ then the convolution above defines a weighted average of the values of f along the curve.

Now, let $v: \mathbb{R}^2 \to \mathbb{R}^2$ be a vector field consisting of normalized vectors. Then, for the vector field's stream lines, we have $\|\gamma'(t)\| = \|v(\gamma(t))\| = 1$, which is equivalent to an arc length parameterization. Overlaying the vector field with an image, the convolution along the stream line passing through the pixel can be computed for each pixel. This operation is known as *line integral convolution* and increases the correlation of the image's pixel values along the stream lines. When the convolution is performed over white noise, this yields an effective visualization technique for vector fields [Cabral and Leedom 93]. If the vector field is closely aligned with the image features, such as the minor eigenvector field of the smoothed structure tensor, convolution along stream lines effectively enhances the coherence of image features, while at the same time simplifying the image.

In order to implement line integral convolution, Equation (12.5) must be discretized. For the smoothing function, a one-dimensional Gaussian function G_{σ_s}

with standard deviation σ_s, is chosen. Since the stream lines become less accurate the longer they are, a comparatively short cutoff for the Gaussian function is used. The stream lines are truncated after two times the standard deviation rounded down to the next integer, $L = \lfloor 2\sigma_s \rfloor$, corresponding to approximately 95% of the weights. The integral is approximated by a sum of rectangle functions using the midpoint rule. Sampling of the image is thereby performed using bilinear filtering. Thus, if $x_L^-, \ldots, x_0, \ldots, x_L^+$ denote the stream line points obtained with step size h, as described in the previous section, then the result of the line integral convolution at x_0 is given by

$$\frac{1}{|G_{\sigma_s}|} \left[\sum_{k=1}^{L} G_{\sigma_s}(kh) f(x_k^-) + G_{\sigma_s}(0) f(x_0) + \sum_{k=1}^{L} G_{\sigma_s}(kh) f(x_k^+) \right],$$

where

$$|G_{\sigma_s}| = \sum_{k=1}^{L} G_{\sigma_s}(kh) + G_{\sigma_s}(0) + \sum_{k=1}^{L} G_{\sigma_s}(kh)$$

denotes the corresponding normalization term. The implementation is shown in Listing 12.5.

12.3.3 Adaptive Smoothing

In the previous section, the length of the stream lines used for smoothing was globally defined and proportional to the standard deviation of the Gaussian filter kernel. This may lead to issues in high-curvature regions, as illustrated in Figure 12.9(c). If the stream lines are too long, they may wrap around, resulting in some pixels being sampled more often than others. Moreover, due to rounding errors and inaccuracies in the stream line computation, adjacent isophotes may be sampled, which introduces additional blurring. To avoid these issues, the length of the stream lines and, correspondingly, the size of the Gaussian filter kernel must be controlled adaptively on a per-pixel basis. To this end, in [Kyprianidis and Kang 11] the standard deviation of the filter kernel was adjusted in relation to an anisotropy measure derived from the smoothed structure tensor. While this approach works reasonably well in practice, it is purely heuristic and its exact behavior is difficult to analyze. An alternative and more intuitive approach is therefore presented here.

Instead of adjusting the length of the stream lines in advance, their parameterization is adjusted by slowing down the parameter's velocity if necessary. To this end, the angle between the previous and the current steps' minor eigenvectors is computed:

$$\theta_k = \arccos \langle t_{k-1}^\pm(x_{k-1}^\pm), t_k^\pm(x_k^\pm) \rangle.$$

Taking the sum $\Theta = \sum_{i=1}^{k} \theta_i$ of the angles measures the cumulated angular change of the stream line. If $\Theta \geq \pi$, the stream line is likely to wrap around or is

```
inline __device__
float3 st_integrate_rk2( float2 p0, float sigma,
                         unsigned w, unsigned h,
                         float step_size, bool adaptive )
{
    float radius = 2 * sigma;
    float twoSigma2 = 2 * sigma * sigma;
    float3 c = make_float3(tex2D(texSRC, p0.x, p0.y));
    float sum = 1;

    float2 v0 = st_minor_ev(tex2D(texST, p0.x, p0.y));
    float sign = -1;
    float dr = radius / CUDART_PI_F;
    do {
        float2 v = v0 * sign;
        float2 p = p0;
        float u = 0;

        for (;;) {
            float2 t = st_minor_ev(tex2D(texST, p.x, p.y));
            if (dot(v, t) < 0) t = -t;

            float2 ph = p + 0.5f * step_size * t;
            t = st_minor_ev(tex2D(texST, ph.x, ph.y));
            float vt = dot(v, t);
            if (vt < 0) {
                t = -t;
                vt = -vt;
            }

            v = t;
            p += step_size * t;

            if (adaptive) {
                float delta_r = dr * acosf(fminf(vt,1));
                u += fmaxf(delta_r, step_size);
            } else
                u += step_size;

            if ((u >= radius) || (p.x < 0) || (p.x >= w) ||
                (p.y < 0) || (p.y >= h)) break;

            float k = __expf(-u * u / twoSigma2);
            c += k * make_float3(tex2D(texSRC, p.x, p.y));
            sum += k;
        }
        sign *= -1;
    } while (sign > 0);
    return c / sum;
}
```

Listing 12.5. Implementation of the flow-guided smoothing using second-order Runge-Kutta stream line integration.

comparatively noisy. In both cases, further extending it in the current direction is undesirable. However, simply stopping the tracing process corresponds to truncating the filtering operation and may introduce sampling artifacts. Instead, a better approach is to modify the stream line's parameter. To this end, the fraction traveled on a half-circle with arc length L can be considered for θ_k:

$$\Delta L_k = \frac{\theta_k}{\pi} L.$$

If ΔL_k is larger than the step size h, this indicates that the parameter of the arc-length parameterized stream line moves too fast, such that a larger step size is required, for which ΔL_k is used:

$$u_{k+1}^\pm = u_k^\pm + \max(h, \Delta L_k).$$

12.4 Shock Filter

The flow-guided smoothing discussed in the previous section is very aggressive. As shown in Figure 12.10(c), the overall shape of the image features is well preserved, but transitions between color regions are smoothed as well. In order to obtain sharp transitions at edges (Figure 12.10(d)), in this section deblurring by shock filtering will be discussed.

12.4.1 PDE-Based Shock Filter

In image processing, shock filters were first studied by [Osher and Rudin 90]. The classical shock filter evolution equation is given by

$$\frac{\partial u}{\partial t} = -\mathrm{sign}(\mathcal{L}(u))|\nabla u|,$$

with initial condition $u(x,0) = I(x)$ and where $\mathcal{L}$ is a suitable detector, such as the Laplacian Δu or the second derivative in direction of the gradient. In the influence zone of a maximum, $\mathcal{L}(u)$ is negative, and therefore a local dilation with a disc as the structuring element is performed. Similarly, in the influence zone of a minimum, $\mathcal{L}(u)$ is positive, which results in local erosion. This sharpens the edges at the zero-crossings of Δu, as shown in Figure 12.11. Shock filters have the attractive property of satisfying a maximum principle and, in contrast to unsharp masking, therefore do not suffer from ringing artifacts.

Instead of the second derivative in the direction of the gradient, the second derivative in the direction of the major eigenvector of the smoothed structure tensor may be used. This was first proposed by [Weickert 03]. To achieve higher robustness against small-scale image details, the input image can be regularized with a Gaussian filter prior to second-derivative or structure-tensor computation.

Weickert's shock filter achieves excellent results in combination with the flow-guided smoothing, but one limitation is its performance. The filter is typically implemented using an explicit upwind scheme. In order to guarantee stability, the time step size has to be small and multiple iterations have to be performed.

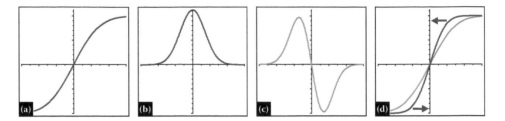

Figure 12.11. Illustration of shock filtering. (a) A smooth step edge. (b) First derivative of the edge. (c) Second derivative of the edge. (d) A shock filter applies a dilation where the second derivative is positive, and an erosion where it is negative, resulting in a sharpening effect.

For each iteration, first- and second-order derivatives, as well as the smoothed structure tensor, have to be calculated. Another limitation is that Weickert's shock filter introduces shocks in almost smooth regions, resulting in maze-like artifacts. The next section discusses an alternative approach.

12.4.2 Gradient-Directed Shock Filter

The idea in obtaining a fast shock filter implementation is to approximate the general working principle discussed earlier and illustrated in Figure 12.11. First, whether a pixel is in the neighborhood of a minimum or maximum is detected. Then, correspondingly, either an erosion or dilation is performed. Both operations are guided by the structure tensor.

Derivative operators are highly sensitive to noise, and sensitivity increases with order. Therefore, the second=derivative operator for the sign computation must be regularized to avoid artifacts. In addition, the regularization allows for artistic control over the resulting line thickness. Two strategies are at hand. First, the image can be isotropically smoothed prior to derivative computation, using a Gaussian filter with standard deviation σ_i. This helps to remove noise and allows for aggressive image simplification. Secondly, the smoothing and derivative operators can be consolidated into a single operator,since convolution and differentiation commute. Inspired by the flow-based difference of Gaussians filter, and its separable implementation [Kyprianidis and Döllner 09], the second-order derivative in direction of the major eigenvector is implemented by convolving the image locally with a one-dimensional (scale-normalized) second-order Gaussian derivative,

$$\sigma_g^2 G_{\sigma_g}''(t) = \sigma_g^2 \frac{\mathrm{d}^2 G_{\sigma_g}(t)}{\mathrm{d}t^2} = \frac{x^2 - \sigma_g^2}{\sqrt{2\pi}\sigma_g^3} \exp\left(-\frac{t^2}{2\sigma_g^2}\right),$$

in the direction of the minor eigenvector. This operation will be referred to as *flow-guided Laplacian of Gaussian* (FLoG). More specifically, let L be the input

```
__global__ void flog( const gpu_plm2<float4> st, float sigma,
                      gpu_plm2<float> dst )
{
    const int ix = blockDim.x * blockIdx.x + threadIdx.x;
    const int iy = blockDim.y * blockIdx.y + threadIdx.y;
    if (ix >= dst.w || iy >= dst.h) return;

    float2 n = st_major_ev(st(ix, iy));
    float2 nabs = fabs(n);
    float ds = 1.0f / (( nabs.x > nabs.y)? nabs.x : nabs.y);
    float2 uv = make_float2(ix + 0.5f, iy + 0.5f);

    float halfWidth = 5 * sigma;
    float sigma2 = sigma * sigma;
    float twoSigma2 = 2 * sigma2 ;

    float sum = -sigma2 * tex2D(texL, ix + 0.5f, iy + 0.5f);
    for( float d = ds; d <= halfWidth; d += ds ) {
        float k = (d*d - sigma2 ) * __expf( -d*d / twoSigma2 );
        float2 o = d*n;
        float c = tex2D(texL, uv.x - o.x, uv.y - o.y) +
                  tex2D(texL, uv.x + o.x, uv.y + o.y);
        sum += k * c;
    }

    sum = sum / (sqrtf(2*CUDART_PI_F) * sigma2 * sigma);
    dst(ix, iy) = sum;
}
```

Listing 12.6. Implementation of the FLoG filter.

image converted to grayscale, let $v = G_{\sigma_i} * L$, and let x_0 be the current pixel; then the convolution is computed by

$$z(x_0) = \sigma_g^2 \int G''_{\sigma_g}(t)v(x_0 + t\eta(x_0))\mathrm{d}t,$$

where $\eta(x_0)$ denotes the major eigenvector. The implementation is shown in Listing 12.6. Evaluation of the integral is performed using a constant step size that has a unit size, along either the x- or the y-axis (Figure 12.12), and using bilinear

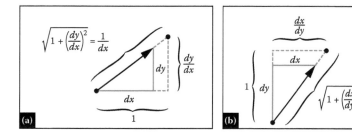

Figure 12.12. Computation of a step vector that has unit size in either horizontal or vertical directions. Two cases must be distinguished: (a) $dx > dy$ and (b) $dy > dx$.

```
__global__ void grad_shock( const gpu_plm2<float4> st,
                            const gpu_plm2<float> sign,
                            float radius,
                            gpu_plm2<float4> dst )
{
    const int ix = blockDim.x * blockIdx.x + threadIdx.x;
    const int iy = blockDim.y * blockIdx.y + threadIdx.y;
    if (ix >= dst.w || iy >= dst.h) return;

    minmax_impl_t mm(make_float2(ix + 0.5f, iy + 0.5f));
    float2 n = st_major_ev(st(ix, iy));
    float s = sign(ix, iy);
    if (s < 0) {
        mm.run<MAX_FLT>(n, radius);
    } else if (s > 0) {
        mm.run<MIN_FLT>(n, radius);
    }
    dst(ix, iy) = tex2D(texSRC, mm.p_.x, mm.p_.y);
}
```

Listing 12.7. Implementation of the gradient-directed shock filter.

interpolation. Due to the unit step size, this results in a linear interpolation of two neighboring pixels and allows for efficient implementation on GPUs using texturing hardware.

The erosion and dilation operations are implemented as directional neighborhood filters as well. Let f denote the input image, and let x_0 be the current point, then the gradient-directed shock filter is defined as

$$\begin{cases} \min_{x \in \Lambda_r(x_0)} f(x) & \text{if } z(x_0) > +\tau_s, \\ \max_{x \in \Lambda_r(x_0)} f(x) & \text{if } z(x_0) < -\tau_s, \\ f(x_0) & \text{otherwise.} \end{cases}$$

Determination of the minimum and maximum is performed based on the corresponding gray values. The filter neighborhood Λ_r is defined as the set of pixels with a distance less than r from x_0 intersecting the line $\{x_0 + \lambda\eta(x_0)\}$ defined by the major eigenvector. The implementation is shown in Listings 12.7 and 12.8. Again, a constant step size with a unit size in either horizontal or vertical direction is used. Bilinear interpolation, however, is not appropriate for the computation of the minimum or maximum; therefore, the two neighboring pixels are sampled explicitly, using nearest-neighbor sampling. Through a small correction of the sampling offset, the correct sampling of horizontal, vertical, and diagonal lines is assured as well.

For the radius, typically $r = 2$ is used. The parameter τ_s controls the sensitivity to noise and is typically set to $\tau_s \in [0, 0.01]$. Since a scale-normalized LoG is used, τ_s does not depend upon σ_g. The threshold effectively prevents

```
enum minmax_t { MIN_FLT, MAX_FLT };

struct minmax_impl_t {
    float2 uv_;
    float2 p_;
    float v_;

    __device__ minmax_impl_t(float2 uv) {
        uv_ = p_= uv;
        v_ = tex2D(texL, uv.x, uv.y);
    }

    template <minmax_t T>
    __device__ void add(float2 p) {
        float L = tex2D(texL, p.x, p.y);
        if ((T == MAX_FLT) && (L > v_)) {
            p_ = p;
            v_ = L;
        }
        if ((T == MIN_FLT) && (L < v_)) {
            p_ = p;
            v_ = L;
        }
    }

    template <minmax_t T>
    __device__ void run( float2 n, float radius ) {
        float ds;
        float2 dp;

        float2 nabs = fabs(n);
        if (nabs.x > nabs.y) {
            ds = 1.0f / nabs.x;
            dp = make_float2(0, 0.5f - 1e-3);
        } else {
            ds = 1.0f / nabs.y;
            dp = make_float2(0.5f - 1e-3, 0);
        }

        for( float d = ds; d <= radius; d += ds ) {
            float2 o = d*n;
            add<T>(uv_ + o + dp);
            add<T>(uv_ + o - dp);
            add<T>(uv_ - o + dp);
            add<T>(uv_ - o - dp);
        }
    }
};
```

Listing 12.8. Implementation of the gradient-directed minimum and maximum filters.

the creation of shocks in almost smooth regions. The quality of the output is comparable to that of the coherence-enhancing shock filter, but computationally the gradient-directed shock filter is much more efficient. It only requires the smoothed structure tensor and the input image converted to grayscale. For the sake of simplicity, the FLoG and the minimum and maximum filters have been implemented independently, but they obviously could be implemented in a single pass as well. Moreover, the gradient-directed shock filter provides finer artistic control. The parameter σ_g restricts smoothing to the major eigenvector direction. This is especially useful for preserving small image features. To achieve a stronger abstraction, the isotropic smoothing parameter σ_i is useful.

12.5   Conclusion

In this chapter, an automatic technique for image and video abstraction, based on adaptively controlled flow-guided smoothing and directional shock filtering, was presented. It aggressively smooths out unimportant image regions, but it protects important features by enhancing contrast and directional coherence, providing a good balance between content abstraction and feature enhancement consistently across the image. For abstraction at the level of the anisotropic Kuwahara filter, the GPU implementation processes video in real time and creates temporally coherent output without further processing.

12.6   Acknowledgments

Original photographs from flickr.com kindly provided under Creative Commons license by Tambako the Jaguar (Figure 12.2(a)) and Ivan Mlinaric (Figure 12.10). Original photograph in Figure 12.2(b) courtesy of Phillip Greenspun.

Bibliography

[Briggs et al. 00] W. L. Briggs, V. E. Henson, and S. F. McCormick. "A Multigrid Tutorial." Presentation, SIAM Annual Meeting, Rio Grande, Puerto Rio, July 2000.

[Brox et al. 06] T. Brox, R. van den Boomgaard, F. Lauze, J. van de Weijer, J. Weickert, P. Mrázek, and P. Kornprobst. "Adaptive Structure Tensors and Their Applications." In *Visualization and Processing of Tensor Fields*, edited by Joachim Weickert and Hans Hagen, pp. 17–47. Berlin: Springer, 2006.

[Cabral and Leedom 93] B. Cabral and L. C. Leedom. "Imaging Vector Fields Using Line Integral Convolution." In *Proceedings of the 20th Annual Conference on Computer Graphics and Interactive Techniques*, pp. 263–270. New York: ACM, 1993.

[Goldberg 91] D. Goldberg. "What Every Computer Scientist Should Know about Floating-Point Arithmetic." *ACM Computing Surveys* 23:1 (1991), 5–48.

[Horn and Johnson 85] R. A. Horn and C. R. Johnson. *Matrix Analysis.* Cambridge, UK: Cambridge University Press, 1985.

[Kang and Lee 08] H. Kang and S. Lee. "Shape-Simplifying Image Abstraction." *Computer Graphics Forum* 27:7 (2008), 1773–1780.

[Kyprianidis and Döllner 09] J. E. Kyprianidis and J. Döllner. "Real-Time Image Abstraction by Directed Filtering." In *ShaderX7: Advanced Rendering Techniques*, edited by W. Engel, pp. 285–302. Hingham, MA: Charles River Media, 2009.

[Kyprianidis and Kang 11] J. E. Kyprianidis and H. Kang. "Image and Video Abstraction by Coherence-Enhancing Filtering." *Computer Graphics Forum* 30:2 (2011), 593–602.

[Kyprianidis et al. 10] J. E. Kyprianidis, H. Kang, and J. Döllner. "Anisotropic Kuwahara Filtering on the GPU." In *GPU Pro: Advanced Rendering Techniques*, edited by W. Engel, pp. 247–264. Natick, MA: A K Peters, 2010.

[Osher and Rudin 90] S. Osher and L. I. Rudin. "Feature-Oriented Image Enhancement Using Shock Filters." *SIAM Journal on Numerical Analysis* 27:4 (1990), 919–940.

[Weickert 99] J. Weickert. "Coherence-Enhancing Diffusion of Colour Images." *Image and Vision Computing* 17:3 (1999), 201–212.

[Weickert 03] J. Weickert. "Coherence-Enhancing Shock Filters." In *Pattern Recognition: 25th DAGM Symposium, Magdeburg, Germany, September 10–12, 2003. Proceedings*, Lecture Notes in COmputer Science 2781, pp. 1–8. Berlin: Springer, 2003.

[Wikipedia 12] Wikipedia. "Expressionism". *Wikipedia—The Free Encyclopedia.*, http://en.wikipedia.org/wiki/Expressionism, 2012.

[Winnemöller et al. 06] H. Winnemöller, S. C. Olsen, and B. Gooch. "Real-Time Video Abstraction." *ACM Transactions on Graphics* 25:3 (2006), 1221–1226.

Screen-Space Grass

David Pangerl

13.1 Introduction

Grass is a fundamental part of any outdoor nature scene. Unfortunately, grass is also a difficult and complex thing to render realistically due to its abundance. (See, for example, Figure 13.1.)

In this chapter we present a novel technique for realistically rendering midground and background grass in screen space. This technique was developed for the games *Agricultural Simulator 2013* and *Industry Giant 3*.

13.2 Motivation

The usual approach for rendering grass in the distance requires generating and processing a large amount of geometry or instances, and this consumes a lot

Figure 13.1. An example scene from *Agricultural Simulator 2013* showing Screen-Space Grass in action. Notice distant grass areas with a shivering grass effect.

of CPU and GPU resources. This approach has been covered in many articles, but its main limitation is that it is not well suited for covering vast amounts of terrain. In order to solve this problem, we considered the question: what does one actually see when they look at grass in the distance? You do not see many individual blades of grass nor any detailed grass movement. What you do see is some general noisy movement, wind patterns, and some grass blades only at boundary regions (where the grass stops and the terrain changes to some other material). From these observations we decided to implement our grass using noise in screen space.

The beauty of this technique is that it is extremely cheap, it is very realistic, it does not require any additional resources or preprocessing, it scales beautifully over an entire terrain, and it can extend to vast distances into the scene. It is also very easy to integrate into existing rendering pipelines.

This technique does not cover nearby grass rendering, where individual grass fins are actually visible. Near grass rendering is a very well covered topic, and we encourage the reader to see [Pelzer 04] and [Whatley 05].

13.3 Technique

Screen-Space Grass (SSG) is rendered in post-processing as a fullscreen quad. It requires some kind of per-pixel depth information that we get from *camera-space position*, but it could also be used for rendering pipelines without it (by reading depth information some other way or by ignoring obstruction detection).

The complete algorithm consists of two stages:

1. terrain stencil masking,

2. post-process fullscreen pass.

When rendering the terrain, we must stencil-mask it with a unique stencil value. We use a stencil mask value of 2 for terrain and 1 for everything else.

During post-process, we execute a fullscreen pass with our SSG shader. The SSG shader samples two textures: the scene's *color* buffer and a *position* texture (or a depth buffer from which a position may be derived). The *color* texture is used for color sampling and a smudge effect, and the *position* texture is used for grass scale and object obstruction detection.

SSG should be computed after the opaque rendering stage and lighting are complete, so that we have a final framebuffer color, but before edge detection, fog, and other post-processing effects.

13.3.1 Generating Realistic Grass Noise

To generate grass noise we use a simple vertical up-down smudge. It is a very simple idea that produces realistic grass noise and edge fins.

Figure 13.2. Grass smudging effect.

In reality, grass grows upward but in our case "smudging" the grass downward simplifies our stencil masking because it allows us to use our original terrain geometry to generate the stencil mask (in the same pass). To create an upward smudge, we would need to somehow extend the stencil mask upward.

For our smudge function we used a simple modulated screen-space quantization:

```
float xx=inSPos.x / TDeviceSize[0].x;
float yy=inSPos.y / TDeviceSize[0].y;

float d     =_blend( len , 0 , 500 , 100 , 500 );
float dclose=_blend( len , 0 , 20 , 30 ,   1 );

d*=dclose;

yy+=xx * 1000 / d;

float  yoffset=frac( yy * d ) / d;
```

The *source pixel* from `inTex0.xy - float2( 0 , yoffset )` is going to be smudged to the *target pixel* (output pixel) `inTex0.xy`, as in Figure 13.2.

With this formula we get a straight vertical grass smudge effect, as in Figure 13.3.

To break up the regular vertical lines and to add a bit of noise, we change the modulation to

```
yy+=xx * 1000
```

However, for some games straight vertical lines may actually be desirable to achieve a certain visual effect (e.g., *Industry Giant 3* uses straight lines; see Figure 13.4).

Figure 13.3. Base smudge grass noise function producing straight vertical lines.

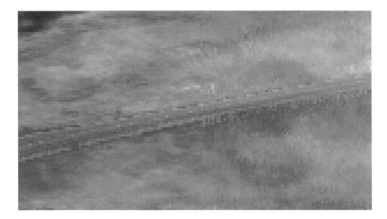

Figure 13.4. Regular terrain rendering on the left. Screen-Space Grass rendering used in *Agricultural Simulator 2013* on the right.

The terrain pixels on the upper edge of the stencil masked area are going to be smudged by pixels outside of the stencil masked space, creating the effect of grass blades on the top of terrain ridges, as in Figure 13.5.

13.3.2 Is It Really Grass?

The whole terrain is not necessarily composed of grass. We would also like to be able to render roads, dirt and sand patches, and other areas that are not covered in grass. We would also like to support objects that are rendered on top of the grassy terrain. Such objects are, of course, masked by a stencil; however, the grass smudge effect can mistake them for grass pixels (*source pixel*) even if they are just outside the stencil marked area (stencil-marked-area pixels are only guaranteed not to be the *target pixels* for the SSG effect). See Figure 13.6.

Figure 13.5. Correct grass fins on edge of stencil marked area.

Figure 13.6. Road and sign are ignored by SSG.

Regions of the stencil masked terrain that do not contain grass may be filtered out with a simple test that checks if the pixel is green. While this may seem too simplistic, we found it to work perfectly for detecting grass:

```
int     isgreen=backcolor.g > backcolor.r + 0.01f &&
                backcolor.g > backcolor.b + 0.01f;
```

This simple test for detecting green pixels is the main reason for requiring a stencil mask. If we had no stencil masking, then all green pixels on the screen would be treated as grass (e.g., all green trees and all green objects). Of course, with stencil masking, we also get a little speed optimization since only terrain pixels are processed by a SSG shader. Other games may find it more convenient

Figure 13.7. Left: fins bleed from undetected obstructed object. Right: obstructed object detection.

to mark their grass using a spare alpha channel instead of relying on pixel color to detect grass.

It is worth mentioning that a similar noise effect would also be great for simulating micro leaf movement on distant trees.

Visual artifacts can result from smudging *source pixels* that are not part of the terrain. This can happen when an object is rendered on top of the terrain (e.g., trees and other props). To detect these pixels, we must take an additional sample from the *position* texture of the *source pixel*. If the *source pixel* is closer to the camera than the target pixel, then it should not be smudged to the *target pixel* (see also Figure 13.7):

```
float4 poscs2=tex2D( Color1SamplerPoint , uvoffset );

if( poscs2.z < poscs.z ) return backcolor;
```

13.4 Performance

The SSG compiled for pixel shader model 3.0 uses approximately 51 instruction slots (4 texture and 47 arithmetic). The measured performance cost without stencil mask (SSG shader was forcefully executed on the entire framebuffer) was 0.18 milliseconds at 1920×1200 on our tests with a GeForce GTX 560 (drivers 320.18).

13.5 Conclusion

We presented a novel technique for post-process screen-space grass that can be applied over vast terrain areas. The technique is extremely cheap, it is very realistic, it does not require any additional resources or preprocessing, it scales efficiently over a large terrain even at vast distances, and it is very easy to integrate into an existing rendering pipeline. See the gallery of results in Figures 13.8–13.15.

Figure 13.8. SSG example 1 from *Agricultural Simulator 2013*.

Figure 13.9. SSG example 2 from *Agricultural Simulator 2013*.

Figure 13.10. SSG example 3 from *Agricultural Simulator 2013*.

Figure 13.11. SSG example 4 from *Agricultural Simulator 2013*.

13.6 Limitations and Future Work

The smudge effect is implemented to be perfectly vertical since it does not use camera tilt and is as such not convenient for a game that tilts the camera. We need to develop another smudge function for such cases.

Figure 13.12. SSG example 5 from *Agricultural Simulator 2013*.

Figure 13.13. SSG example 6 from *Agricultural Simulator 2013*.

We would also like to add realistic wind movement into the grass noise function. One very interesting effect comes from just using *target pixel* color as an additional noise modulator:

```
yy+=backcolor.g * 0.04f;
```

Figure 13.14. SSG example 7 from *Agricultural Simulator 2013*.

Figure 13.15. SSG example 8 from *Agricultural Simulator 2013*.

As mentioned before, a similar effect could also be used to simulate micro leaves noise for trees in the distance.

13.7   Screen-Space Grass Source Code

This is the source code for the SSG.fx effect.

```
float4 TDeviceSize[2]; // rtt size in TDeviceSize[0].xy
float4 TTimer[1];       // game time in TTimer[0].w

void vsmain(float3        inPos         : POSITION,
            float3        inTex         : TEXCOORD,
            //
            out float4    outPos        : POSITION,
            out float4    outTex0       : TEXCOORD0 )
{
   outPos=inPos;
   //
   outTex0=inTex;
   // half pixel offset
   outTex0.xy+=TDeviceSize[1].zw; // 0.5f / rtt size in [1].zw
}

float _blend(float val, float val0, float val1, float res0,
    float res1)
{
   if( val <= val0 ) return res0;
   if( val >= val1 ) return res1;
   //
   return res0 + (val-val0) * (res1-res0) / (val1-val0);
}

float4 psmain(float4 inTex0       : TEXCOORD0,
              float2 inSPos       : VPOS) : COLOR
{
   // get target depth
   float4    poscs=tex2D( Color1SamplerPoint,
                          inTex0.xy);
   //
   float     len=length( poscs.xyz );
   //
   float4    backcolor=tex2D( Color0SamplerPointClamp,
                              inTex0.xy );
   // check if color is green (aka grass)
   int    isgreen=backcolor.g > backcolor.r + 0.01f &&
                  backcolor.g > backcolor.b + 0.01f;
   //
   if( isgreen )
   {
       float4    color=0;
       // rtt size in TDeviceSize[0].xy
       float xx=inSPos.x / TDeviceSize[0].x;
       float yy=inSPos.y / TDeviceSize[0].y;
       //
       float d=_blend( len , 0 , 500 , 100 , 500 );
       float dclose=_blend( len , 0 , 20 , 30 , 1 );
       //
       d*=dclose;
       //
       yy+=xx * 1000;

       // add a little wind movement
       yy+=TTimer[0].w * 0.004f;
       //
       float    yoffset=frac( yy * d ) / d;
       //
       float2 uvoffset=inTex0.xy - float2(0,yoffset);
       //
       color=tex2D(Color0SamplerPointClamp,uvoffset);
```

```
                   // check if obstructed
                   // get source depth
                   float4 poscs2=tex2D( Color1SamplerPoint,
                                        uvoffset );
                   // check if source is closer to camera than target
                   if( poscs2.z < poscs.z ) return backcolor;
                   // blend a bit
                   return lerp( backcolor , color ,
                                saturate( 1-yoffset * d / 3.8 ) );
               }
               //
               return backcolor;
          }

          technique defaultshader
          {
               pass p0
               {
                   CullMode       = None;
                   ZEnable        = false;
                   ZWriteEnable   = false;
                   //
                   StencilEnable  = true;
                   StencilFunc    = Equal;
                   StencilPass    = Keep;
                   StencilFail    = Keep;
                   StencilZFail   = Keep;
                   StencilRef     = 2;      // stencil mask is set to 2
                   //
                   VertexShader   = compile vs_3_0 vsmain();
                   PixelShader    = compile ps_3_0 psmain();
               }
          }
```

Bibliography

[Pelzer 04] Kurt Pelzer. "Rendering Countless Blades of Waving Grass." In *GPU Gems*, edited by Randima Fernando, Chapter 7. Upper Saddle River, NJ: Addison-Wesley, 2004.

[Whatley 05] David Whatley. "Toward Photorealism in Virtual Botany." In *GPU Gems 2*, edited by Matt Pharr, Chapter 1. Upper Saddle River, NJ: Addison-Wesley, 2005.

14

Screen-Space Deformable Meshes via CSG with Per-Pixel Linked Lists
João Raza and Gustavo Nunes

14.1 Introduction

In this chapter we describe a deformable mesh method that utilizes an implementation of the Constructive Solid Geometry (CSG) algorithm in real time through the usage of a per-pixel linked list data structure stored in the GPU memory. Via this method, the proposed CSG algorithm manages to have a constant number of passes. This contrasts with standard image-based CSG implementations in which the number of required rendering passes increases linearly with the scene's depth complexity.

Although the union, intersection and difference CSG operations can be rendered via this approach, this chapter focuses on the difference operation, since it yields a deformable mesh scenario. Moreover, a modification to the CSG algorithm behavior is made in a particular case to properly target the deformable mesh scenario. The solution presented here is generic, does not make any assumption on the scene's topology, and works for any concave, convex, or flat mesh.

14.2 Mesh Deformation Scenario

Games and real-time applications utilize deformable meshes as a mechanism for enhancing the user experience and providing immediate feedback to their actions. Common scenarios are for deforming car models when they hit obstacles, or altering walls as explosions impact them. Mechanisms to enable mesh deformation vary from altering the vertices in the mesh structure to utilizing parallax mapping. Although these algorithms succeed in presenting a deformable mesh to the end user, they usually are not general enough so that the deformation mechanisms are applicable in any particular scenario and/or any particular mesh. Parallax mapping does not work well with curved surfaces, while altering the vertices structure in a mesh requires a high polygon count to look smooth.

Methods to circumvent this limitation use screen-space rendering techniques to assess which pixels should be clipped. Clipping pixels in screen space to deform meshes is not in itself a new concept for games [Vlachos 10]. The Sequenced Convex Subtraction algorithm [Stewart et al. 00] and the Goldfeather algorithm [Goldfeather et al. 86, Goldfeather et al. 89] are part of this group of implementations, for example. However, these traditional CSG techniques are usually implemented on the GPU [Guha et al. 03] through some sort of depth peeling method [Everitt 01]. This has the disadvantage of relying on multiple rendering passes proportional to the scene's depth complexity.

To address these limitations, this chapter presents a solution that allows meshes to deform with a high degree of flexibility, by utilizing another mesh that acts as the deforming component. Our solution is independent of the scene's depth complexity, since it requires a constant number of passes. In addition, departing from other CSG rendering methods [Stewart et al. 02] that assume a particular scene topology, the proposed solution is generic and works for any given scene. The algorithm still works even when deforming flat meshes, which in the common use for CSG leaves a hole in the mesh, as opposed to deforming it.

14.3   Algorithm Overview

14.3.1   Creating the Per-Pixel Linked List

Initially the entire scene must be rendered using a shader that stores each incoming fragment into a per-pixel linked list. This section will give a quick overview of this concept; for a more comprehensive explanation, see [Thibieroz 11].

To create the linked list we use two unordered access view buffers (UAVs). One is the head pointer buffer, while the other is a node storage buffer of linked lists. The head pointer buffer is equivalent in dimensions to the render target. Each pixel in the render target has an equivalent pixel in the head pointer buffer. These two pixels are correlated by the pixel's (x, y) coordinate in the render target. What this means is that each pixel in the render target will have only one equivalent address in the head pointer buffer. All pixels in the head pointer buffer either point to a location in the node storage buffer or to an invalid value. If a pixel in the head pointer buffer points to a valid location in the node storage buffer, then the node it points to is considered the first node in the per-pixel linked list. Each valid node in the node storage buffer may point to another node in the node storage buffer, thus creating a linked list of nodes.

As a new pixel is rendered, a lookup is made in the head pointer buffer for its equivalent address. If it points to any valid location in the node storage buffer, then a new node is added in the node storage buffer, while adjusting the corresponding linked list to point to it. If the pixel doesn't point to any valid location in the node storage buffer, meaning this is the first pixel to be added for its equivalent render target pixel, then a new node in the node storage buffer is added. The head pointer buffer is then updated to point to that node.

Via this method, one is able to keep track of all rendered fragments for each pixel on-screen. For simplicity, we will collectively refer to these two UAV buffers throughout this chapter as a per-pixel linked list, since their end-product yields exactly that.

14.3.2 The Scene vs. Deformer Mesh

For clarification, throughout this chapter we will refer to the scene as any mesh that has to be rendered to the end user that could be deformed. In Figure 14.3, the cube would be considered the scene. Any and all pixels that were derived via rendering calls from the scene are thus referred to as pixels from the scene. For simplicity, we will also refer to pixels from the scene as M+ pixels.

In contrast, for generating the CSG algorithm, we will also utilize a deformer mesh. The deformer mesh will not appear in the final image that is displayed to the user. Its sole purpose is to have its pixels as part of the heuristics in constructing a deformed mesh to the end user in the final image. Any and all pixels that were derived via rendering calls from the deformer mesh are thus referred to as deforming pixels. For simplicity, we will also refer to pixels from deforming mesh as M− pixels.

14.3.3 Per-Pixel Linked List Node

Each node in the per-pixel linked list will contain the rendered pixel RGB color, its depth value, and a flag indicating if it is a back-facing or front-facing generated pixel, as well as a flag indicating if the pixel belongs to M+ or M−.

14.3.4 Rendering the Scene and the Deformer Mesh into the Per-Pixel Linked List

The first step in the algorithm is to render the front-facing pixels of the entire scene plus the front-facing pixels of the deformer mesh into the per-pixel linked list. The second step is to render the back-facing pixels of the entire scene plus the back-facing pixels of the deformer mesh into the per-pixel linked list. Two constant buffer variables are used in these two rendering passes. One buffer is used to express to the shader storing the pixels into the linked list that the incoming fragments are either front facing or back facing. The other buffer provides information to the shader that the incoming fragments belong to M+ or M−. All this data is then stored in each node in the linked list.

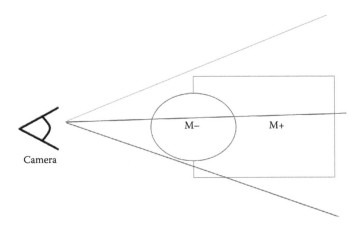

Figure 14.1. Three lines of sight from the camera. The linked list on the green line of sight will contain no nodes, the red line of sight will have [M− front, M+ front, M− back, M+ back] in its list, and the blue line of sight will have [M+ front, M+ back] in its list.

14.3.5 Sorting the Linked List

Once the linked list contains all pixel information, a shader program will sort all pixels in each of the linked lists based on their depth values. The result is that each linked list will contain a list of pixels sorted from closest to farthest depth from the camera. To help illustrate the result of this step, take as an example Figure 14.1. In it we have a camera that's positioned in world coordinates, a scene mesh (M+), and a deforming mesh (M−) that intersects the scene mesh. Both M+ and M− are inside the camera's frustum.

Look at the three lines of sight (red, green, blue) from the camera. Once sorted, the per-pixel linked list on the green line of sight will have no nodes in it. The red line of sight will have [M− front, M+ front, M− back, M+ back] in its list. The blue line of sight will have [M+ front, M+ back] in its list.

14.3.6 Determining M+ and M− Intersections

For the next set of steps, we will need to assess if M+ and M− intersected, that is, if any given M+ pixel is inside M−, as well as if any M− pixel is inside M+. To assess if any given M+ pixel is inside or outside M−, we linearly traverse the sorted per-pixel linked list starting from the closest pixel. If a front-facing M− pixel is found, then any subsequent M+ pixels are inside M− until a back-facing M− pixel is found. In addition, if the first M− pixel found on the list is a back-facing one, this means that all previously found M+ pixels were inside M−, since this is a case where the camera is inside M−. One can also determine if an M− pixel is inside M+ by utilizing the same steps described but switching the keywords of M− for M+ and vice versa.

14.3.7 Saving the Right Pixel Depth for Lookup

Once the per-pixel linked list is sorted based on depth, the algorithm needs to assess what is the correct pixel to be rendered on screen for each pixel in the list. We begin traversing the linked list from the closest pixel to the farthest one. If any front-facing pixel of M+ is found that is currently outside of M−, then that is the pixel to be rendered on screen. If any back-facing pixel of M− is found that is currently inside of M+, then that is the pixel to be rendered on screen. If there is a valid M+ and M− pixel to be rendered, whichever is closest to the camera wins. The front-facing M+ or back-facing M− pixel to render will be referred to in this chapter as the eligible rendered pixel for consistency. If we used the per-pixel linked lists exemplified in Figure 14.1 to retrieve the set of eligible rendered pixels, we would have none for the green line of sight, the first M− back-facing pixel for the red line of sight, and the first M+ front-facing pixel for the blue line of sight.

The eligible rendered pixel case described above works when M+ is a non-flat mesh (such as a cube). When M+ is a flat mesh (such as a wall), then the eligible rendered pixel is either any front-facing pixel of M+ that is outside of M−, or the first back-facing pixel of M− that lies behind a M+ front-facing pixel.

Via this heuristic, the method to communicate to the final render pass (the next step in the algorithm) the eligible rendered pixel, is by storing the eligible rendered pixel depth value in an auxiliary texture buffer. The final pass rendering step will then use that auxiliary texture buffer as a lookup table. Please see the book's website for the code that executes all of the steps outlined in this section.

14.3.8 Final Pass Render

In the final render pass, we re-render the front-facing pixels of M+, as well as the back-facing pixels of M−, with a final pass shader. This final pass shader will compare the incoming fragment's depth value with what is stored in the auxiliary texture buffer. If the fragment's depth value is equal to the one stored in the auxiliary texture buffer, then that means that the incoming fragment is the eligible rendered pixel. It then gets rendered in the render target. All other fragments are clipped. Figure 14.2 displays how Figure 14.1 would look after

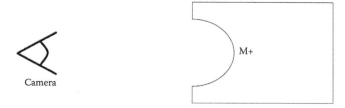

Figure 14.2. The final scene once M− is subtracted from M+.

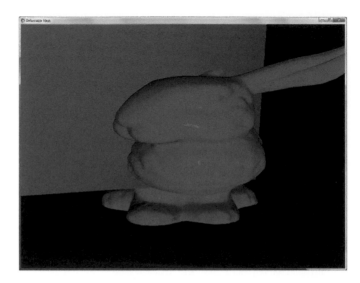

Figure 14.3. The Stanford bunny acts as M− and the cube acts as M+ (prior to the algorithm having run).

the final rendering pass. Figure 14.3 is a display of the algorithm in which the Stanford bunny acts as M− and the cube acts as M+, with the algorithm turned off. Figure 14.4 is the same point of view, but with the algorithm turned on. Figure 14.5 is a close up of Figure 14.4.

Figure 14.4. The same point of view as Figure 14.3 but with the algorithm enabled.

Figure 14.5. A zoomed-in view of the scene while the algorithm is enabled.

14.4   Optimizations

Areas of potential optimization involve knowing beforehand the topology of the rendered scene (such as if M+ and M− are colliding or not) or determining beforehand if M− is convex or not. Further, one might leverage the D3D 11.2 fixed function overlay hardware technique [Sorbo 13] to minimize the memory consumption of the GPU by having a lower dimension swap chain. This means one could use a lower dimension set of buffers to generate the per-pixel linked list. We leave these areas of optimization up to the reader, since our goal for the sample code and code snippets in this chapter was to focus on readability, as well as providing a generic framework for end developers to work on.

14.5   Conclusion

Deformable meshes are a common scenario in several contemporary games, and being able to produce a flexible environment in which artists have a greater degree of freedom is always useful. The algorithm discussed in this chapter aims to provide a solution for this space. As elaborated previously, there are several ways to optimize the proposed algorithm, but we hope this serves as a building block for whoever is interested in the deformable mesh scenario.

14.6 Acknowledgments

João Raza would like to thank his family and wife for all the support they've provided him. Gustavo Nunes would like to thank his wife and family for all their help. Special thanks goes to their friend F. F. Marmot.

Bibliography

[Everitt 01] C. Everitt. "Interactive Order-Independent Transparency." White Paper, NVIDIA Corporation, 1999.

[Goldfeather et al. 86] J. Goldfeather, J. P. M. Hultquist, and H. Fuchs. "Fast Constructive Solid Geometry Display in the Pixel-Powers Graphics System." *ACM Computer Graphics (SIGGRAPH '86 Proceedings)* 20:4 (1986), 107–116.

[Goldfeather et al. 89] J. Goldfeather, S. Molnar, G. Turk, and H. Fuchs. "Near Realtime CSG Rendering Using Tree Normalization and Geometric Pruning." *IEEE Computer Graphics and Applications* 9:3 (1989), 20–28.

[Guha et al. 03] S. Guha, S. Krishnan, K. Munagala, and S. Venkatasubramanian. "Application of the Two-Sided Depth Test to CSG Rendering." In *Proceedings of the 2003 Symposium on Interactive 3D Graphics*, pp. 177–180. New York: ACM, 2003.

[Sorbo 13] B. Sorbo. "What's New in D3D 11.2." BUILD, Microsoft, 2013.

[Stewart et al. 00] N. Stewart, G. Leach, and S. John. "A CSG Rendering Algorithm for Convex Objects." *Journal of WSCG* 8:2 (2000), 369–372.

[Stewart et al. 02] N. Stewart, G. Leach, and S. John. "Linear-Time CSG Rendering of Intersected Convex Objects." *Journal of WSCG* 10:2 (2002), 437–444.

[Thibieroz 11] N. Thibieroz. "Order-Independent Transparency Using Per-Pixel Linked Lists." In *GPU Pro 2*, edited by Wolfgang Engel, pp. 409–431. Natick, MA: A K Peters, Ltd., 2011.

[Vlachos 10] Alex Vlachos. "Rendering Wounds in Left 4 Dead 2." Presentation, Game Developers Conference 2010, San Francisco, CA, March 9, 2010. (Available at http://www.valvesoftware.com/publications/2010/gdc2010_vlachos_l4d2wounds.pdf.)

Bokeh Effects on the SPU
Serge Bernier

15.1 Introduction

Graphics programmers work hard to spend their per-frame millisecond budget wisely—by ensuring the color buffer gamma is correct, using a true high dynamic range pipeline, or trying to have the best antialiasing technique possible. Therefore it can be surprising to actually spend more milliseconds to produce a blurred image! Many games use depth of field (DOF) to focus the player's attention on a particular part of the frame, as well as to reinforce the depth illusion in the rendered image. Depth of field has a natural home in cutscenes, which typically have a more cinematographic feel, using framing and focus on a particular character or object to deliver a critical plot line for the game.

Of course, the use of depth of field is mainly driven by the artistic direction of a game, and this can differ dramatically from game to game. Typically, to create the in-game depth-of-field lens effect, we blur a copy of the framebuffer and interpolate between the blurred and non-blurred version depending on the distance of each pixel to the focal plane. For many years the blurring technique used was just a simple Gaussian blur to approximate the lens effect; however, a new technique is around the corner that allows us to achieve a much more real, filmic DOF effect. It is called *bokeh*, a Japanese word meaning "confused" or "dizzy." In our context we use it to qualify the aesthetic quality of the blur applied to the out-of-focus part of the image. Typically the bokeh effect will make highlights or light sources blur out into discs, or shapes that show the number of iris blades in the camera lens. A DirectX11 implementation was shown at GDC 2011 in the Samaritan tech demo driven by the Unreal Engine. This technique enhanced the DOF effect, giving something much closer to the look that we often see in a movie. (See Figure 15.1.) Many techniques can be found on the web to implement the bokeh effect, but in this chapter I will focus on the sprite-based approach [Pettineo 11], applied to the Playstation 3 with a *Synergistic Processing Unit* (SPU) twist! Instead of using the compute shader, geometry shader, or the

Figure 15.1. Bokeh example from a real camera.

`DrawInstancedIndirect` call feature in the DX11 API, this chapter will explain how to use the SPUs to analyze the framebuffer luminance and generate bokeh draw calls.

15.2   Bokeh behind the Scenes

To understand what the bokeh effect is, we need to first understand depth of field. Depth of field is the distance from the focal plane in which objects appear in focus. (See Figure 15.2.)

Objects outside this region are considered out of focus and will appear blurred. In film or photography, depth of field is mainly a characteristic of the lens and

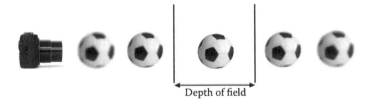

Figure 15.2. Depth of field is the distance between the nearest and farthest objects in a scene that appear acceptably sharp in an image.

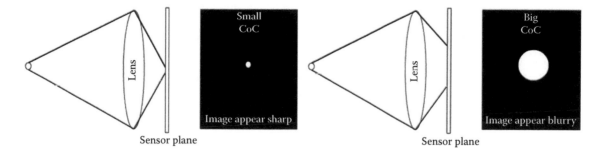

Figure 15.3. Variation of the CoC for a combination of subject distances.

focus distances. One important thing to understand is that objects don't go from sharp to unsharp abruptly. It gradually goes out of focus as it gets farther from the focal point. Since it is a gradient, we quantify the blur amount with the size of the *circle of confusion* (CoC). The bigger the CoC value for a particular pixel, the more blur you apply to it. Conversely, the smaller the CoC value, the sharper the pixel should appear. (See Figure 15.3.)

The CoC value will vary in the range $[0, 1]$ and will indicate how much in or out of focus the pixel is. The blur amount, generally in pixel size, will be multiplied by the CoC of the pixel to find the blur amount for a particular pixel in the framebuffer. The maximum blur value will be game driven and is something that artists can tweak to achieve the desired DOF effect.

So what does bokeh have to do with all this? Well, bokeh is intimately connected to the lens aperture, or more precisely, the aperture shape. On a real camera the quantity of light passing through the lens is controlled by the aperture. A set of blades mounted into the lens controls the light entering the camera, as shown in Figure 15.4.

We can now see how the lens design affects the shape of out-of-focus highlights. (See Figure 15.5.) Typically, you will have a nice circular bokeh shape with a fully opened aperture. Some lens manufacturers have iris blades with curved edges to make the aperture more closely approximate a circle rather than a polygon.

Figure 15.4. Aperture shape depending on the f-stop. We can see now where the bokeh shape is coming from!

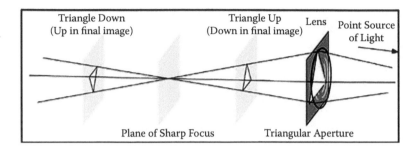

Figure 15.5. Aperture shape affecting out-of-focus detail in the image.

15.3 The Sprite-Based Approach

Sprite-based bokeh effects are pretty simple to understand and are very flexible, allowing artist modification to achieve the desired result. The main idea is to take each pixel of the framebuffer and analyze its luminance:

$$L_{i,j} = 0.2126R_{i,j} + 0.7152G_{i,j} + 0.0722B_{i,j},$$

$$\text{average pixel luminance} = \frac{\Sigma_i^m \Sigma_j^n L_{i,j}}{m \times n}.$$

To analyze each pixel of the framebuffer, you start with a filter kernel, to analyze the pixels surrounding the current pixel. The bigger the kernel size is, the more expensive the luminance calculation is. (See Figure 15.6.) In my tests I

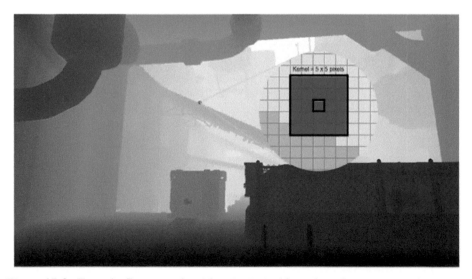

Figure 15.6. Framebuffer example with a 5×5 pixel kernel used to compute the average luminance of the pixel.

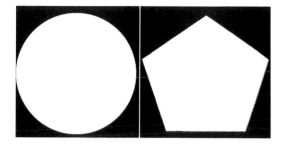

Figure 15.7. Examples of bokeh shape textures.

decided to go with a simple case, so kernel size equaled 1, with a buffer downscaled by a factor of 2. The result was quite good in performance and quality. Using the filter kernel, calculate the luminance for each pixel and simply spawn a texture sprite (see Figure 15.7) at the pixel screen space position if the luminance pixel is higher than a certain threshold. This luminance threshold value can be editable by the artist so they can adjust at which luminance value the pixel will produce a bokeh sprite when the pixel is out of focus. Performing the threshold test on each pixel will give you a list of pixels that will spawn a bokeh sprite. The last step is to calculate a proper scale for the bokeh sprite. The scale typically has a maximum size, which is also editable by artists. In this step, the depth value of the pixel is used to determine how much the pixel is out of focus. This represents the circle of confusion mentioned earlier and at its maximum value it represents a fully open aperture.

In short you need to calculate how much the pixel is out of focus and apply a pixel scale to the 1×1 bokeh sprite that you will spawn. The more the pixel is out of focus (remember that in the DOF explanation a pixel is gradually out of focus), the bigger the sprite will be on screen. If the scale value is 20 pixels, the bokeh sprite spawned at a pixel fully out of focus will be 20×20 pixels. (See Figure 15.8.)

At the end of this process you end up with a list of sprites containing

- x screen-space position of the pixel,

- y screen-space position of the pixel,

- z linear value of the pixel needed to depth test the bokeh sprite in the pixel shader,

- UV coordinates of the bokeh texture,

- CoC value of the pixel needed to adjust the blending amount to preserve energy conservation,

- color value of the pixel.

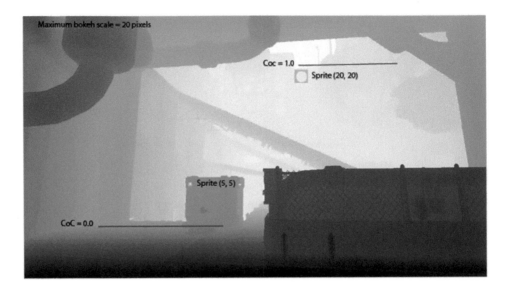

Figure 15.8. CoC across the framebuffer.

Now, depending on the platform you are developing for, this process can be done by different work units. On DX11, all this is realized in the compute shader with the color and depth buffer used as textures. On PS3, we don't have this stage available, but we do have the SPUs!

15.4 Let's SPUify This!

On PS3 the memory is split in two: main and video memory. Typical pipelines have the main color buffer placed in video memory for performance and memory footprint reasons. Since the SPUs like to work on buffers placed in main memory (read/write mode), the first step is to transfer the main color buffer into main memory. SPUs can work on buffers placed in video memory but the write speed will be slower.

After the reality synthesizer (RSX) transfers the color buffer to main memory, the SPU can start analyzing the scan lines to find each possible location where a bokeh sprite should be spawned. Basically, SPUs will write sprite information in a vertex buffer reserved in main memory that the RSX will process to display the bokeh sprites. The SPU program then patches the draw call previously reserved in the command buffer and removes the Jump To Self (JTS). During this process we calculate the average luminance of the color buffer needed in the tone mapping step, allowing us to save the Graphics Processing Unit (GPU) downscaling steps to find the average luminance of the color buffer.

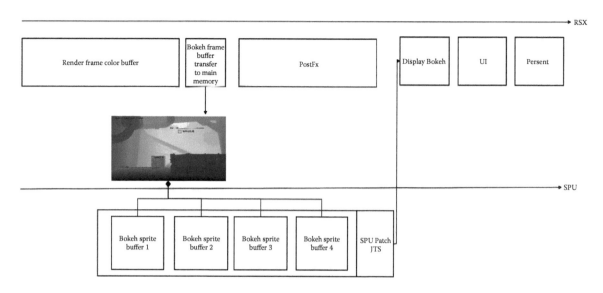

Figure 15.9. Bokeh effect timeline example.

The effect is very similar to the bokeh effect available from the DirectX 11 API, using the compute shader.

Let's detail the different steps (see also Figure 15.9):

1. Transfer the color buffer to main memory. You can transfer at full resolution or half resolution depending on the budget or quality of the bokeh effect you want.

2. Prepare (n) SPU jobs working on a sub-part of the color buffer to analyze the pixel luminance.

3. Each SPU fills a vertex buffer with the bokeh sprite information.

4. On the PPU, reserve space in the command buffer for the `SetDrawArrays`. Since the command `SetDrawArrays` has a variable size in the command buffer depending on the number of vertices, we must declare a maximum number of vertices and reserve that space in the command buffer. JTS commands are inserted before each `SetDrawArrays` so that the RSX waits until the SPUs are done.

5. On the PPU we issue (n) draw calls working on (n) vertex buffers depending on the number of SPU jobs we decided to spawn to process the framebuffer: for example, if we decided to create two SPU jobs, both jobs would work on half of the framebuffer, and we would need to issue on the PPU two draw calls each using their own vertex buffer (so two vertex buffers) and patched

by the SPU jobs. Note that the sprites are rendered in additive blend mode on top of the color buffer.

6. On the SPUs, each bokeh job analyzes the pixels and spawns a bokeh sprite for each pixel passing the luminance threshold, scaled by the CoC factor. The scale is clamped to a maximum bokeh scale size (in pixel space).

7. Each sprite is written in the vertex buffer (x, y, z position in screen space + UVs + color) and the `SetDrawArrays` is patched with the correct number of vertices. The rest of the reserved space is filled with NOPs.

```
void SetDrawArrays( ContextData *thisContext, const uint8_t
    mode,
const uint32_t first, const uint32_t count)
```

where `mode` = QUADS, `first` = 0, and `count` = the number of pixels that passed the luminance threshold with a valid CoC value.

8. The SPU patches the JTS so RSX can consume the graphic commands.

9. RSX draws each batch of bokeh sprites using additive blending.

10. Depth test is done in the pixel shader since we have the z position of the sprite in the vertex buffer.

11. The blend amount is adjusted to respect energy conservation for the bokeh sprite.

There are various ways to hide the luminance analysis and bokeh draw call generation steps done by the SPUs. In my case I decided to kick the RSX transfer right after the blended objects. This leaves enough time for the SPUs to analyze the framebuffer and fill the vertex buffer that the RSX will use to display the bokeh sprites on top of the framebuffer. The important thing to remember is to be careful not to stall the RSX. One nice thing about all this is that by doing the luminance computation on the SPUs you can have the total frame luminance for free! Normally, a game will have some kind of luminance/tone mapping adaptation of the framebuffer at the end of the frame. Adaptation effects usually involve the GPU by adding the work of doing a cascade of downscale passes to find the average luminance of the framebuffer. This obviously has some cost on the GPU and can be removed if you analyze the framebuffer on the SPUs.

15.5 Results

15.5.1 SPU

The present metrics are done on a half resolution 720p color buffer in main memory:

- 1 SPU working on a 640×360 buffer = **2.8ms**.

- 5 SPUs working on a 640×360 buffer = **0.65ms**!

The computations are done in a *Structure of Array* (SoA) manner, allowing the processing of four pixels at once. The SPU could certainly be more optimized by better balancing the odd/even pipes and reducing instruction latency.

15.5.2 RSX

On the RSX the cost is totally dependent on the number of bokeh sprites you decide to spawn and the screen coverage each sprite has (this is dependent on the bokeh maximum scale in pixels).

- Transfer to main memory with a draw call: 1280×720 to a 640×360 surface (untiled) = **0.44 ms**.

For the bokeh sprite draw calls, I will use a capture to show performance but remember that the number is dependent on the number of sprites per SPU job and the bokeh maximum scale.

Figure 15.10 shows a test case to analyze the cost of bokeh sprites on the RSX.

Total cost of the draw calls of the bokeh sprites = **0.56ms** for 5660 vertices with a 10 pixel maximum bokeh scale factor. (See Figure 15.11.)

Figure 15.10. Bokeh effect with a pentagon bokeh shape.

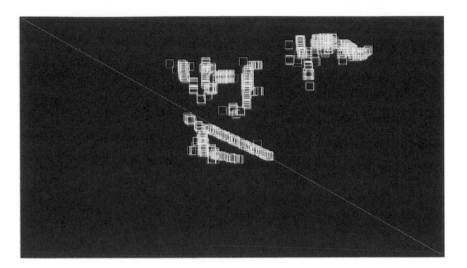

Figure 15.11. Wire frame view of the bokeh sprite draw calls.

15.6 Future Development

- Optimize SPU code by distributing the instructions evenly between the odd and even SPU pipelines.

- Since the SPU computes the luminance for each pixel we could have the total luminance of the color buffer without involving the RSX (downsampling and reading the final target on PPU). This could save the downsampling step on the RSX if you have some sort of Eye Adaptation post-process in your pipeline.

- Try to remove or push the vertex maximum number.

- Maybe spawn one SPU job working on the whole color buffer and sort the bokeh sprites to use only the brightest ones.

- Work with a bigger kernel size to generate fewer bokeh sprites.

- SPU's could write the bokeh sprite directly in the framebuffer. Instead of writing the vertex buffer, SPU's calculate for each sprite the 2D transfers representing lines contained in the Bokeh sprites. The RSX would use this buffer in additive blend mode to add it on top of the framebuffer.

Bibliography

[Pettineo 11] Matt Pettineo. "How to Fake Bokeh (And Make It Look Pretty Good)." http://mynameismjp.wordpress.com/2011/02/28/bokeh/, February 28, 2011.

About the Contributors

Serge Bernier is a lead graphics engineer at Eidos Montreal, where his main focus is to work on rendering algorithms and graphics architecture. He has been involved with graphics-related optimizations for various projects on Playstation 3 since the platform was launched. Passionate about graphics innovations, what he loves the most is the fast evolving pace of specialization, where art and engineering meet to create great-looking worlds.

Michael Bukowski graduated magna cum laude with a BS in computer systems engineering from Rensselaer Polytechnic Institute. After a brief stint with IBM as a hardware designer, he jumped head first into the games industry. He has spent the last ten-plus years in game development, where he has shipped six-plus titles working as a lead engineer and as a production engineer in a range of areas such as audio, systems, and graphics. He has handled IPs such as *Doom 3*, *Marvel Ultimate Alliance*, and *Guitar Hero*. He also has a number of publications at conferences such as SIGGRAPH, I3D, and HPG. Currently he is an engineering specialist at Vicarious Visions where he leads the Visual Alchemy Team, a research and development group focused on creating and supporting industry-leading graphics technologies for a variety of gaming platforms.

Carsten Dachsbacher is a full professor at the Karlsruhe Institute of Technology. His research focuses on real-time computer graphics, global illumination, scientific visualization, and perceptual rendering, on which he published articles at various conferences and journals including SIGGRAPH, IEEE VIS, EG, and EGSR. He has been a tutorial speaker at SIGGRAPH, Eurographics, and the Game Developers Conference.

Jürgen Döllner is a full professor at the Hasso Plattner Institute at the University of Potsdam, where he is leading the computer graphics and visualization department. He studied mathematics and computer science at the University of Siegen, Germany and got his PhD in computer science from the University of Münster, Germany, in 1996. He also received there his habilitation degree in 2001. His major research areas are in information visualization, software visual analytics, and geospatial visual analytics. In particular, his research is focused on concepts, tools, and techniques for complex software systems and graphics-based systems. He is an author of more than 200 papers in computer graphics and visualization (for an overview of publications, see http://www.hpi3d.de). He serves as a reviewer to a number of international and national journals, conferences, and workshops.

Thomas Engelhardt received his MS in computer science from the University of Erlangen-Nuremberg and is now a PhD student in computer graphics at VISUS (Institute for Visualization), University of Stuttgart, Germany. His research interests focus on efficient GPU techniques and rendering algorithms for interactive global illumination.

Diego Gutierrez is a tenured associate professor at the Universidad de Zaragoza, where he got his PhD in computer graphics in 2005. He now leads his group's research on graphics, perception, and computational photography. He is an associate editor of three journals, has chaired and organized several conferences, and has served on numerous committees, including the SIGGRAPH and Eurographics conferences.

Padraic Hennessy is a senior graphics engineer at Vicarious Visions, an Activision Blizzard Studio. He is a primary member of the Studio's Visual Alchemy Team. Work from this team has been published at SIGGRAPH, I3D, and HPG. The team has also worked on AAA franchises such as *Skylanders*, *Doom*, *Marvel Ultimate Alliance*, and *Guitar Hero*. While graphics is his main focus at the studio, he has contributed as a core engine architect, tools engineer, network engineer, and gameplay systems engineer. When not working on developing new graphics techniques, he strives to improve artist workflow and to help artists understand complex graphics techniques through training seminars. He received a BS in computer engineering from Binghamton University in 2006.

David Illes is a PhD student at the Budapest University of Technology and Economics. His research interests include distributed fluid simulation, GPU-related algorithms, and tools development for computer animated productions. He has been working as a freelancer software developer for several animation studios, including Next Limit Technologies, Axis Animation, Digic Pictures, and GYAR Post Production.

Jorge Jimenez is a real-time graphics researcher at the Universidad de Zaragoza, in Spain, where he received his BSc and MSc degrees, and where he is pursuing a PhD in real-time graphics. His passion for graphics started after watching old school demos in his brother's Amiga A1000. His interests include real-time photorealistic rendering, special effects, and squeezing rendering algorithms to be practical in game environments. He has numerous contributions in books and journals, including *Transactions on Graphics*, where his skin renderings made the front cover of the SIGGRAPH Asia 2010 issue. He loves challenges, playing games, working out in the gym, and more than anything, breaking in the street.

Henry Kang received the BS in computer science from Yonsei University, Korea, in 1994 and his MS and PhD degrees in computer science from the Korea Advanced Institute of Science and Technology (KAIST) in 1996 and 2002, respectively. He is currently an associate professor of computer science at the University of Missouri-St. Louis, USA. His research interests include nonphotorealistic rendering and animation, illustrative visualization, image and video processing, image-based modeling and rendering, and facial expression animation.

Kaori Kubota is a graphics programmer in the technical development department at KOEI in Japan. She began shader programming six years ago and has written various shaders for KOEI's games. Recently she has been involved with a shader development system.

Jan Eric Kyprianidis graduated in mathematics from the University of Hamburg, Germany, in 2005. Until 2007 he was a senior software engineer at Adobe Systems. He is currently a research scientist with the computer graphics group of the Hasso-Plattner-Institut at the University of Potsdam, Germany. His research interests include non-photorealistic rendering and digital image processing.

Hugh Malan is a principle tech programmer at Guerrilla Games. Previously, he worked for CCP on Dust 514, and before that at Realtime Worlds, as graphics lead on *Crackdown*. He developed the "Realworldz" real-time procedurally-generated planet demo for 3Dlabs. He has an MSc in computer graphics from Otago University, New Zealand, and a BSc in physics with honors in mathematics from Victoria University, New Zealand.

Pavlos Mavridis is a software engineer at the Foundation of the Hellenic World, where he is working on the design and implementation of real-time rendering techniques for virtual reality installations. He received his BSc and MSc degrees in computer science from the University of Athens, Greece. He is currently pursuing his PhD in real-time computer graphics at the Department of Informatics of the Athens University of Economics and Business. His current research interests include real-time photorealistic rendering, global illumination algorithms, texture compression, and texture filtering techniques.

Morgan McGuire teaches game design and computer graphics at Williams College and works on new products in the games industry. His industry work includes *Skylanders: SWAP Force* and *Marvel Ultimate Alliance 2* at Vicarious Visions, *Titan Quest* at Iron Lore, the EInk display for the Amazon Kindle, and designs for recent GPUs at NVIDIA. His academic publications include *The Graphics Codex for iOS* (2012), *Creating Games: Mechanics, Content, and Technology*

(2008), *Computer Graphics: Principles and Practice* (Third Edition, 2013), and SIGGRAPH papers on video and GPU ray tracing. He received his PhD from Brown University.

Gustavo Nunes is a graphics engineer in the Engine team at Microsoft Turn 10 Studios. He received his BSc in computer engineering and MSc in computer graphics from Pontifícia Universidade Católica do Rio de Janeiro, Brazil. He has several articles published in the computer graphics field. He is passionate about everything real-time graphics related. Gustavo was part of the teams that shipped Microsoft Office 2013, Xbox One, *Forza Motorsport 5*, *Forza Horizon 2*, and *Forza Motorsport 6*.

Brian Osman is a senior software engineer at Vicarious Visions, where he specializes in rendering and engine technology. He has spent over ten years working on games in a variety of genres and for a wide range of platforms. He received his BS and MS in computer science from Rensselaer Polytechnic Institute.

David Pangerl is the CEO of Actalogic, where he is working as a lead researcher and engine architecture designer. He has been involved in computer graphics and engine research for over a decade.

Georgios Papaioannou is currently an assistant professor of computer graphics at the Department of Informatics of the Athens University of Economics and Business. He received a BSc in computer science and a PhD degree in computer graphics and pattern recognition, both from the University of Athens, Greece. In the past, he has worked as a research fellow in many research and development projects, and as a virtual reality software engineer at the Foundation of the Hellenic World. His research is focused on real-time computer graphics algorithms, photorealistic rendering, virtual reality systems and three-dimensional pattern recognition. He has contributed many scientific papers in the above fields and has coauthored one international and two Greek computer graphics textbooks. He is also a member of IEEE, ACM, SIGGRAPH, and Eurographics Association and has been a member of the program committees of many computer graphics conferences.

Emil Persson is the Head of Research at Avalanche Studios, where he is conducting forward-looking research, with the aim to be relevant and practical for game development, as well as setting the future direction for the Avalanche Engine. Previously, he was an ISV Engineer in the Developer Relations team at ATI/AMD. He assisted tier-one game developers with the latest rendering techniques, identifying performance problems and applying optimizations. He also made major contributions to SDK samples and technical documentation.

João Raza is a program manager at Microsoft's 343 Industries, where he works in the services cloud compute systems. Previously he was in the Windows Phone division, where he helped ship the SDK for game developers. An avid gamer, he has worked in the game industry for over five years. He holds a bachelor of computer science from Universidade Federal de São Carlos (UFSCar). He runs the blog www.versus-software.com, where he writes about his main interests in graphics, networking, and game design.

David C. Schedl received his master's degree in the program of Interactive Media at the University of Applied Sciences Upper Austria Campus Hagenberg in 2011. He worked as a scientific researcher at the Institute of Computer Graphics and Algorithms at the Vienna University of Technology until 2012. He is currently a project assistant at the Institute of Computer Graphics at the Johannes Kepler University Linz. His research interests include real-time rendering, image processing, and light fields.

László Szécsi is an associate professor at the Technical University in Budapest, Hungary. He gives lectures in programming, computer graphics, and computer game development. His research revolves around global illumination, real-time rendering techniques, and the combination of the two. László has published numerous scientific papers and has been a regular contributor to the *ShaderX* book series.

Michael Wimmer is an associate professor at the Institute of Computer Graphics and Algorithms of the Vienna University of Technology, where he received an MSc in 1997 and a PhD in 2001. His current research interests are real-time rendering, computer games, real-time visualization of urban environments, point-based rendering, and procedural modeling. He has coauthored many papers in these fields, was papers cochair of EGSR 2008, and is papers cochair of Pacific Graphics 2012.